THE ENERGY GRID

DIAGRAM 1

Showing relationship of grid structure to the geographic poles. Each of the two grids has a similar pattern, the interaction of which sets up a third resultant grid. The poles of the three grids are positioned at three different latitudes and longitudes.

C, D, E, F = Corner aerial positions of grid polar square. Similar to aerial discovered by the survey ship *Eltanin*.

J — K = Polar axis.

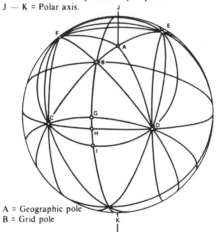

A = Geographic pole
B = Grid pole

Distance C — G — D = 3600 minutes of arc.
Distance C — H — D = 3418.6069 minutes of arc.
Distance C — I — D = 3643.2 minutes of arc

(3600 — 3418.6069) = 181.39308
(181.39308 x 4) = 725.57233
$\sqrt{725.57233}$ = 26.93645 = 2693645 harmonic.

Write for our free catalog of exciting books and tapes.

THE ENERGY GRID

Adventures Unlimited Press
One Adventure Place
Kempton, Illinois

The Energy Grid
by Bruce Cathie

This edition published 1997

ISBN 0-932813-44-5

Printed in the United States of America

Adventures Unlimited Press
303 Main Street
Kempton, ILLINOIS 60946 USA
Phone: 815-253-6390
Fax: 815-253-6300

The Lost Science Series:
The Anti-Gravity Handbook
Anti-Gravity & the World Grid
Anti-Gravity & the Unified Field
The Free-Energy Device Handbook
The Energy Grid by Bruce Cathie
The Bridge To Infinity by Bruce Cathie
The Harmonic Conquest of Space by Bruce Cathie
Vimana Aircraft of Ancient India & Atlantis
Tapping the Zero Point Energy
The Fantastic Inventions of Nikola Tesla
Man-Made UFOs: 1944-1994

AUTHOR'S NOTE

THIS BOOK IS A REVISED COMBINATION OF MY second and third books, "Harmonic 695, the UFO and Anti-gravity" and, "The Pulse of the Universe, Harmonic 288". The contents have been up-dated in relation to my present Knowledge.

To do this I have deleted a small amount of material which I now believe to be inaccurate, or covered in a more comprehensible form in my later works; corrected, or added, material necessary to explain my theories as clearly as possible.

I realise that I cannot be one hundred percent correct at all times in my speculations, but if some progress is being made in new concepts, then I am more than satisfied. A fantastic future awaits us if we can unravel the secrets underlying the basic structure of the universe.

ACKNOWLEDGMENTS

For the quotations from published material reproduced in the text and the illustrations in this book I am indebted to the following:

Definitions:
Britannica World Standard Dictionary.

The New Zealand Scientific and Space Research Organization, Auckland.

Behind the Flying Saucers by Frank Scully, Holt, Rinehart and Winston, Inc., New York.

The City of Revelation by John Mitchell. Garnstone Press Ltd., London.

John Tunstall: article in *The Times*, London, July, 1969.

The Great Pyramid: Its Divine Message by D. Davidson and. Aldersmith. William Rider and Son Ltd., London.

The Pyramid and its Relationship to Biocosmic Energy by G. Patrick Flanagan.

Physics, Part 1 by Robert Resnick and David Halliday. John Wiley and Sons Ltd., New York and London.

Flying Saucers Have Landed by Desmond Leslie and George Adamski. Werner Laurie, London.
The Story of the Laser by John Carroll. The Scientific Book Club, London.

A Beam of Light by Gaston Burridge. *Rosicrucian Digest*, March, 1961.

The Secret of Life by G. Lakhovsky. Health Science Press, Sussex.

The Changing Universe by John Pfeiffer. London.

"New Home for America's Doomsday Radio": *New Scientist.* 16 August, 1973.

Blast the Bush by Len Beadell. The Griffon Press, Rigby Ltd., Adelaide.

The Marshall Cavendish Dictionary of Medicine. Marshall Cavendish.

"Antarctic Base for N-Testing" by Gilbert Sedbon, *Sunday Herald,* Auckland, 7 October, 1973.

APRO Bulletin: March/April 1973.

The Prodigal Genius by John J. O'Neill. Neville Spearman, London.

"Pyramids Versus the Space Age" by John Tunstall. *The Times.* London, 26 July, 1969.

"Proceedings", Volume 10, 1974, No. 6 by George W. Van Tassel, Yucca Valley, California.

I also thank my colleague Mr. Donald Offwood for permission to reproduce his report "On an Investigation into Electroculture 1972, 1973".

Bruce Leonard Cathie

CONTENTS

CONTENTS (CONTINUED)

LIST OF DIAGRAMS

LIST OF TABLES

PHOTOCOPY

LIST OF MAPS

PREFACE

THE UNIVERSE IS A LIVING INTELLIGENCE

ITS HEARTBEATS THUNDER AT THE CENTRE OF galaxies and whisper in the nucleus of atoms. With the spiraling wave-forms of its own essence it creates from within its infinite depths the matter which constitutes all physical substances, living or inanimate. It was-it is-it always will be-timeless.

We are created by this intelligence from the same myriad of wave-forms that interlace the depths of space, connecting all things. We and it are one. For all truth and wisdom look within, for we are a shimmering mass of miniature stars and worlds, with emerald seas and sandy shores, which in their turn provide home for intelligence.

DEFINITION OF TERMS

Harmony and *harmonic* etc. as defined by the *Britannica World Standard Dictionary:*

1. **HARMONY:** A state of order, agreement, or completeness in the relations of things, or of parts of a whole to each other.

2. **HARMONIC:** Producing, characterised by, or pertaining to harmony.

   (a) **MUSIC:** Pertaining to a tone whose rate of vibration is an exact multiple of a given primary tone.

   (b) **MATHEMATICAL;** Derived from, or originally suggested by, the numerical relations between the vibrations of the musical harmonies, or overtones, of the same fundamental tone: Harmonic functions.

   (c) **PHYSICS:** Any component of a periodic quantity, which is an integral multiple of the fundamental frequency. In this book we discuss the fundamental harmonies of the vibrational frequencies which form the building-blocks of our immediate universe: and that of the theoretical anti-universe which modern scientists have postulated as existing in mirror-like image of our own. We theorise that the whole of physical reality which is tangible to us is formed from the basic geometric harmonies, or harmonics, of the angular velocities, or wave forms of light. From these basic harmonies, or resonating wave forms, myriads of other waves are created which blend in sympathetic resonance, one with the other, thus forming the physical structures. Einstein stated that the geometric structure of space time determines the physical processes.
   We theorise that space and time manifest from the geometric harmonies of the wave motions of light. The fundamental harmonic of light in geometric terms being an angular velocity of 144,000 minutes of arc per grid second. There being 97,200 grid seconds to one revolution of the earth.

The reciprocal harmonic of light, or 1/144,000 being 694444, repeating. It was found that to calculate the values of harmonic wave forms that have sympathetic resonance, it was possible to disregard zero's to the right, or left, of whole numbers and extract the values direct from the mathematical tables. Harmonic 69444 therefore refers to the geometric reciprocal of light, which in theory forms the basic building-block of the anti-universe, or region of negative reality.

3. **ANTI-MATTER:** A hypothetical form of matter in which all the component particles, as protons, electrons, etc., are assumed to carry charges opposite to those associated with the corresponding particles of the known universe.

4. **ANTI-GRAVITY:** In the known universe all physical matter has a common gravitational attraction or tendency to coalesce together. As the word itself suggests, a body under the influence of antigravitational fields would be repulsed or tend to move away from normal physical matter.

It has been found in later research that the harmonic of the speed of light varies in relation to the geometric distance from the centre of the earth. The value at various levels, from the centre to the edge of the atmosphere, is demonstrated in my fourth book, "The Bridge to Infinity, Harmonic 371244."

INTRODUCTION

WAKE UP EARTH! THE SIGNALS HAVE BEEN received. First, in 1927 by American experimenters Taylor and Young, from apparent distances of 2,900 to 10,000 Km. Halls, an engineer, reported to Carl Stormer of Oslo that echoes of 3 seconds delay had been heard at Eindhoven, Holland. On 11th October 1928 Carl Stormer, with Halls, helped by Van der Pol transmitting from Eindhoven, picked up 3-second echoes on 31.4 meters, which changed to echoes varying from 3 to 15 seconds. The signal pulses were transmitted at 20 second intervals. Echoes were received in the following delay sequence: 8, 11-15, 8,13,3,8,8,8-12,15,13,8,8. In two cases echoes were heard 4 seconds apart.

The consensus was: that the signals were saying — Here I am in the orbit of your Moon.

And nobody wanted to listen.

More than twenty years have passed since I presented the manuscript for my first book, HARMONIC 33, for publication. In it I related the findings — up to the time — of my investigations into the mystery of unidentified flying objects.

Amongst other interesting facts, I had discovered evidence of a world energy grid system and little did I know then that I had opened up a line of enquiry which would cause me to get attention from the intelligence agencies of several of the major countries around the world. It soon became obvious that I had discovered something that many of the worlds power groups preferred to remain unknown to the general public. As time went on it was admitted that the world grid did exist, but it was considered that it was not yet time to openly admit to a source of almost free energy. Energy means power in more ways than one.

As my work has progressed I have found more than enough evidence to convince me that the public is not being informed of the most fantastic and advanced scientific discoveries in the history of man. After forty years of sightings, scientists, and government agencies, are still trying to convince the public that Unidentified Flying Objects are figments of the imagination. I state, without any doubt whatever, that the public is being conned. UFOs do exist; they are interdimensional anti-gravity machines.

I believe that many of the machines sighted are visiting us from outer space, but a great number of sightings are of machines produced by our own scientists on Earth. The secrets of anti-gravity and free energy production are known in top scientific circles and they will go to any length to keep this knowledge from us. Many reasons could be given for the suppression but I believe that one of the main ones is the financial consequences of complete release of such advanced technology on the world economy. This would certainly be a problem, but the longer things are left the way they are the greater the problem is going to be.

Whatever the reasons are, we have the right to know the truth and it is up to every one of us to demand that the truth be given.

Every day, somewhere in the world, there are verified sightings of UFOs. While the sceptics continue to assert that such normal circumstances as marsh gas, eye floaters, the rising and setting of Venus, or the flashing of car headlights against banks of low clouds, account for UFO sightings, they have nothing to say about the growing number of radar reports which indicate that physical objects, not always visible to the human eye, are continuing to frequent our airspace. Vehicles in the sky appear to watchers in the far corners of the globe; they carry out elaborate manoeuvers, then fade from sight; or they leave the area at fantastic speed, leaving bewilderment, excitement, confusion or outright fear behind them.

Within the last week there has been an incident which has hit the headlines worldwide. The event occurred in the early morning hours of January 20 1988, about 40 Km west of Mundrabilla, near the western Australian border.

Fay Knowles and her three Sons, Patrick (24), Sean (21), and Wayne (18), watched a glowing object which resembled a giant egg in an egg cup, chase a truck and a car, which were travelling in the opposite direction, before it turned and hovered over their own vehicle. They said it picked the car up off the road, shook it quite violently, turned it in the opposite direction, then forced it down again with such pressure that one of the tyres was blown. Crime investigators from Port Lincoln examined the car, which was covered in an ash-like substance and sent samples from the interior and exterior to Adelaide for forensic examination.

It was reported that a similar incident involved a police officer in the United States some years ago.

The explanations for the occurrence have been more bizarre than the story itself. One academic said it could have been caused by a carbonaceous meteorite, "which could do this sort of thing." I wonder how much longer the public will accept such obvious nonsense.

As long as there are inexplicable activities in the skies and on the ground and as long as my existing theories continue to be supported by facts and reports from many parts of the world, I will not be satisfied until I am able to approach one of the vehicles closely, examine it in detail, and if possible communicate with one of the beings who control it.

The knowledge I now possess is far in advance of that which I had when I was preparing my earlier works. A great deal has happened that has tended to confirm my basic calculations and theories. Moreover, the acceptability gap is constantly narrowing; thousands of people who have never given serious thought to UFOs are suddenly turning to all the available reference material in search for a glimmering of the truth.

During my many years of research I have uncovered a considerable body of evidence pointing to the existence of projects being carried out on a world-wide basis which have direct connections with UFOs. From this evidence the logical conclusion is that top scientists and electronic engineers have direct contact and communication with UFOs.

I also believe it is most probable that a Moon-base has already been established by our own scientists. The advanced technology would give them this capability. When the rocket program was wound down years ago, it was probably because it was obsolete.

As I continued making my discoveries — the existence of a vast power grid, the devises contrived to establish communication between some groups on this planet and the UFOs — I made a point of keeping interested parties in government aware of them, fully expecting to be either dismissed as a crank, or at least, to be told to stop my activities. Much to my surprise I was given every encouragement to continue with my probing and to publish whatever information came to light. Possibly this is the first time that any government has ever authorised a civilian to pursue unrestricted research into UFO phenomena.

Among other things, I have discovered a series of Harmonic geometric equations which, when put into practical application, will cause reactions in space-time.

During the 1968 series of nuclear explosion tests by the French at Mururoa Island in the Pacific, it was requested by the head of a government department that I provide a list of pre-calculated explosion dates. In my earlier publications I had indicated how geometric factors determined any possibility of a nuclear explosion, or reaction. I supplied the dates, as requested, and later on I was informed that my calculations had been passed on from Auckland to the heads of four other government departments before the actual tests were carried out. My calculations proved correct. This information is now in the files of the government authorities concerned.

If they are not already aware, then events of this order must sooner or later command the attention of international scientific organizations. One day the scientists will no longer be able to turn their backs on the basic precepts of true science. They will have to examine all evidence impartially before they reach their conclusions — and instead of offering only ridicule, carry out a full world-wide investigation into all the phenomena related to UFOs, and the world grid energy system. Facts cannot be ignored forever; although it is obvious to all thinking people that there are interests that would very much prefer the world to be kept in ignorance and in cultivated indifference for as long as possible.

My investigations have led me into many by-ways, not all of them of great moment, or interest to others than myself. The workload of my studies has increased enormously; and yet there are facts, as well as hypotheses, which I feel must be brought to the notice of the public urgently.

Some of the information will be found in the following pages of this updated book.

1> THE BRANCHING AREAS FOR INVESTIGATION

WHAT IS HAPPENING TO THE CLASSICAL IDEAS of scientific research? It has always been my understanding that the basic attitude towards any scientific investigation should be one of non-bias. The scientist, I understood, was a person who collected all available data on the subject of his study, weighed it and interpreted it, and reached certain conclusions about it without prejudice and without preconceived notions.

Today Science is up on a pedestal. A new god has appeared; his high priests conduct the rituals, with nuclear reactors, moon-probing rocket ships, cathode tubes and laser beams. And their territory is sacrosanct; laymen are denied entry.

A letter to an Auckland newspaper signed by Robert Adams, chairman of the Institute of Electrical and Electronics Engineers of the USA, New Zealand section, referring to the proposed installation of an Omega station, states with supreme satisfaction: "It is not for laymen to pass comment on such installations."[1]

As the more advanced nations lead the way into a state of technocracy, it becomes more and more apparent that the laymen of the world will have no more say in this planet's affairs than did the slaves of Pharaoh. Already there are clear indications that the scientific Establishment in a number of countries is able to operate, and to conduct activities with government funds without having to account scrupulously to government or citizenry just what those activities are. There is an open and manifest activity in certain directions, but there is reason to suspect that this often cloaks an inner, secret activity — an activity in which government and people have no say. Already scientists speak among themselves in a language that is no longer public property. Have they, despairing of the muddled state of the world's affairs, banded together in a modern — day monastic order of their own, with the aim of taking over entirely the affairs of the earth?

There is an enormously vast mass of data that has never been explained satisfactorily, ranging through every branch of every recognized science; the indefatigable Charles Fort referred to this body

---

[1]*New Zealand Herald, 17 January, 1969*

1

of data as the "damned" — damned by science because it did not fit in anywhere, and so in order to preserve the status quo of the scientific Establishment, had to be rejected and ignored.

UFOs are in the category of the damned. Never before has public interest been so high in flying saucers, strange aerial lights and objects, reported landings, unidentified submarine objects, alien voices speaking no known earthly language on low-frequency radio bands, unexplained explosions which coincide very often with sightings of UFOs, and a host of related phenomena. There is no existing science capable of neatly fitting in all this data and offering a consistent explanation. To acknowledge what millions of laymen around the world already know — that UFOs do exist — would result in a complete upset of the scientific Establishment. The facts are all there, staring blind science in the face. But the facts are unacceptable; therefore, UFOs don't exist.

There is nothing new in this attitude; the only thing new is that the establishment itself has changed. In medieval times "Establishment" meant the ruling families of Europe, in the West; the knowledge then being built up and explored by people known as "witches" and "alchemists" was contrary to accepted theories about reality. The penalty for these seekers of truth was frequently a lingering death.

Today science is on the throne, but nothing else has changed. Uncomfortable data are still rejected and filed away somewhere, at best as "curiosities."

In examining his data, with a clear, unbiased attitude, the true researcher must correctly reject all those which are clearly not free of doubtful accuracy; but after all his sifting, if even one datum remains that cannot be ignored, it is obviously his duty to come to grips with it.

UFOs are notoriously nothing more than "hallucinations," but even if we allow for all the unwitting or otherwise human errors of observation, there is still the implacable scientific and impersonal evidence of radar to be accounted for.

Radar is not subject to hallucinations. It records the presence of solid objects, establishes their movement patterns, tracks their flight. Auckland's radar station at Mangere is only one such station of thousands throughout the world which is habitually recording the presence in the sky of unidentified moving objects — moving too fast to be explained as birds or aircraft and moving in flight patterns impossible for any kind of earth-made craft. There have been

2

many occasions when radar control has directed incoming aircraft to areas nearby where objects are "seen" by radar; frequently the pilots have been unable to detect anything visible. While they search for the object, the radar follows the search; the unseen object's "blip" is watched on the radar viewing screen; it plays leapfrog with the searching aircraft, bobs up and down like a yo-yo, or veers away and moves off at a fantastic speed. Inexplicable, yes — by our present understanding. But does evidence of this kind also have to be rejected, ignored, tucked away for "future reference"? It would appear so.

In January 1969 the University of Colorado issued a report on a UFO investigation endorsed by a panel of "leading scientists" convened by the National Academy of Sciences.

"Our general conclusion," according to the bulky report, "is that nothing has come from the study of UFOs in the past twenty-one years that has added to scientific knowledge." This is of course double-talk; it does not deny the existence of UFOs outright, but merely publicly admits that science has failed to come to grips with the world-wide phenomena.

The panel of scientists noted that the report concedes a residue of "perplexing episodes."

At England's Lakenheath airbase, used by both the USAF and the RAF in 1956, radar operators on the ground detected "one or more" targets moving apparently at speeds as great as 2000 or 4000 mph, although there were no sonic booms. They made right-angle turns at a "few hundred miles an hour" (an impossible manoeuvre for terrestrial craft).

Two RAF fighters were sent out, and one obtained radar gunlock on the target. But the object, whatever it was, circled the fighter's tail and remained there in spite of all evasion attempts. The plane eventually had to land in order to refuel, and ground staff saw "one or more white rapidly moving objects."

This is but one example of the inexplicable residue which flatly refuses to be categorised or classified into some convenient pigeon-hole of knowledge. There were fifty-nine cases cited by the report as being of "special interest from several hundred" that were reviewed.

Mr. William Ryan (Democrat, New York), the congressman in Washington who is also the voice of the National Investigations Committee on Aerial Phenomena (NICAP), which has about 10,000 members in some forty countries, told the House of Representatives:

3

"A Federal UFO surveillance programme should be set up. UFOs cannot be wished away, and reported sightings will persist."

And NICAP added a bombshell of its own: it claimed to have proof that the Colorado investigation team had never intended to study UFOs objectively, but had intentionally fitted its data into a negative report.

Reading of this, I was inevitably reminded of a document in my possession. It is a copy of a directive to USAF investigators of UFO reports; it is signed by General Curtis LeMay, who was at the time of its publication chief of the USAF. In effect it instructs investigating officers of UFO reports how to denigrate UFO reports, how to play them down and how to offer logical explanations for various phenomena. It does not suggest that UFO sightings are to be considered worthy of a fuller study.

I wonder: can scientists really be as hollow as they appear to be? Do they really imagine the much-despised laymen of the world will settle for shrugged shoulders and a shroud of marsh gas?

I wonder: couldn't it be that the scientists already have the full explanation of UFOs — and for reasons not yet clear, are deliberately keeping the knowledge as a jealously-guarded secret within their own closed ranks?

Incredible as it may seem, this appears to be the truth. I have amassed a considerable amount of evidence which strongly suggests that scientists in a number of countries not only know a great deal about UFOs, they also know how to keep in contact with them. I believe that from such contacts there has already been a considerable exchange of information. I believe that the Establishment has gone through a phase of shock, amounting to severe trauma, as new knowledge has been revealed, and that there is not one science, not one major industry, that can remain unaffected by what the scientists have already learned. The rocket programmes of the Soviet Union and the United States, the transportation systems of the world, the power supply authorities and every conceivable kind of industry would be rendered obsolete if a new, unsuspected yet universally available system of power were to become available. I believe the earth is on the brink of having access to that power source.

I am neither a naive fantasy fan, nor a proselytizer of any particular brand of faith. I am in complete accord with the French authors, Louis Pauwels and Jacques Bergior[1], in that I declare: it is

---

[1] *The Dawn of Magic, 1963*

not necessary to believe everything; it is only necessary to look at everything, to study and to examine everything; to explore with an unbiased mind, free of bigotry; to sift evidence and known facts, and upon these to reach certain tentative conclusions which are not the product of preconcieved notions. I hope that at least a large number of readers will feel the same way.

The road towards an equation began with the discovery that there exists on this globe an all-encompassing grid, the interlocking lines of which correspond to the lines of flight of verified UFO appearances. It would be in order here to recapitulate briefly, the theories and calculations regarding the nature of that grid.

First of all, a geometric pattern of UFO activity was discovered which indicated a definite purpose in the presence of UFOs about our planetary surface. Having established the pattern of the grid, the next step was to break it down into mathematical co-ordinates. When this was done, it was found that all the values represented in the grid had direct harmonic relationships with the speed of light, gravity and earth mass.

Once these relationships became clear it was possible to theorise on the method of propulsion employed by the UFOs. It would appear that by setting up a harmonic imbalance of gravitational forces, the UFOs are able to reposition themselves in space-time; that is, the UFO moves from one point to another in order to restore the balance of the forces caused by space-time geometrics. I hope the full meaning of this concept will become completely clear as we proceed.

The thinking up to this point followed rationally from the theories of Einstein which state, in part, that the geometric relationships of space and time control all physical processes.

My findings led me to conclude, further, that volcanic activity, atomic disruption (nuclear bomb detonations) and earthquakes could all be related to the grid structure, an atomic bomb being a space-time geometric device, and volcanos and earthquakes occurring on geometric points of the grid system, due to disturbances at these points.

A correlation of all these different phenomena led me to conclude that all major changes of physical state, anywhere in the world, are brought about by the harmonic interactions of those manifestations which we refer to as: light; gravity; mass; and electrical and magnetic forces.

The controlled manipulation of these resonant factors would, in my hypothesis, make it possible to move mass from one point to another in space-time (that is, to the eye of a theoretical observer, instantaneously); or to change the form of mass to a more, or to a less, tangible state. The contraction or expansion of time could also be controlled by the same manipulations of harmonic pulsations, or resonances, since time has a direct relationship with the speed of light. The "speed of light", as we call it, is not a constant, contrary to all the declarations of the scientific establishment. In theory, for this is yet to be demonstrably proven, there is no limit to the speed of light.

The concept of relativity has been with us for a long time; it reached its clearest expression at the hands of Albert Einstein. Now, a study of UFOs can show us some of the practical applications of the theory.

It is commonly believed that Einstein expressly declared that the speed of light was an absolute, and that nothing could exist beyond this speed. Biologist Ivan T. Sanderson states in a recent book[1] that shortly before his death, Einstein denied that he had ever made any such statement: "What he did say was that around 186,000 miles per second mass would become infinite — that your backside would become your frontside, and time (as we conceive it) would come to a stop — in other words, there is no reason, theoretical or otherwise, why that particular speed cannot be exceeded."

There is also a widely-held belief, possibly one that has been deliberately encouraged, that Einstein's work on his "unified field theory" had not reached its final stage when his death left this work to be completed, presumably, by still other brilliant minds yet to develop. But Sanderson asserts that Dr. B. Russell has privately stated that Einstein completed his theory before his death. There is evidence to suggest that Dr. Russell might be correct.

In 1945 secret experiments were carried out in the mid-Pacific by American scientists. A unified force field was created, and a ship of the US Navy, fully crewed, was made to disappear. Ivan Sanderson and others have brought forward further detailed evidence in their own books.

Over the past few months I have found evidence which strongly suggests that the unified field concept has been incorporated in the UFO grid system, in a harmonic sense. By doubling the C, or light values in the harmonic unified field equation based on the famous

---

[1]*Uninvited Visitors, 1968*

Einstein equation ($E = MC^2$), a gravitational effect becomes possible. But I will leave the full explanation of this to another place.

In *Harmonic 33* it was my endeavor to establish that the harmonic equivalents of light, gravity and mass and so on are built into the global UFO grid system as geometric, or angular, units, and are expressed as minute of arc values. Some of these values are as follows:

Speed of light harmonic: 1439
Anti-speed of light harmonic: 695
Harmonics associated with the earth's magnetic field: 2545.5 and 3930.
Earth mass harmonic: 1703

Logarithmic and radian values as well as trignometrical values were also found to be harmonically tuned to the geometric pattern of the system.

At that time my calculations were taken only to four-figure accuracy, chiefly because this enabled me to carry out my calculations more easily. My log tables only run to four figures in any case, and it would have taken many months of additional work to find all the correlations if I had had to work with, say, seven- or eight-figure harmonics.

But in recent months, thanks to the receipt of much new information coming to me, as I shall explain later, I did extend my harmonics to five figures. I then found a harmonic unified field equation.

The main lattice type pattern of the grid, I had found, consisted of areas of 30 minutes of arc oriented approximately north-south (006° true) and 30 minutes of arc approximately east-west (276° true). Subsequently, it has been my discovery that these areas are further divisible into sixteen smaller areas, measuring 7.5 by 7.5 minutes of arc.

Note:

For all practical purposes the orientation of the system has been stated as 006 degrees true, according to the accuracy of the plotted grid on my original maps. Recent computer work allows the possibility that the actual orientation could be: 5.90165 degrees.

The harmonic reciprocal of this value is 0.169444. This would create a direct harmonic relationship with mass, as discovered in later research.

Recent radar and verified visual sightings of UFOs, plus a large volume of evidence coming to light in the New Zealand area alone, have verified the existence of the grid in the pattern. I have described it beyond any shadow of reasonable doubt.

Furthermore, the creation of a complex network of manned radio stations within the structure of the UFO grid system proves not only that the system is there, but also that our technical experts have a knowledge of it, an understanding of it, and through it, direct communication with the UFOs themselves.

Incredible? In the framework of conventional thinking, and in the light of concepts which we have been conditioned to accept as the cornerstones of what we euphemistically call reality, my statements may indeed seem beyond belief. I do not intend to allow my incredible statements to remain hovering in mid-air, as it were.

In this book I shall be presenting a variety of evidence, facts and hypotheses. I hope to answer at least some of the important questions that must arise; and I hope to point the way in which other investigators, perhaps infinitely more competent than myself, may travel in the search for truth.

Meanwhile, I must at this stage offer some evidence to the doubtful that the grid really does exist.

I am satisfied that there is an overwhelming body of evidence that provides all the proof necessary, and that establishes that the harmonic radiations emanating from it are in turn causing certain physical effects at specific localities. Moreover, the activities of scientists in certain key areas indicate that there is feverish, government or otherwise backed, activity going on in connection with research into the basic structure and character of the grid.

My grid system, drawn up on a map of New Zealand, was completed in 1965. As verified sighting reports came to hand, I plotted on this map the precise positions of the sightings, and not to my surprise found that invariably the UFO positions fell with uncanny precision on the grid's lines of longitude or latitude — never in the intervening spaces.

In September 1967 reports came of four accurate fixes of UFO sightings a few minutes apart in the Hawke's Bay area (Map 1). Here were no isolated sightings, but four, all within a short period of time and in a relatively small area.

When I plotted the position of these four verified sightings on the grid map I found they fell exactly on four parallel lines of grid latitude. One was over the city of Napier, one to the north-west, one to the north-east, and one to the south-east. As I told an Auckland

MAP 1

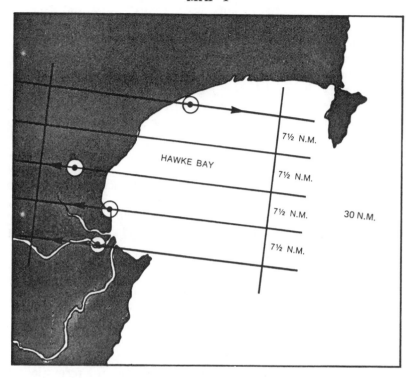

A portion of the grid superimposed on the Hawke's Bay area where UFO sightings were reported. The four sightings (ringed) coincide perfectly with the lines of the grid which had been drawn up three years previously on the basis of confirmed sightings throughout New Zealand.

reporter at that time: "The Hawke's Bay sightings provide the most impressive evidence to date in support of my grid theory."

The UFO, or UFOs, incidentally, were seen on 3 September 1967 by residents of Hastings, Pakowhai, Wairoa and the Esk Valley.

Did I somehow employ ESP when I constructed the grid map three years earlier - predicting, as it were, by means of lines on a map just where future sightings would be made?

We are told by the scientists that, theoretically, there should be a region of negative matter in the universe. This would constitute a negative reality that would consist of matter made up of anti-protons, anti-electrons and anti-neutrons etc. If any particle of matter from the negative reality were to drift into, and come in contact with, a particle in our positive reality there would be instantannihilation of both particles. A Cosmic atomic explosion. This sounds all very well and would create some sort of symetry in the Universe, but they never explain where the boundary is between the two regions. Space is not empty, as most people imagine. There are all sorts of particles drifting round in space which could light the fuse of such a system. If this were so I believe the Universe would be a very dangerous place to live in.

My fundamental theory concerning the formation of particles of matter and anti-matter is as follows:

First, matter and anti-matter are formed by the same wave motions in space. The waves travel through space in a spiralling motion, and alternately pass through positive and negative stages. Matter is formed through the positive stage, or pulse, and anti-matter during the negative pulse.

An electron is formed by three spiraling wave motions in space. These waves pass through each other at 90⁰. The point of intersection in space causes the manifestation of what we term electrons.

The electron thus formed carries out a spiraling motion.

Each spiral of 360⁰ forms a single pulse. The circular motion of an electron about the nucleus of an atom is therefore an illusion. The relative motion of the nucleus and electrons through space give the illusion of circular motion. The period during the formation of anti-matter is completely undetectable, since obviously all physical matter is manifesting at the same pulse rate, including any instruments or detectors used to probe atomic structures.

The period or frequency rate between each pulse of physical matter creates the measurement which we call time, as well as the speed of light, at the particular position in space of which we are aware, at any given moment. (See Diagram 1).

Note:

Recent research has indicated that the electron could possibly move through 371.27665 degrees. This being the radius multiplied by 3.24, which I call spiral Pi. The harmonic of 37127665 would be a reciprocal value of that derived from the unified equations. (26934) approx.

If the frequency rate of positive and negative pulses is either increased or decreased, then time and the speed of light vary in direct proportion.

10

DIAGRAM 1

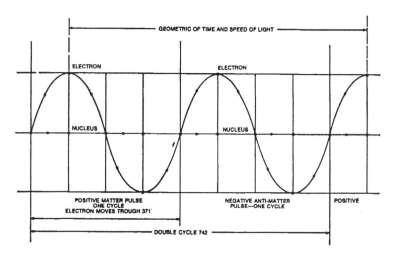

Formation of matter and anti-matter in alternate positive and negative cycles. The frequency rate between each pulse of physical matter determines the rate of flow of time, and the speed of light, at any particular point in space.

The path of the nucleus through space would also be a spiral, but for the sake of simplicity it has been shown as a straight line in this diagram.

This concept would explain time as a geometric, as Einstein theorised it to be.

A rough analogy of physical existence can be made by reference to a strip of motion picture film. Each frame or static picture on the film strip may be likened to a single pulse of physical existence. The division between one frame and the next represents a pulse of anti-matter. When viewed as a complete strip, each frame would be seen as a static picture and, in a sense, by comparing two of these static pictures — say one at either end of the strip — then the past and the future can be viewed simultaneously. However, when the film is fed through a projector, we obtain the illusion of motion and the passage of time. The divisions between the static pictures are not detected by our senses because of the frequency, or speed, of each projection on the movie screen. But by speeding up or slowing down the projector, we can alter the apparent time rate of the actions shown by the film.

To continue this analogy: our consciousness is the projector. The conscious "I am" part of our individuality passes from one pulse of physical matter to the next within the framework of the physical structure which we term our body, thus giving the illusion of constant reality, and the passing of time.

It is logical to assume that we have a twin stream of consciousness on the anti-matter side of the cycle, which in fact creates a mirror-image of our own individual personality. (This postulate has already been put forward by scientists.) The frequency of manifestation of both streams of consciousness, that is, the plus and the minus "I am" would position our awareness of the illusion of reality at a particular point in space and time. In other words, if the frequency of pulse manifestation is altered, even fractionally, our awareness of reality, in the physical sense, will shift from one spatial point to another. In fact, we would travel from one point in space to another without being aware that we had traversed distance in the physical sense. This would be space travel in the truest sense.

Let's look at another analogy: we can consider a simple spiral spring as representing the wave motion of an electron through space. Every second 360° spiral of the spring represents the path of the electron in physical matter, while the opposite applies to anti-matter.

The theory outlined above explains why light has been described as being caused by both a wave motion and a pulse. Both explanations are correct.

A pulse of light is manifested when the energy level of the atomic structure is altered by outside influences (theory of Max Planck). In the physical plane, the electron of the atomic structure appears to jump from its orbit. According to my belief, the electron *does not jump orbit*. But this is the illusion we obtain, since we are not equipped to perceive the path of the electron during the anti-matter cycle. What actually happens is that the radius of the spiralling motion is increased or decreased in order to absorb or release the energy imparted to, or removed from, the atomic structure. If the energy is imparted, then the electron must extend orbit in order to maintain balance in the system; and vice versa. Light, or any other radiant energy above or below light frequency, is therefore manifested by undetectable changes in the radius of the spiral motion of the electron during the anti-matter cycle.

If this hypothesis is correct, movement from one point in space to another point, regardless of apparent distance — in other words, true space travel — is completely feasible. By manipulating the frequency rate of the matter-anti-matter cycle, the time and speed of light can be varied in direct proportion to any desired value.

This, I believe, is the method of propulsion used by UFOs, and it is at the core of the theory upon which I have constructed the global UFO grid system.

This is the basis. I am aware that considerable refinement will have to be undertaken. But I believe that the completed concept will be quite simple. As our technocracy advances, you will find from a casual examination of many examples (printed circuits, for example) that equipment and apparatus become simplified rather than more complex.

And now, to round off this section of my mathematical theories, a word or two about the equation which I believe will set up a reaction in space-time.

$$\frac{1}{2545.56} = \left(2C + \sqrt{\frac{1}{2C}}\right)(2C)^2$$

The classical Einstein equation is contained in this, but the speed of light factor, C, has been doubled.
Furthermore:

$\left(C + \sqrt{\frac{1}{C}}\right)$ is equal to M, or the volume or mass of any

unit body in space.

By calculation of the diameter of any spherical mass and the rate of its rotation, the value of the speed of light, time and gravity accelerations should be capable of being determined. If the volume of irregular bodies can be determined, then by calculation of the equivalent spherical volume the other values can also be determined.

There is a corollary: the linear speed of light in any particular point in space determines the volume of the body precipitated at that point. Therefore, relative to earth values of light, a lesser speed will determine smaller masses, and larger speeds will determine larger masses — such as that of Jupiter, for example. The angular acceleration of light will remain constant.

Corollary: for any unit body, once precipitated, then the rate of rotation, or spin, and its volume will directly determine its rate of acceleration in space (i.e., its movement in space relative to other

13

bodies). This movement will maintain a constant balance of the angular acceleration of light at the point in space in which the body may be at any given instant.

If these theories seem to be complex and abstruse, bear with us. They are presented here as a means of establishing the foundation of other theories in support of which evidence will be offered.

2> MATHEMATICS OF THE WORLD GRID

MY INTEREST IN THE INCREASING UFO ACTIVITY in the New Zealand area led me to the discovery that the surface of the world was crisscrossed with an intricate network of energy grid lines. I began my research in 1965.

In a general way I was convinced that UFOs were actively engaged in a survey of the earth for some definite reason. I felt that their visits were not haphazard; they were not just on casual sightseeing tours. Quite a number of investigators around the world had come to the conclusion that the sightings were beginning to form a pattern. At this period, however, this pattern was so complex as to defy any definition, or solution. By the correlation of sightings small sections of track had been identified, and some saucers had been seen moving along these set paths. Some of these had hovered over certain spots at set intervals. But these bits and pieces of tracklines were so scattered around the surface of our planet that it was quite impossible to fit them together into any semblance of order.

I was certain that if an overall pattern could be found and plotted, it might be possible to establish the reason behind UFO activity. I considered that the pattern would be geometric if these things were intelligently controlled, and that if somehow I could find the key to one section then I might solve the rest by duplication and inference. I had sighted a number of unidentified objects in the sky over a period of several years, and by correlating two of these with other data, I was eventually able to construct a grid system which covered the whole world.

One of these sightings was in 1956. I was a DC3 co-pilot crewing a flight from Auckland to Paraparaumu. It was about 6pm, conditions were calm, and there was unlimited visibility. We were just south of Waverley at 7000 feet when I saw this object at an extremely high altitude in the east. I drew the captain's attention to it and together we watched it travel in a curved trajectory from east to west across our track until it disappeared in a flash of light at about 10,000 feet in the area of D'Urville Island. It appeared to travel across New Zealand in the vicinity, or slightly to the north, of Cook Strait, and it was so large that two streaks, similar to vapour trails, were seen to extend from either side of its pale green disc.

When about halfway across the Strait a small object detached itself from the parent body and dropped vertically until it disappeared. It looked almost as if the main disc was at such a high temperature that a globule had dripped from it. I thought about this later and decided that if that were so, the small object would also have a curved trajectory in the direction of the parent body. But this was not so; it detached and dropped vertically down at great speed. There could be only one answer from this action: the small body must have been controlled.

Calculations at a later date proved this UFO to have been between 1500-2000 feet in diameter. A report in a Nelson newspaper on the following day described an explosion at a high altitude to the north of the city. The shock-wave broke windows in some local glasshouses.

The other sighting occurred on 12 March 1965. This was the best and most interesting of them all, and from then my investigations were pressed on with all speed until they culminated in my present findings.

I had always expected to see UFOs in the sky, and that was where my attention was usually focussed. When I was flying I was alert and ready to analyse any object sighted from the aircraft. I never expected to find a saucer landing at my feet and so far this has never happened. This sighting however was different from all the others because I observed it lying under thirty feet of water.

I was scheduled to carry out a positioning flight from Whenuapai, Auckland's main airport at that time, to Kaitaia. Departure was at 11 am and as no passengers were involved and the weather was perfect, I decided to fly visually to Kaitaia along the west coast. An officer from the operations department was on board and this was a good opportunity to show him some of the rugged country to the north. (I must stress that air-traffic regulations were strictly observed during the flight.)

On leaving Whenuapai I climbed to clear the area and when approaching the southern end of the Kaipara Harbour, just north of Helensville, I dropped to a lower altitude to have a better look at anything in the flight path. The tide in the Harbour was well out, and the water over the mudflats and estuaries was quite shallow.

I suppose we were about a third of the way across the harbour when I spotted what I took to be a stranded grey-white whale. I veered slightly to port, to fly more directly over the object and to obtain a better look.

I suppose a pilot develops the habit of keeping his emotions to himself. As far as I can remember I gave no indication of surprise, and I said nothing as I looked down. My "whale" was definitely a metal fish. I could see it very clearly, and I quote from the notes I made later.

A. The object was perfectly streamlined and symmetrical in shape.
B. It had no external control surfaces or protrusions.
C. It appeared metallic, and there was a suggestion of a hatch on top, streamlined in shape. It was not quite halfway along the body as measured from the nose.
D. It was resting on the bottom of the estuary and headed towards the south, as suggested from the streamlined shape.
E. The shape was not that of a normal submarine and there was no superstructure.
F. I estimated the length as 100 feet, with a diameter of 15 feet at the widest part.
G. The object rested in no more than 30 feet of clear water. The bottom of the harbour was visible and the craft was sharply defined.

Inquiries made from the navy confirmed that it would not have been possible for a normal submarine to be in this particular position, due to the configuration of the harbour and coastline.

The chief engineer of the Ministry of Works, Auckland, checked this spot on the harbour with a depth-sounder in September 1969. He informed me afterwards that a hole had been detected in the harbour bed approximately one eight of a mile wide and over 100 feet deep, which I consider would indicate that some activity had been carried out in this position some five years previously. (See photocopy of the report — page 246).

I had a further key to the puzzle in April 1965. My wife saw an advertisement in the local paper seeking members for a UFO organisation called New Zealand Scientific and Space Research. I contacted this organisation and found that a vast amount of information had been very efficiently compiled. Material had been collected from twenty-five different countries over a period of twelve years. I was invited to study the information at leisure.

Amongst this mass of data I discovered the reports of a UFO that had been seen from several different localities in both islands of New Zealand on 26 March 1965. People in Napier, New Plymouth,

Palmerston North, Wanganui, Feilding and Otaki Forks in the North Island; Nelson Coast Road, Blenheim and Westport (Cape Foulwind) in the South Island, had all reported sightings. It was decided that I try to plot the track of this UFO. From the considerable amount of information available I found that the maximum variation in the times of sightings from all areas was 15 minutes. Most reports gave the time as 9:45 pm. This proved that the object must have been very large and at high altitude during the greater part of its trajectory.

Here is a brief description of each sighting taken from the original reports:

1. *New Plymouth*
   About 9:40 pm Mr. A. Nixon went outside his home to put out the milkbottles. He had a clear view over the sea to the north. A glow first appeared on the horizon and as he looked at it he saw a light that was approaching slowly. Then it came nearer at tremendous speed, lighting up the clouds in a red glow as it passed through them. As it passed overhead in a clear patch of sky, the object was sharply defined. It was bright white in colour, and was ball-shaped with a silvery edge. After passing overhead the rear emitted a red glow. It sped to the west of Mt Egmont and disappeared. According to Mr. Nixon "his hair stood on end".

2. *Napier*
   A bright object was seen by a resident to curve through the sky at 9:45 pm. It was visible in the north-west and changed colour from white to a vivid green, then to a vivid red before it disappeared behind some trees.

3. *Wanganui*
   Between 9:30 pm and 10:00 pm Mr. M. F. C. Grotenhuis was looking out of a window when he saw a flash similar to lightning. Then he observed a fireball which appeared to fall towards the south. It began as a bright white light, changed to greenish blue, then to a sizzling red before it disappeared like a shooting star. The sky was clear at the time.

4. *Feilding*
   While cycling up a hill Miss Ralda Campbell heard a swishing sound. It was followed by a blinding blue- white light, similar to a flash of sheet lightning. The whole area was lit by this, then she saw a huge orange ball that "looked like a dinner-plate". The ball seemed to emanate from the left edge of the blue-white light. After a few seconds it exploded and three orange balls, like tennis

balls and very dense, appeared at the right-hand edge and disappeared.

Miss Campbell said the three smaller balls seemed to emerge from the larger ball when it vanished. The apparent track was from north-east to south-west.

5. *Palmerston North*

A woman witness saw an object in the sky at about 9:30 pm. It was a vivid green with a long comet-like tail issuing from a deep orange centre. It descended and disappeared from view behind a nearby building.

6. *Otaki Forks*

This is a position in the tararua mountain range. While tramping in the area, five Venturer Scouts saw an enormous bluish-white ball of light in the sky at 9:45 pm. This was surrounded by what looked like sheet lightning. The sighting was brief; the ball seemed to be stationary and apparently far away to the west, and about half the size of a full moon. One of the scouts, Mr Parnell, said that later the size of the object worked out trigonometrically by the group and the diameter arrived at was about 2000 feet.

7. *Nelson*

Over the mudflats of Tasman Bay, a resident saw a very bright flash in the sky. Immediately afterwards, three bright green balls descended at a 45° angle. This was 9:45 pm (a flying pawnshop?).

8. *Nelson Coast Road*

At 9:45 pm a Nelson resident driving towards Wakapuaka saw a big white ball with a bluish tail light up the place like day. It then burst in a shower of bright particles.

9. *Westport*

Mr. L.H. Keay, a farmer, saw a bright object in the sky. It was far brighter than the moon, and lit up the sky with a bright white light that changed to green, and then to red. It apparently fell eastwards. The time was "somewhere around 10 o'clock".

10. *Blenheim*

Mr. and Mrs. Bell and their daughter Linda, Margaret White, and many other people, saw a great green ball of light that seemed to explode over their heads. A small brightly-coloured ball broke away and whizzed off to the east. It was 9:45 pm. Mrs. M. Christensen observed a green ball, about the size of a cricket ball. It descended steadily from the sky, and appeared to be very close and dull in colour. Time 10:15 pm.

There was nothing of any great significance or originality in these accounts, and they followed the pattern of many other sightings. However from the mass of detail supplied by so many different people over so wide an area, it was possible to plot the track of the object with reasonable accuracy. I started work on a Mercator's plotting chart, and after several hours of checking one report against the other and calculating possible elevations and trajectories, I felt I had refined the plot sufficiently to draw in the final track of the object, or objects. The result is shown on Map 2.

The track began about seventy nautical miles north of New Plymouth, passed just to the west of Mt. Egmont, and finished at D'Urville Island. When first seen the altitude would have been about 30,000 feet curving down on a flight path to somewhere around 10,000 feet when it disappeared.

Some time after those sightings on 26 March 1965 I had another look at the plot I had made. I could find no flaws in my thinking, but I needed more information. As I was to discover many times later, the clues were quite obvious, but I was then not sufficiently expert in realising their significance. In point of fact this first trackline was to be the starting point of a whole string of discoveries of which I have yet to find an end.

I pored over that plot for a long time before it suddenly occurred to me that the track appeared in line with the position where I had sighted the unidentified submarine object, or USO, on 12 March 1965. On extending the line back I found it was in line with the sightings of 26 March. I was positive there had to be a connection — but to prove it was a different matter.

I checked my report files again and found that on 2 March some fishermen just north of the coast at New Plymouth had seen a large object plunge into the sea and disappear. They thought it was an aircraft and reported the incident to the appropriate authorities, but no aircraft or personnel were missing. I checked this position on the map and found that it also fitted the established trackline. Was this connected with the USO of 12 March, and could the two sightings be of the same object, sighted twice in ten days? Could it be working slowly up this track carrying out some project on the sea bed? I tucked this thought away for future reference and carried on with the search.

It was some days later that I remembered the UFO I had seen in 1956. This object was similar and, most significant of all, both objects had apparently travelled at 90^0 to each other, and finished

MAP 2

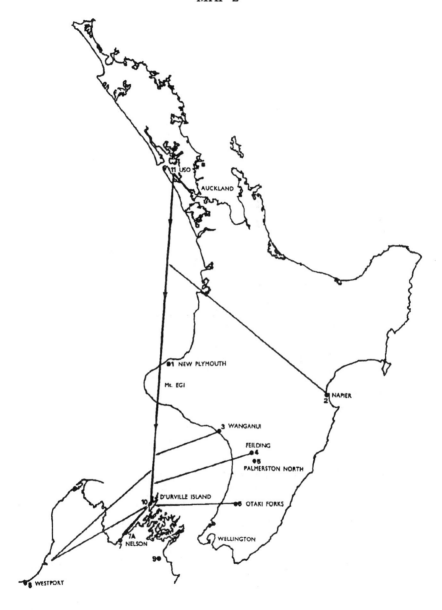

Showing path of UFO from Kaipara Harbour to D'Urville Island.

in the same grand all illuminating flash in the area of D'Urville Island.

If these objects were *not* controlled, how could anyone explain such coincidences? No two meteors or other natural phenomena could coincidentally carry out similar manoeuvres, travel at 90⁰ to each other, and both decide to end their existence at the same point in space, within nine years of each other. Also, in both cases, objects had been seen to emerge from the parent bodies. Was this irrefutable evidence that they were intelligently controlled vehicles.

I plotted the track of the 1956 UFO on the map at 90^0 to the north-south line. I realised that I had no definite proof that they were at exactly 90^0 to each other or that the 1956 track was not a few miles north or south of this position — still, I had to start from somewhere, and I would assume this to be correct unless and until other evidence proved me wrong.

Two track lines at 90^0 meant little on their own. If I found several at 90^0, I might have something — a grid perhaps? These two lines hinted at this, and I believed that if I could solve the system of measurement, then I had two readymade baselines to work from.

Once again I went to the UFO files and found that a Frenchman by the name of Aime' Michel had been studying UFOs for a number of years and had found small sections of tracklines in various areas of Europe. Saucers had been seen hovering at various points along these tracklines, and Mr. Michel had observed that the average distance between these points was 54.43 kilometres. By itself this was only a small grain of information but, like a starting gun, it set me off again.

Using the Kaipara Harbour as a starting point, I marked off the 54.43 kilometre intervals along the trackline I had found. I was disappointed when I was unsuccessful in obtaining an even distribution of positions to the D'Urville Island disappearing point. I checked and re-checked, but nothing worked out. I slept on the problem, and at some time during the night inspiration turned up the wick; once more the light grew bright.

I remembered that a great number of sightings had occurred around the Blenheim area. Even before the advent of ordinary aircraft in New Zealand, this area had been visited by UFOs. I had read about them in old copies of the local papers, and many recent sightings suggested again that this area had something special about it.

So I dragged out my map and extended the trackline until it cut a 90° coordinate from the town of Blenheim. The distance from this point to the Kaipara position I found to be exactly 300 nautical miles. So far so good. I stepped off the 54.43 kilometre intervals — and swore. *Still* the thing didn't fit! Frustration was always my companion in this business, and we had many, many arguments! Sometimes it was a protracted battle of wits...a fiddle with my computer and I was off again.

The distance of 54.43 kilometres found by Michel was only an average estimate. I found that 55.5955 kilometres was equal to 30 nautical miles, and this divides exactly into 300 nautical miles, ten times. Was this the system of measurement used by the UFOs? There was no proof of course, but it seemed a reasonable assumption. A minute of arc is a measurement which could apply to the whole universe. It just so happens that a minute of arc, from the earth's centre subtends, at the surface, what we call a nautical mile. So be it.........

Since I made that statement in my first book I have been attacked repeatedly by university personnel and others in the academic field. They have maintained that degrees and minutes of arc are arbitrary values set up by the ancient mathematicians and that therefore my calculations are meaningless. I believe the evidence shown in this book will now convince them that my original assumptions were correct. The angular values of 360° and 21,600 minutes of arc which constitute a complete circle have direct geometric associations with the speed of light.

The fifth interval of 30 nautical miles from the Kaipara position coincided with the position off the coast of New Plymouth where the mysterious object had plunged into the sea. The plotted points of disappearance of the two large UFOs at D'Urville Island did not quite match up with the ninth interval, but this did not worry me unduly as I expected that a small percentage of error must be expected in my original plot. I readjusted this position to the ninth interval, and carried on the search to see how many other sightings I could fit into this pattern.

The results exceeded my expectations. I found that by using units of 30 minutes of arc latitude north-south, and 30 minutes of arc longitude east-west, on my Mercator's map, a grid pattern was formed into which a great number of UFO reports could be fitted. I eventually had a map with sixteen stationary and seventeen moving UFOs plotted on grid intersections and tracklines.

MAP 3

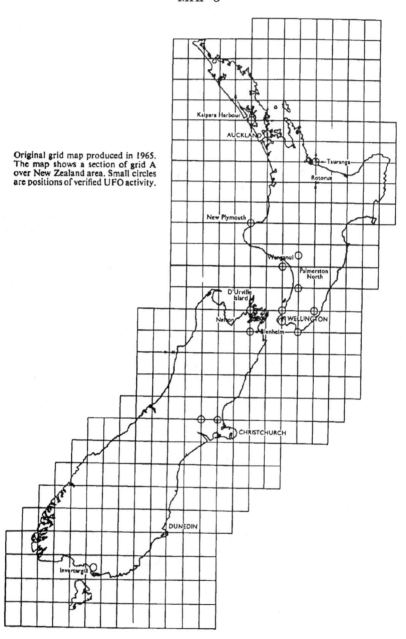

Original grid map produced in 1965. The map shows a section of grid A over New Zealand area. Small circles are positions of verified UFO activity.

Having satisfied myself that my reasoning and plotting were not false, I considered that I had good proof that New Zealand, possibly other countries, and probably the whole world, were being systematically covered by some type of grid system (see grid map 3).

I subsequently discovered that the grid lattice could be further divided. It is now evident that the grid lines in the main system are spaced at intervals of 7.5 minutes of arcnorth-south, and east-west. The importance of this will prove itself when compared with the rest of the calculation in this book. There are 21,600 minutes of arc in a circle, and when this is divided by 7.5 we get a value of 2880. The grid lattice therefore is tuned harmonically to twice the speed of light(288), as will be shown in other sections.

It appeared that I had found a section of a geometric grid pattern in the New Zealand area. I now had to form some theory of construction for the whole world. I could then possibly fit the New Zealand section into it.

By drawing a series of patterns on a small plastic ball I finally found a system which could be used as a starting point for a global investigation. (The basic pattern is shown in diagram 2.)

I was sure I was on the right track, but I now had to superimpose this pattern on the world globe. It was essential that I find a point position somewhere on the earth upon which to orientate the geometrical pattern. I finally came upon an item of news that gave me a very important clue on how to proceed.

On 29 August 1964 the American survey ship *Eltanin* was carrying out a sweep of the sea-bed off the coast of South America. A series of submarine photographs was being taken of the area by means of a camera attached to a long cable. A surprise was in store when these photographs were developed. On one of the points, in marvellous detail, was an aerial-type object sticking up from an otherwise featureless sea-bed.

The object appeared to be metallic and perfectly symmetrical in construction. The array consisted of six main crossbars with small knob-like ends and a small crossbar at the top. Each cross looked to be set at angles of 15° to the others, and the whole system stood about 2 feet in height. The position where this object was found was given as latitude 59°08' south, longitude 105° west.

As this bit of ironmongery was situated at a depth 13,500 feet below the surface, I was certain that no human engineers had placed it there.

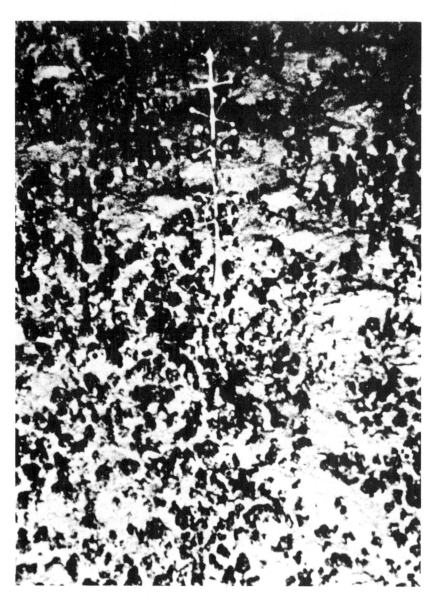

Aerial type object photographed by the survey ship "Eltanin"

DIAGRAM 2

Showing relationship of grid structure to the geographic poles. Each of the two grids has a similar pattern, the interaction of which sets up a third resultant grid. The poles of the three grids are positioned at three different latitudes and longitudes.

C, D, E, F = Corner aerial positions of grid polar square. Similar to aerial discovered by the survey ship *Eltanin*

J–K = Polar axis

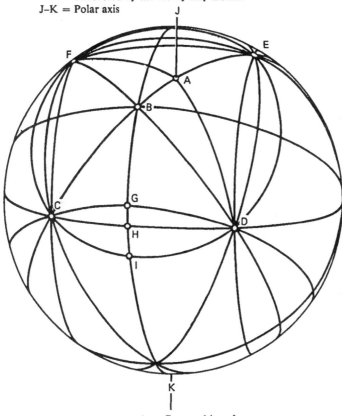

A = Geographic pole
B = Grid pole
Distance C–G–D = 3600 minutes of arc
Distance C–H–D = 3418.5 minutes of arc
Distance C–I–D = 3643.2 minutes of arc

(3600 − 3418.5 = 181.5) (181.5 × 4 = 726) ($\sqrt{726}$ = 26944)

27

Scientists may be able to descend to those depths in specially constructed bathyspheres, but I don't think they could work as deeply as that on a precision engineering problem. In view of my earlier sightings in the Kaipara Harbour, I was willing to accept that the aerial-type object had been placed there by a unidentified submarine object, or USO.

Since this photo was taken there has been a determined attempt by the scientific world to label this object as nothing more that a plant of some sort. A journalist friend and I managed to visit the *Eltanin* during one of its few visits to New Zealand and when we discussed this object with some of the scientists on board, the comment was that it was classed as an artefact. This was before the great hush-up but, regardless of that, I believe that the mathematical proofs will show without doubt that the object is artificial, and most probably an aerial of some sort.

The form of this aerial-like structure also fitted in with the general pattern of the grid as I had envisaged it on the plastic ball. The six main crossbars denoted the radiating points of six or twelve great circles which form the main structure of the grid.

I centred the grid on the position of the object found by the *Eltanin*, and the 180⁰ reciprocal of this is in Russian Siberia, lining the whole thing up with the section I had found in New Zealand. I found the system to be lined up very closely with the magnetic field of the earth. The equator of the grid followed very closely the line of zero dip around the world. (That is, the positions on the earth's surface where a magnetic compass needle has only a horizontal and no vertical component.)

In my earlier works I discussed the methods I used to line up the system and calculate the first estimates of the grid pole positions, and the major focal points of the grid similar to the *Eltanin* "aerial" placement.

The reciprocal position of the *Eltanin* "aerial" is at latitude 59⁰08' north, longitude 75⁰ east, in Siberia. I calculated the length of the diagonal of what I call, for simplicity, the "polar grid square" and found it to be 5091.168825 minutes of the arc long. I plotted a track from the Siberian position through the north geographic pole and measured off this distance to locate another corner "aerial" of the polar square. (Square is not technically the right word to use as the four sides are formed by sections of small circles which are in different planes to each other. When the "polar square" areas are transferred from the surface of the earth sphere on to a flat plane such as a map, then a perfect square is formed with sides 3600 minutes long and diagonals of 5091.168825 minutes of arc.)

In my first two books I stated, in error, that the sides of the "polar squares" were formed by sections of GREAT circles 3600 minutes of arc long, instead of SMALL circles. The great circle distance between these points is in fact 3,418.5 minutes of arc, which is very confusing to any investigator attempting to reconstruct the grid. I apologise to my readers for this error, which was caused by my lack of access to calculators during my earlier research. In the grid pattern there are actually two small circle segments, and one great-circle segment connecting each of these points which form the polar squares. Each of the segments has a different path over the earth and some tricky calculating is necessary to ascertain the true length. Although I used the wrong term in my earlier publications, the actual calculations derived from the grid system are not altered in any way, and still stand the test of time. Over the last few years I have slightly refined the values I demonstrated previously, derived from a mixture of practical and theoretical studies. I have now set up what I see as a completely theoretical system, discovered by working entirely by calculator. Time will prove how close my calculations are. I have no doubt that I, and others, will continue further to perfect the system as more facts come to light.

Once I had established this first baseline I found it quite easy to construct the main skeleton of the grid over the whole surface of the earth.

As my work progressed I found that there were in fact two similar grids, interlocked with each other. The poles of the grids were spaced at different distances from the north geometric pole, and this arrangement set up a series of geometric harmonics which were directly related to the speed of light, mass, and gravity. The interaction of the two grids created a harmonic resonance which in turn, formed a third resultant grid.

The theoretical position for the three grid poles in the northern hemisphere are a follows:

Grid pole "A" = Latitude 72.4266°/longitude 90° west 1054.4 minutes of arc from the North Pole.

Grid pole "B" = Latitude 78.4266°/longitude 105° west 694.4 minutes of arc from the North Pole.

Resultant grid

       pole "C" = Latitude 75.6°/longitude 97.5° west 864 minutes
                of arc from the North Pole.

Reciprocal positions will give similar values for the southern hemisphere.

DIAGRAM 3

Showing the relationship of a grid polar square to the geographic pole. Each grid has a similar pattern.
The pole of each grid is set at a different latitude and longitude.

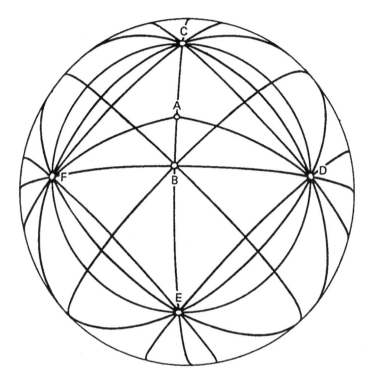

A = Geographic pole
B = Grid pole

$\left.\begin{matrix} C \\ D \\ E \\ F \end{matrix}\right|$ = Corner aerial positions of grid polar square

$\left.\begin{matrix} B–C \\ B–D \\ B–E \\ B–F \end{matrix}\right|$ = 2545.584412 minutes of arc

A–B   Grid "A" = 1054.4 minutes of arc
A–B   Grid "B" = 694.4 minutes of arc
A–B   Grid "C" = 864 minutes of arc (resultant grid)

DIAGRAM 4

Showing the relationship of grid polar squares A, B, and C. The polar squares are oriented in reciprocal positions around both the north and south geographic poles.

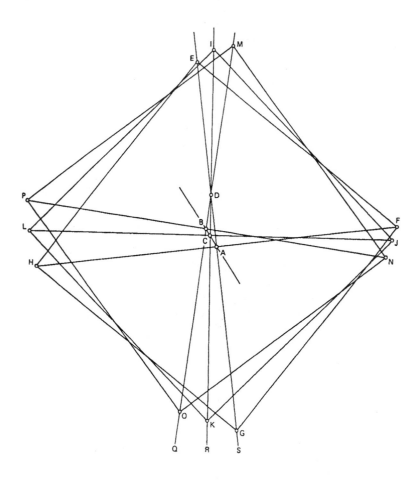

A: Grid pole "A": 1054.4 minutes of arc from geographic pole
B: Grid pole "B": 694.4 minutes of arc from geographic pole
C: Grid pole "C": 864 minutes of arc from geographic pole

D: North geographic pole
E, F, G, H: Polar square "A"
I, J, K, L: Polar square "C"
M, N, O, P: Polar square "B"

Q: Longitude 105° 00' west
R: Longitude 97.5° west
S: Longitude 90° west

32

3> THE UNIFIED EQUATIONS

PACE TRAVEL, THANKS TO THE AMERICAN AND Russian rocket programmes, is a reality. By using great masses of hardware, miles of wiring and plumbing, Newton's law of motion and some not inconsiderable beginner's luck, the first man on the moon has stepped out of the pages of Jules Verne into history. Probes have been sent out to study Venus and Mars at close quarters. Considering the brief time in which man has taken serious notice of ways to bridge the gap between earth and sky, these are remarkable achievements.

During the 1939-45 war German scientists were carrying out experiments in rocketry; their experiences gained in directing doodlebugs towards London made them the leaders in this field; Werner von Braun and other German experts subsequently passed on their knowledge and experience to others on both sides of the Iron Curtain. Those Model T's of rocketry, the V-2s, have given rise to the sophisticated Apollo and Vostok power units which thrust comparatively tiny pay-loads into the void of space.

They work. And they have enabled man to venture far away from his own planet.

Yet, before the first space vehicle built on this planet thrust its snout beyond the ultimate atom of air in the envelope which clings as a life-sustaining wrapper about our planet, the method was already out of date. It may have been out of date centuries ago. As a means of propulsion rockets are obsolete — as obsolete as a propulsion method as the sling-shot is out of date as a weapon. In both cases brute force is the criterion; in both cases the law of diminishing returns rules the game. As the power of the prime mover is increased, the size and cost of the system becomes less and less practicable, and the pay-load must eventually fail to give sufficient returns in relation to the effort expended in moving it through space.

A rocket allowed mankind to take the first essential step; but it is obvious, if we stop to think about it, that rocket propulsion cannot be the answer to exploration of the star systems that surround our galaxy.

Even if we could eventually achieve speeds approaching that of light itself, we could never hope to venture far from the solar system in one lifetime. The distances are vast; rockets the size of small cities would be necessary, so that several generations could live out their lives during the journey through space in order that there would be colonists for the far planet destinations.

It might be possible to do this. It would not be very practicable. As a theme for science fiction writers it has been a bountiful source of stories.

The first glimmerings of how true space travel might be achieved came to me when I uncovered the first clues that led me to the UFO grid which laces about our globe. I published my findings and hoped that someone with greater scientific knowledge than I possess would carry on from that point — and finally discover every secret locked into the system.

I was aware that my calculations were not precisely accurate — in the strict mathematical sense — but I could see that the system was based on space-time geometrics, and at least there was the best possible support for this none less than the theories of Einstein.

Somewhere, I knew, the system contained a clue to the truth of the unified field which, he has postulated, permeates all of existence. I didn't know at the time that this clue had already been found by scientists who were well ahead of me in the play. I know now that they must have understood something of the grid system years ago. They knew that Einstein's ideas about the unified field were correct. What's more, for many years they have been carrying out full-scale research into the practical applications of the mathematical concept contained in that theory.

I believe, and with good reason, that the full facts have been known to at least some scientists for many years.

The very fact that man-made scientific equipment has been built into the UFO grid system, which I put forward as a theory years ago, is evidence that at least some people had prior knowledge of the grid and its workings. It must have taken them years to build up the network of stations which now exists. But as far as they or their masters are concerned, it is not *our* right to know.

The only way to traverse the vast distances of space is to possess the means of manipulating, or altering, the very structure of space itself; altering the space-time geometric matrix, which to us provides the illusion of form and distance. The method of achieving this lies in the alteration of frequencies controlling the matter-antimatter cycles which govern our awareness or perception of position in the space-time structure. Time itself is a geometric, just as

Einstein postulated; if time can be altered, then the whole universe is waiting for us to come and explore its nooks and crannies.

In the blink of an eye we could cross colossal distances; for distance is an illusion. The only thing keeping places apart in space is time. If it were possible to move from one position to another in space, in an infinitely small amount of time, or "zero time", then both the positions would coexist, according to our awareness. By speeding up the geometric of time we will be able to bring distant places within close proximity. This is the secret of the UFOs — they travel by means of altering the spatial dimensions around them and repositioning in space-time..

When I had completed my first book I was not aware of just how close I had come to this truth. The answer was literally staring at me from the pages of my own work for nearly three years, before a visit from a stranger brought it into my grasp.

A year after the book was published I had a telephone call from a man who had just arrived in New Zealand from England. He explained that he was a textile salesman and would be here for only a few days on business. He said he had heard of my research, and was most insistent that he should see me. He said that he had very little knowledge of UFOs, but that he would like to talk to me about my theories. Could he come out to my home for a visit?

On that particular evening I was busy with some affairs of my own; I wasn't anxious to entertain a stranger, but in the end I agreed to see him.

He arrived in a rented car, and at once began questioning me about my activities and my research. It was soon obvious that he knew a great deal more about the subject of UFOs than he was prepared to admit; and he was quite demanding about getting his questions answered. He had an air of nervous tension about him as he checked through pages of my calculations; then he wanted to know where I kept all of my data, and if there were many people who knew about my studies.

I make no secret of whatever findings I turn up, and I showed him everything he asked to see. Finally he insisted that there was something I hadn't shown him — an equation which knitted all my calculations together. In some surprise I told him I knew of no such equation; his expression was eloquent of disbelief.

As this discussion proceeded I informed him that there were probably others who thought as he did — that I had some such equation up my sleeve, because I was being watched and on several occasions my car had been followed. I added that since he had come to my home he would most likely have unwanted company on his way back into the city. Whoever it was that was keeping an eye on me, I told him, would probably believe him to be a contact man from abroad and would therefore be interested in his movements.

I must admit that I told him this intriguing little tale to see what his reaction might be. I was fascinated to see his apparent nervousness become increased, and in some agitation he decided it was time to leave. His departure was hurried; I have neither seen him nor heard of him since.

For the next two or three days I found myself going over and over his questions. The more I thought about it, the more convinced I became that the stranger had known far more about my calculations than I did myself. Was there something there which he could see — but which I had missed? If there was an equation buried somewhere in my figuring, then I would have to find it.

Reworking the math, I finally decided to concentrate specifically on three harmonic values which appeared to have a close relationship with one another. Previously, I had shown this connection, and had truthfully pointed out that I did not know why the relationship was there at all. These were the harmonic values that now fully occupied my attention:

1703 — This is the four-figure harmonic of 170,300,000,000, which is the expression in cubic minutes of arc of the mass or volume of the planet Earth and its surrounding atmosphere.

1439 — A four-figure harmonic of 143,900 minutes of arc per grid second, representing the speed of light in grid values.

2640 — This figure, expressed in minutes of arc values, is built into the polar portion of the grid structure as a geometric co-ordinate.

Now I found that when I matched these values harmonically the results were as follows. Zeros to the right-hand side can be ignored in this form of harmonic calculation:

$$
\begin{array}{r}
1703 \\
-264 \\
\hline
1439
\end{array}
$$

In other words the difference between the harmonic of mass and the harmonic of light is the harmonic of 264(or 2640). It was now apparent that if any calculations were more accurately worked out it should be possible to find out just what the 2640 figure referred to.

After several hours of work the following was what looked up at me from my paper:

$$17025 \text{ earth mass harmonic}$$
$$\underline{-2636} \text{ unknown harmonic}$$
$$\underline{14389}$$

Checking through the five-figure mathematical tables I found to my surprise that 2.6363 is the square root of 6.95 (from the 1-10 square root tables). In harmonic calculations of this kind decimal points as well as zeros to the right of a figure can be ignored; so it could be said that the square root of 695 was 2636. Now I could perceive the first steps necessary to solving the elusive equation. I had long established that 695 is the harmonic reciprocal of the speed of light, or 1/1439. The calculations were now sufficiently accurate for algebraic values to be substituted — although obviously a computer would be necessary to solve the true values to extreme accuracy.

So—

17025(earth mass)
-2636(square root of speed of light reciprocal)
14389(speed of light)

If C = the speed of light, and
M = mass
Then

$$\left(C + \sqrt{\frac{1}{C}} \right) = M$$

Now at last I had the first part of a unified field equation in harmonic values. To take the next step I first had to go back to Einsteinian theory, particularly the famous equation, $E=MC^2$, where E is energy, M is mass and C the speed of light.

Einstein declared that physical matter was nothing more than a concentrated field of force. What we term physical substance is in reality an intangible concentration of wave forms. Different combinations and structural patterns of waves unite to form the myriads of chemicals and elements which in turn react with one another to form physical substances. Different wave forms of matter appear to us to be solid because we are constituted of similar wave forms which resonate within a clearly defined range of frequencies — and which control the physical processes of our limited world.

Einstein believed that M, the value for mass in the equation, could eventually be removed, and a value substituted that would express the physical in the form of pure energy. In other words, by substituting for M, a unified field equation should result which would express in mathematical terms the whole of existence — this universe, and everything within it. As I have already said, it seems that before his death Einstein did indeed produce this equation. What the mathematical terms were which he used, I do not know; but I couldn't help wondering what results I might get if I were to tackle the problem from the point of harmonic math. If an equation could be found which had a harmonic affinity with all substance, one which showed a resonance factor tuned to matter itself, then the problem, perhaps, would be solved.

Einstein maintained that the M in his equation could be replaced by a term denoting wave form. I had now found a substitute for M in terms of wave form of light. So the obvious step, to me, was to replace Einstein's M with the values of C, found from the UFO grid. These are the results I obtained:

Einstein: $E = MC^2$

UFO grid: $M = \left(C + \sqrt{\dfrac{1}{C}} \right)$

Therefore: $E = \left(C + \sqrt{\dfrac{1}{C}} \right) C^2$

I now had before me a harmonic unified field equation expressed in terms of light - or pure electromagnetic wave form — the key to the universe, the whole existence; to the seen and the unseen, to form, solids, liquids, gases, the stars and the blackness of space itself, all consisting of visible and invisible waves of light. All of creation is light; that was the answer that had been right within my grasp for four years.

Now it was necessary to check the validity of the equation; to accomplish this I needed a computer and the help of an expert in pure mathematics.

A young man who had attended one of my lectures said he was willing to put a small computer at my service and a friend of his, an excellent mathematician who had a larger computer was willing to programme it harmonically to give me assistance should I need it. I was deeply appreciative of both offers and the subsequent calculations proved the initial equation to be valid. Throughout all my research I have always been at the limits of my own knowledge, for ever frustrated by my slow rate of progress. I could always see much further ahead than my technical ability would allow me to travel.

In my earlier publications I had stated that I believed that the value of 2545.58, the geometric distance in minutes of arc, from the grid poles to the main corner aerial positions, in the grid polar squares, was a harmonic of gravity acceleration. I am now aware that this assumption was incorrect and that the true value for the harmonic of gravity acceleration is derived from the speed of light.

The diagonal of the "polar square" of 5091.168825 units can be broken down into a series of values:

$$5091.168824 \div 2 = 2545.584412$$
$$2545.584412^2 = 6480000$$

The number 648 is a harmonic factor of great importance, as will be demonstrated in other sections of this book. The many other harmonic factors centred around the "polar square" corner aerial positions, form a series of complex mathematical associations and this can be left for those who wish to carry out their own research.

The reciprocal of 2545.58, rounded off to four-figure accuracy, was given as a harmonic of 3930, (Now corrected to 3928371). When I made my initial discovery of the unified equations, the harmonic of 3930 was thought to be that of anti-gravity. It is now known that this value is related to the earth's magnetic field. Although I labelled them wrongly the actual values have stood the test of time and still fit into the equations as originally demonstrated.

The harmonic equations are those from which an atomic bomb is developed. By setting up derivatives of the equation in geometric form, the relative motions of the wave forms inherent in matter are zeroed, and convert from material substance back into pure energy.

By reversing the process, physical substance in any desired shape or form could be produced from pure energy.

While practical applications of the latter possibility may still be far in the future, we are nevertheless at least capable, now, of destroying matter. As I have stated elsewhere — scientists can make a bang from a bomb, but as yet they are still unable to get the bang back into the bottle.

Although I was much happier with progress when I arrived at this point in my calculations, there were still some important answers missing. As far as they went, the equations explained the workings of a nuclear explosive device, but they still had not yielded the secrets of UFO propulsion. The UFO grid was undoubtedly constructed on the basis of the equation, yet a UFO does not disintegrate when it moves within the resonating fields of the system. There had to be an extension of the equation, which so far I had missed, that would produce the necessary harmonics for movement in space-time. But I felt close to the solution, and I was determined to find it.

It has often been my experience that when a stalemate is reached it is best to throw aside one's work for a time and take a rest. For the next few weeks I deliberately forgot everything even remotely connected with UFOs. But one evening, unheralded and unexpected, a thought flashed into my mind. Why only deal with single values of C?

The key was turned and a sequence of doors swung open, one after another, to reveal secrets of space and time.

In the polar area of the UFO grid the geometric valuesof some of the co-ordinates appear to be doubled up.

The diagrams of the "polar squares," as I have termed them, incorporate twice the value of 2545.56.

In the resultant grid polar square the speed of light reciprocal harmonic of 695 is incorporated in a harmonic of 2695. These coordinates are the same from corner aerial positions to the geographic poles. It appears that the factor 2 preceding the 695 serves to harmonically double the reciprocal of the speed of light.

I reasoned that a way to check this idea was to increase the values of C in my equation, and observe the changing harmnonic of E. In a few hours in pursuit of this line of thought, I was able to say: "I have found something extremely interesting".

It was apparent that one only had to double the value of C. Once I had done this, it was possible to produce two different equations, through the use of the tables relating to the square root portion of the equation. The results differed according to whether square roots 1-10 or 10-100 were employed. In equation No.1, I found that the resulting harmonic was: 3926991712050.

This was the value calculated by the computer after we had fed the equation in, and gradually corrected from one side of the equation to the other. I was only too well aware that my calculations were only of "near-enough" accuracy up to this point, and had been sufficient only to form a general basis for the theories I had developed. Four-figure accuracy in fact is just not nearly good enough, as any pure scientist will be quick to agree. By feeding in the harmonics on either side of the equation and gradually correcting, the 12-digit value was finally arrived at.

This harmonic is not yet completely accurate; larger computers will be necessary to carry on the correction to the ultimate of precision. Nevertheless, the result is now "good enough" as far as I am concerned, and it may at least start off a scientist of an independent nature to carry out further investigations of his own.

I had shown previously that the four figure harmonic of 3930(rounded off to four figures) was the close reciprocal of 2545.58. In a practical sense the values were near enough to demonstrate what I was trying to establish. Therefore I considered that the harmonic of 392699171205, derived by doubling the C component of the equation, was also indicating a reciprocal of the 2545.58 value found in the grid polar square areas. With slight corrections the equation could nowbe expressed thus:

$$\frac{1}{2545.56} = \left(2C + \sqrt{\frac{1}{2C}}\right)(2C)^2$$

The second equation is derived by using the square root of the 10-100 tables. This equation is as follows:

$$\text{Double harmonic of the speed of light reciprocal} = \sqrt{\left(2C + \sqrt{\frac{1}{2C}}\right)(2C)^2}$$

The nearest we have brought this to accuracy, using a small desk computer, is as follows:

$$2695 = \sqrt{\left(2C + \sqrt{\frac{1}{2C}}\right)(2C)^2}$$

$$= \sqrt{\left(28777620 + \sqrt{\frac{1}{28777620}}\right)28777620^2}$$

$$= \sqrt{\left(28777620 + \sqrt{34749200}\right)82815141}$$

$$= \sqrt{\left(28777620 + 58948452\right)82815141}$$

$$= \sqrt{\left(87726072\right)82815141}$$

$$= \sqrt{72650470}$$

$$= 26953$$

The speed of light harmonic accurate to four figures is equal to 1439, as I have said elsewhere. The value used in this calculation according to the more accurate computer check equals 1438881. As I have already stated, the true value will only be derived by the use of highly sophisticated computers.

Another possible lead for mathematician readers is the fact that the natural tangent of 36^0 is 72654. The square of 26953 from the equation is 726504, which is very close.

The fact that the harmonic of light has only to be doubled in order to obtain anti-light fields must be related to the matter and antimatter cycles of the physical and the non-physical worlds. If the two, plus and minus, fields are interlocked, as I have postulated, and matter and anti-matter manifest in alternate pulses, then a double cycle must occur between each pulse of matter and anti-matter. The anti- matter pulse cannot be perceived by us, for fairly obvious reasons; but when calculating the frequency interaction between the two, both cycles must be taken into account.

By stepping up or slowing down the frequency of C between the two cycles, a shift in space-time *must* occur.

4> FURTHER EVIDENCE OF THE UFO GRID

A ND NOW TO LOOK AT SOME EVIDENCE OF THE existence of the global grid which is used by UFOs, either for propulsion, navigation or both.

In the early part of 1968 I was approached by a co-pilot of a National Airways Corporation Viscount. He had an interesting account for me:

The previous day he had been a crew member of a Viscount flying north to Auckland from Wellington. Between New Plymouth and Auckland, with the aircraft at 19,000 feet, a request was received from Air Traffic Control to divert slightly starboard of track. Radar operators at Auckland airport had three stationary objects on their screen, spaced at intervals down the west coast between Raglan and New Plymouth.

The Viscount was vectored towards these positions by radar control, and the crew was asked to scan the area, to check whether the objects causing the radar blips were visible to the human eye.

The manoeuvre was carried out accurately, but there was no sight of anything unusual in the sky. Although the presentation of the objects on the radar screen was clear and pronounced, the operators, in view of the crew's negative report, prepared to dismiss the incident. And suddenly the blips disappeared, disposing of the problem anyway.

Until the next day, when I appeared in the radar room with my grid map under may arm.

I discussed the incident with the radar crew, and one of them then plotted the positions of the three unknown objects on the radar map on the display board. When these positions were compared with my grid map, it was immediately apparent that the UFOs were spaced along one of the north-south grid lines running down the coast, and that the intervals between the UFOs were thirty nautical miles and fifteen nautical miles — a spacing that coincided with track lines running east-west on the grid.

Clearly our visitors were active again; some project was in progress on this section of the system occupying their attention when they had been disturbed by the approach of the Viscount.

Recently I have been able to correlate this particular incident with other human activity off the coast of New Zealand, which strongly suggests that our close-lipped scientists are not only aware of the actual existence of alien visitors, but are indeed working in close co-operation with them. We shall enlarge upon this point later.

By now my old, original grid map, which I completed in 1965, is showing signs of wear and tear; but it still helps me to prove to anyone interested that the grid is no myth, not something I have just dreamed up in order to confuse an already baffled public. I could not possibly have predicted the positions of those three blips seen on an airport radar screen, long before they actually made their appearance; yet, unless the grid map is in fact accurate and reliable, that is the only alternative explanation. At least one of my critics has dismissed my work with an amusingly contemptuous "Oh well, you can prove anything by numbers!" Forecasting the future by numbers and lines may or may not be possible, but I have neither the training, knowledge nor understanding to attempt that sort of thing. And I'm pretty sure I don't possess second sight; more's the pity!

Another incident which occurred later in 1968 was one that startled the flying fraternity. The RNZAF was in on this one, but as happens with air forces in other parts of the world the authorities quickly hushed the matter up. The lid was slammed down tightly on Pandora's box, which must be pretty full by now; it manages to fly open with increasing regularity, much to the anguish of those who would like to have the whole business of UFOs thought of by the public as a modern fairy-tale.

An Air Force Orion was carrying out a routine exercise mission off the west coast of New Zealand's North Island one cloudy afternoon, when the crew was alerted by radar control. An unidentified object was travelling at the leisurely pace of about forty knots from north to south some thirty miles off the coast. The Orion was requested to check on this intruder, and was vectored on to an intercept course. Approaching closer to the object, the Orion's forward-seeking radar locked on to the visitor, but there was no solid object visible to anyone on board. According to my information the object then lost altitude, and the Orion followed it down. The crew then reported that a whirlpool-like eddy was visible on the surface of the sea. Perhaps the object, whatever it was, had dived into the ocean and escaped in submarine fashion.

This, you may be sure, will not be the last time that UFOs will be tracked by radar in our skies. About once a month I am approached by an aircrew member and am informed of yet another UFO sighting in the New Zealand area. If all these crew members are crazy, then our airlines are a fairly precarious means of travel for the unsuspecting public.

Why is it that none of the reports that reach me are printed in the newspapers? The answer is this: the newspapers never receive them. Aircrew members are, on the whole, a conservative breed, and they jealously guard their image as a sane and level-headed group, dedicated only to the task of flying in a "safe and expeditious manner", as it is termed in the code of regulations. So far I have been one of the few foolish people in commercial flying to stick my neck out and make public what I have seen, theorised and heard. Perhaps in the near future others in my profession will come forward and give support to my statements; there are many who believe, as I do, that the truth is more important than most of the artificial criteria with which we burden ourselves in this so-called civilised society of ours.

Nuclear tests are still with us, and provide a perfect check on the harmonic calculations which I described previously. The French were active at Mururoa Island again in 1968, and gave me a further opportunity to make some predictions on the possible dates on which a nuclear device could be exploded.

Mostly for my own satisfaction I spent one evening calculating all the possible combinations in harmonic values necessary for the detonation of a nuclear bomb, to cover the whole of the testing period.

I was quite aware that I had not yet discovered all of the harmonics involved, but by carrying out constant checks on the activities of the scientists involved, I hoped that in time most of the secrets would eventually be revealed. I doubt if many of the boffins will welcome my constant snooping; but I believe that if the public is under a constant threat of annihilation they at least have the right to know how the mechanics of the operation will be carried out. The more knowledge we have, the better our chances of stopping these idiots from blasting our planet into eternity.

A few weeks after I tucked away my calculations, I was invited to present a lecture on UFOs to the Royal Aeronautical Society in Auckland. Just before the lecture I was taken out to dinner by the president and the secretary of the society. Over the meal conversation turned to my theories regarding the nuclear bomb tests. Not altogether unnaturally, the president was inclined to be skeptical of my methods of calculation, and he asked me quite casually when the next French bomb would be detonated. I told him that the 25th of the month, about a fortnight away, was my bet; the talk then switched to more mundane matters.

The lecture, presented to a capacity audience, was well received, and the bomb discussion forgotten.

On the 25th of the month the peace of Mururoa Island was shattered, and the echoes of the French nuclear explosion rippled around the world. It was another personal victory for me to chalk up.

That afternoon my telephone rang. It was the president of the Royal Aeronautical Society. Could I come into the city for a chat, and could I give further test dates to cover the rest of the current French series?

This I did. The dates I supplied proved to be correct, culminating in the explosion of France's hydrogen bomb. Further tests were cancelled when President de Gaulle found that the French bankers were having a lean year. It was a choice between bread and bombs, and bread won.

I had proved my point that the dates of nuclear tests could be accurately predicted on the basis of harmonic calculations. The president of the Society, who is also the head of a government department, gave me a copy of notes he had made on some of my predictions. He told me that these had been passed on to the heads of other government departments.

This memo is shown in photocopy No. 1. It shows that my prediction for the hydrogen bomb test was very close. For the moment I was quite satisfied with this very small error. I would have been satisfied had I been several hours out.

Newsweek magazine reported: "Drilling for future nuclear tests — Last week's underground test of an 'advanced nuclear weapon' at Pahute Mesa, north of Las Vegas, foreshadows even bigger blasts. The atomic energy commission has drilled several cased holes a mile deep in Central Nevada 100 miles north of the present test site. It has let further contracts for construction of four test holes to a depth of 6000 feet on Amchitka, the fourth island from the end of the Aleutian chain. These holes take a year and a half to drill and mine out at the bottom. In essence the AEC is stockpiling holes in the ground against future test requirements."

Capt Cathie's Predictions
French A Bomb Tests

Explosions can only occur
at the following approximate
times (within an hour or two)

		G.M.T.		
1968 Sept	08 22 50			
ACTUAL	08 19 00			
"	23 15 50			
"	28 21 00	28 N 00		
Oct.	06 15 15	06 05 15		

If any explosion (H Bomb)
between above dates, they
must occur on one or more
of them.

PHOTOCOPY OF ATOM BOMB PREDICTIONS

Photo-copy of predictions of atom tests to be carried out by French scientists at Mururoa Island in the Pacific, in 1968, handwritten and pre-dated by the head of a government department in Auckland City, New Zealand. The actual time shown is that of the hydrogen bomb. I was informed that this note was passed on to four other government departments before the test date.

Recent computer lists of the geometric positions of many atomic tests carried out at the Nevada test site show that a great number of them have been detonated on positions which straddle a latitude of 37.1195^0 north. This would create a reciprocal harmonic of 2694, an average value related to the unified equations discovered in my research.

In my earlier publications I indicated that a mass value was possibly utilized for the Aleutian Island tests. Now that I have computers to work with I believe that a more accurate set of values can be demonstrated which would allow the geometric harmonics, required for successful detonation, to be fulfilled.

A position of 51^0 25' 10.85" north/ 179^0 24' 00" east, on the south east end of the island would be ideal as a test site.

The great circle distance from this point to longitude 180^0, at the same latitude is:

1347 seconds of arc; which is a half harmonic of 2694; the average value derived from the unified equations.

The circumference of the parallel of latitude at 51^0 25' 10.85" is:

13470 minutes of arc, or nautical miles, relative to the Equator. This again is a half harmonic of 2694 (unified equation).

Other harmonics which are associated with this position and grid pole "B" in the north have connections with gravitation. This will be explained more fully in later works.

For interest, the test site of Bikini Island and Eniwetok are 11^0 35' north latitude, which equals 695 minutes of arc. This figure, 695, is the harmonic of the speed of light reciprocal, or 1/1439. Johnson Island is 169.5^0 west longitude.

Note:

It has been discovered in later research that the speed of light is not a constant over the earth's surface. It varies in relation to gravity acceleration. This in turn causes a slight variation of the values derived from the unified equations. This will be more fully explained in future publications.

5> THE MYSTERIOUS AERIALS

O N A BLAZING MORNING OF FEBRUARY 1968 SOME information came my way which was to start off a whole new chain of investigation — and which was to bring me to a number of discoveries so startling that even now their full implications are hard to comprehend.

As a theory, anti-gravity looks all very well. True, it would make obsolete overnight such antiquated forms of transportation as trains, cars, aircraft and rocket-propelled space ships; true, it would revolutionise our thinking about fuel oil resources and basic engineering.

But suppose the theory were not only correct but in actual application today — suppose there were a great many people fully aware of the existence of the UFO grid and its mighty potential as a power source that could be tapped by earth technology; suppose, in fact, that equipment had been set up in many parts of the world, even right here in quiet New Zealand where nothing very earth-shattering ever seems to happen — then would not this mean that in fact anti-gravity was virtually within the grasp of us all?

A group of fellow-pilots and myself had finished preparing our flight plans for the first flight of the day, and we were chatting generally, when a co-pilot came up to me and said he had noticed an odd-looking aerial mast on his way to the airfield. It was, he said, on private property, but its shape was so unusual, and it was so patently expensive-looking, that it had caught his attention.

Like many other aircrew members, this pilot had shown considerable interest in my UFO research and had got into the habit of noting any unusual activities up and down the country which could possibly have a bearing on my investigations. By training and experience pilots are good observers and generally capable of making concise, factual, and impartial reports. In fact I am greatly indebted to pilots and aircrew as a group for a great deal of help and many fascinating leads. Many there present that February morning were aware of some suspicions I had concerning some unusual radio transmitting stations that were springing up around New Zealand. But until this time I had no proof that these stations were anything other than what they purported to be; what had principally stimulated my suspicions was little more than an occasional rumour, and the evasiveness of officials when pointed questions were asked.

The co-pilot wondered if the mast he had seen, with its strangely-shaped array of aerials perched on top, could have any connection with the evidence I was looking for. He made a rough sketch of the mast for me, and I immediately sensed a familiarity about the pattern in which the hardware was arranged. Certainly it was only a rough sketch; the co-pilot, whatever his virtues, is no artist. But the sketch he drew of the side view of the mast had a marked similarity to the polar patterns of the UFO grid system. This intrigued me greatly and I had a hunch that a closer look at this aerial might provide a key to unlock yet another section of the Pandora's box with which I had become involved.

That evening I contacted my journalist friend Peter Temm and we arranged to meet the next day. Armed with a camera equipped with a telephoto lens, we planned to drive to the area in question and quietly obtain a few close-ups of the aerial for closer scrutiny at our leisure.

A few days later we pored over a series of ten, good enlarged photographs which showed the aerial and the house to which it was linked. The aerial was in the shape of a cube, with each side about nine feet long. Supports for the wires forming the box-like shape radiated from a central point. These were eight in number, with each individual support terminating at a corner of the box. The aerial was supported, from the central point of the box shape, on top of a lattice steel mast we estimated to be about thirty feet high.

A check revealed that according to Post Office regulations this expensive and elaborate device was nothing more sinister than a ham radio aerial erected by the owner for communication with hundreds of other technically knowledgeable hams scattered around the world.

Maybe so. We even found that there was a technical name for the general form of aerial in the photographs — neither of us being in any way informed about ham radio, this came as news. But somehow the gear had a slick, sophisticated look about it that gave it a ring of something more than the kind of ham devices one can see almost anywhere. Hams are enthusiastic and inventive folk, skilful at rigging and jury-rigging their own-designed aerials; but a great deal of money is not generally laid out on the mast. In this country, at least, a length of wire stretched from a wooden mast is more the norm. Sometimes the amateur operator will have a few dipoles across the top of his mast for directional purposes: but this one had a decidedly professional look about it.

I decided to check a bit further and, to start off with, I set about plotting the position of the aerial on my Auckland grid map to see if any correlations would show up.

At first nothing unusual presented itself; there seemed to be no connection with the aerial site and the grid system. But something kept nagging at me. I had a very strong feeling that there was a connection and that a thorough search of the facts and figures would bring it out.

At this point I decided to plot co-ordinates from the various positions of known UFO activity already plotted on an Auckland map. The results were immediately interesting. A line plotted through a position where a large, disc-shaped UFO had been observed hovering over Inverary Road, Epsom, and the point where an unexplained explosion occurred in Rutland Street, Auckland, some eleven years previously, passed directly through the location of the North Shore aerial. This was hardly anything conclusive — but it suggested a possible lead. I told Peter of my find, and we agreed that the next step was to search the Auckland area for similar aerials, plot their positions on the map and then look again for correlations of data. In the interim I began to spread the word among some of my associates and fellow pilots that we were hunting for aerials, and asked them to keep an eye out.

Over the next four months I spent my days off work cruising around the Auckland area looking for anything unusual in the way of masts and aerials. Results exceeded all expectations. A surprisingly large number of strange aerials turned up; plotted on the Auckland map, they showed quite clearly that they were more than ham listening-posts — although in every instance they were in fact listed as belonging to ham stations in the official ham radio yearbook. It was clear that the specialised aerials were set up in straight lines in relationship to one another — and in addition were blended into the UFO grid pattern established over the Auckland area.

At this point I was faced with the obvious conclusion that a group of electronics experts knew far more than I did about the grid system — and moreover, that the knowledge must have been in their possession for quite some years. Some of the aerials, we found, had been located on the present sites for periods ranging up to several years.

51

When the implications of this dawned on me, the shock was severe: the grid was no longer just a theoretical possibility. It was a definite fact, and a fact that had been known to an indefinite but clearly large number of people for some considerable time. It looked to me as though electronic equipment was being built into the network, and as though they were carrying out or controlling large-scale experiments. But to what purpose? And who were "they?" Both of these questions cannot yet be answered. However, we shall present some of our speculations and we hope that readers will come to light with further information that will help solve the mystery.

There was another method by which we could prove conclusively that the so-called ham radio stations were established on certain geometric positions for purposes other than for private experiment or simple communication. By a study of the geometric pattern that had emerged from a careful plotting of all the known aerial sites, it should be possible to predict where other odd aerials would show up. If the pattern was right, if our thinking was right, we should be able to extend the pattern, rather like the "series" type of problem sometimes presented in intelligence tests, and declare that therefore another aerial should be located here, there, or over there — on the map.

If, on the other hand, the positions were entirely coincidentally linked with the grid; if in fact there was no connection at all; and if indeed the aerials were genuinely ham stations and scattered in a more or less random order over the countryside, such predictions would simply not be valid.

One Friday night I spent a couple of hours studying the network of aerials and calculated various co-ordinates from their positions. When I had pinpointed what seemed to me to be a most likely position for an aerial as yet undiscovered by us, I called Peter and we arranged for a meeting the following afternoon.

On an ordinary street map we pencilled in the position where I expected an odd aerial should be located. Then with a camera handy, we went off on our hunt.

This was to be the first big test. I was reasonably confident that we would find an aerial where I had plotted it on the map; but at the same time I was horribly aware that I could also be falling flat on my face. I had still been compelled to assume certain geometric relationships in connection with the system; whoever had planned the evident aerial network already knew for certain all the relationships involved, while I had to fumble through a maze of calculations to theorise about them. I was not certain, also, how Peter was reacting to my theories. We hadn't long been working together at that stage, and up to now he had simply had to take my word for many aspects of my research. But if the present excursion proved to be successful, the greatest gain for both of us could be a firming up of confidence.

We approached the street I had circled on the street map, and turned the corner.

And there it was.

I was both relieved and excited. Peter seemed quietly surprised.

The aerial before us, and which we photographed, was a two-way complex of directional components. Co-ordinates from several other aerial positions passed through this point from different directions. My plot had been accurate to within about a hundred feet or so which, considering the quality of the survey maps I use, was fairly close to precision. We found a place from which we could take photographs to add to our growing pile of pictorial evidence for the existence of an aerial network, and went home.

There was still a slim possibility that the finding of an aerial almost exactly where I had predicted it to be could have been by chance alone; I knew that it was by no chance; but at the same time we recognised the fact that sceptics would make this claim. However, a short time later, and on two different occasions, I was able to go through the identical performance for yet another two aerials — first, figuring on the map where they ought to be, in accordance with the emerging pattern and my theories on the factors involved in locating the strange masts; and then with a street map and a car, actually locating them in precisely those positions.

In all honesty I must also admit that on two occasions I drew a blank. One of these spots, where I was certain I would find a mast, is now being kept under observation by some of our helpers; I believe there is a strong possibility that eventually an aerial will appear on this location. One development, and one that we realised would come about, has been that the folk in charge of these aerials are aware of our activities and, probably knowing that we have the place under surveillance, they may be unwilling to construct a mast until it becomes imperative for the network as a whole to have one there.

We have never been reluctant to let people know what we were up to in our searching, and in our conclusions. As soon as new evidence has come along we have passed it along the pipeline which we believe is being tapped by "them." There is nothing secret, classified or underhand about our investigation. The New Zealand Government has been kept up to date with my findings, both thorough correspondence and written reports direct to the Prime Minister. We have made a point of passing on each link in the chain of evidence to key personnel so that there can never be any suggestion made that our investigation is somehow or other "subversive."

Our whole aim has been to bring facts to light so that from the sheer weight of the evidence someone in authority, somewhere, sooner or later, is going to have to admit to the public that not only do UFOs exist but that the grid system on which they operate is also an established fact. And until this happens, our work shall continue. If it should happen that I am stopped, there are many others now with the knowledge that will enable them to continue the investigation, with or without official approval. The information we have patiently garnered over the course of several years has been spread out, and I have personally schooled others so that they can carry on if it becomes necessary. Several journalists, some of them correspondents for overseas organisations, are also kept informed of our progress, and it will now be impossible for the truth to be hidden for much longer.

When the admission is finally made, when it is stated that marsh gas, the rise and fall of Venus and all the other rubbish trotted out by the tame and the not so tame scientists who seemingly have forgotten the first principles of science to "explain" UFO sightings, are *not* the be-all and end-all of UFO phenomena, then our investigation will slow down. Our aims will have been achieved.

Our search for aerials has continued throughout the months, up to the present time, and still the odd mast is drawn to our attention. They can be seen throughout New Zealand, and we know they exist abroad as well from reports from as far afield as Australia, France and America. In this country we have uncovered them from Invercargill to the north of Auckland.

Most numerous are those shaped like boxes. But others have slight variations. One variety is an elongated type that looks something like the framework of a box-kite — presumably for more efficient directional purposes. Some have a highly polished metal sphere placed within the box shape. For some reason these spheres, which are quite large, give off flashes of light, observable from many miles away on a fine day. This type is easily seen from the air — from as far away as fifteen miles. Whether the light is reflected from a prismatic surface or emitted from within the spheres themselves is something we do not yet know.

We do not know what this sphere is, or what it does. One possible explanation was offered by a director of a scientific equipment manufacturing company in the United States: "The needle-like protruding elements on the ball are uni-directional vertical probes. In the ball a transducer, or transistor pre-amp director, directs any signal from above the main antenna down to the main antenna, and this is then relayed from one antenna tower to the next to a main base of receiver operations. This, then, would prevent any accidental reception of the signal from a UFO etc. from being picked up by any, just any, radio that happened to be tuned to the right frequency...I prefer to think that the little ball on top of the receiver receives at a much higher wavelength (frequency) and then the ball's transistorised circuit, acting as a converter, reduces the received signal to a lower frequency, and it is then carried from one tower to the next until it reaches its home receiver station."

Another hint of connection between the strange aerials and UFOs is the fact the grid aerial under the sea off the coast of South America, photographed in 1964 by the US survey ship *Eltanin*, has ball-shaped objects on the extremities of its antennae; moreover, antennae protruding from UFOs have been observed, also, to have ball-shaped ends.

The other main type of aerial which appears to be built into the grid consists of a similar lattice steel mast with heavy-looking aerial elements supported horizontally across the top. Some minor masts within the system are more like ordinary TV aerials.

The pattern produced on a map by pinpointing the aerials is a complex one — especially when positioned on a map that also includes the UFO grid. After a close study of the network it becomes obvious that the man-made aerials have been built into the UFO grid for a definite purpose, and apparently with a full awareness of the existence of the UFO grid. A number of areas in New Zealand where UFO activity has been pronounced are also areas in which the aerials occur.

As our investigation went on, a mass of information was built up from the aerial network, and I have been able to check many of my own theories against it. The discovery that "they" had placed their equipment in specific geometric positions gave me clues which have led me on to new discoveries. "They" are now aware of this, and I imagine I am not too popular with "them" — first, for having stumbled on the aerial network, and then for not having the decency to keep quiet about it.

The discovery of the aerials and our conclusions about their function, plus the new discoveries which we have derived from our understanding of their positioning, have given rise to a cat-and-mouse affair which has sometimes been anything but a game. The following chapters will enlarge upon these matters in detail.

6> SCIENTISTS AND THE UFOS

THE DISCOVERY OF A NETWORK OF MAN-MADE transmitting stations around our city, described in the preceeding chapter, was the most startling tangible fact that we had encountered in our UFO research. We discovered that Auckland city and the surrounding areas were linked with the transmitters by numerous geometric alignments. Further investigation suggests very strongly that the pattern is still incomplete — and that other stations are yet to be added to the system.

Months passed before we were able to determine the positions of all the stations plotted on the survey maps and at that stage we considered that there was enough evidence to prove that secret experiments were being carried out. We decided also that it was now necessary to bring to public attention all the facts so far established, and to fill in further details of the aerial network patterns as each new additional aerial came to our notice. On the basis of the material in this chapter, some readers may wish to carry out investigations of their own into the aerial system. If so, we would certainly be interested in hearing about results.

As each aerial was discovered, its precise position was plotted on the same grid map of Auckland and its surrounding districts which I had used when I established the positions of UFO activity, published in my first book. The question was whether there was some correlation between the positions of known UFO activity and the location of the transmitting aerials. Remember, the UFO positions had been established several years before our investigations into the aerials.

It was soon very clear indeed that there were connections between the UFO positions and the more recently found aerial locations. Straight lines drawn through different combinations of aerial positions produced definite geometric patterns which were clearly linked to the UFO positions.

When these patterns were further analysed it appeared that where the building of a man-made station was not possible for topographic reasons, a UFO may have been brought in to place — or blast — an aerial or similar device into position. One of these positions was, we believe, in the middle of a factory in Rosebank Road in the Auckland suburb of Avondale.

Another such position was, in our opinion, near the corner of Rutland Street, in the central part of the city. If this hypothesis is correct, one is naturally led to the conclusion that scientists were well aware *in advance* that certain locations would be subjected to extensive damage as a result of the placement of aerial devices.

We do not dispute that research of the kind being undertaken in secrecy involving both UFOs and aerials *may* be essential for the advancement of mankind. But it is the secrecy that we feel is wrong. Moreover, the dangers inherent where aerial locations fall upon crowded city areas must be obvious. If the rules of geometry (and the concepts involved are those of geometrics) compel whoever is responsible to construct apparatus of a dangerous nature in densely populated areas, then surely the citizens of those areas have a right to be told — and to be warned of the possible consequences of the experiments to be carried out. If the instigators of the research happen also to be representatives of a foreign country, which we believe to be the case, this is all the more reason for the nature of the experimental work to be made public.

One scientist has told me quite plainly that the aerial network is *not* under the control of the New Zealand Government. I find the implications of that statement rather disquieting. Is it possible that New Zealand, one of the last peaceful sanctuaries on this planet, is being manipulated by a power group operating outside the normal confines of demoratic control? I believe there is a distinct possibility that this is the situation and that no government, large or small, is able to control its activities.

The knowledge possessed already by the group may be so advanced that those who have the secrets may be in a position to dictate action on their own terms, particularly if political leverage is applied at the same time, through normal governmental channels.

It was suggested to me by my informant that this was indeed the case, and that New Zealand would be cut off from certain overseas aid if our government refused to allow the activities of foreign scientists to continue within our territory.

We believe that this is too high a price. If our dealings with overseas interests are not openly and honestly carried out, then we would be much better off not to have this work going on in our midst. Who among us, anywhere in the world, has the right to decide who should and who should not have access to advanced technical knowledge — or to any knowledge, for that matter?

Technological superiority is dangerous only when held by a small group. History shows that groups of this very nature have, in times past, invariably used their superior knowledge for purposes other than for the good of all humanity, eventually destroying themselves and large numbers of their fellow men along with them.

The atomic bomb offers a prime example of the folly of secrecy in the field of advanced technology. I know for certain that my theories regarding the bomb have been proved correct. The bomb is, in short, a geometric device which can only be detonated in accordance with the unbreakable laws of geometry. The device is detonated by the manipulation of the relative motions of the atomic particles enclosed within its casing; and this can only be effected by placing the bomb on, under or over a specific geometric point related to the earths's surface, at a specific time. The relative motions of the earth and sun, at this instant of time, cause the disruption of the unstable particles of uranium, plutonium, cobalt or whatever unstable matter is used to trigger the explosion. Every test of nuclear devices since World War II has been designed to discover all the geometric combinations possible for the detonation of the atom.

Because of the secrecy imposed on this advanced body of knowledge, every major power has been frantically carrying out experimental tests in an endeavour to keep up with, or ahead of, rival powers — in the fear that one or the other will eventually get the upper hand. The computers of each nation concerned are fed with this information so that calculations can be made ahead as to where and when a nuclear device might be triggered. In this way the spiral of insecurity and distrust has increased its momentum until, at this present time, the world has become a mad-house with ourselves its inmates. Unless something is done, a system set up for the pooling of all knowledge, we shall end up as have so many other civilizations, intent on annihilation of the race.

If every intelligent individual had had free access to these secrets immediately after the war, the sheer weight of public opinion alone might have been enough to prevent the insane game now being played the world over in the name of national security. Certainly, at least, the brakes would have been applied to slow down our headlong rush to eternity.

The geometric nature of the bomb makes a nuclear war completely illogical — and perhaps this explains the present concentration of research in the United States, England, Switzerland and elsewhere into bacterial and chemical warfare techniques.

Why is a nuclear war illogical?

Let's take an example: if Russia, let us say, were to launch a missile in an attempt to demolish New York, the Americans would have known months in advance that at such-and-such a time the city would have been a potential nuclear target. Their computers would have told them so. Naturally, all defences would have been alerted for that one target point until the danger period had passed. If a missile managed to get through the defence system and New York was incinerated, America would want immediate retaliation. But again because of the solar geometrics involved, this would not be possible at any unspecified time for any specific Soviet target. It could take hours; days or weeks for a major target in Russia to match the harmonic geometrics of the sun position in order for a missile to be successfully launched towards that point with any certainty of its detonation. And so it would drag on, month after month.

For this very reason it became necessary to arm submarines with nuclear weapons and launching devices so that they could roam the oceans in secrecy and be able to position themselves in such a way that they could launch nuclear missiles at enemy targets as the right times came up.

Meanwhile, those at the top who had started this insane war, and those in control on both sides, would know clearly, and well in advance, where the danger spots were going to be. They would make sure that they themselves were many hundreds of miles away until the danger periods had passed. The general populace, you can be sure, would be blissfully unaware of impending explosions.

An even more dangerous and complex game has now been initiated by the same group. Knowledge obtained from the bomb has opened a door to secrets of anti-gravity; if one group or another obtains supremacy in this field, they could, if they desired, rule the world.

For UFOs are real. They are anti-gravity machines. Someone has advanced knowledge about them. Now we would like to have access to the truth, all of it, and a democratic voice in the control of our own destiny.

My informant declared that his group was not concerned with moral issues. Its representatives are here to carry out certain work, and it is only this task that interests them. It is neither right nor good, he declared, for the public to have knowledge such as this.

My answer was that I was part of the public, a free man in what I believed to be a free country; and that, relying on my own resources, I had been able to discover a considerable amount of information concerning the activities of the people in question.

I often wonder how much worry, how many years of hard work, I could have saved myself if only it could have been possible for me to study all the relevant data in freely available technical publications.

Isn't it the right of all free citizens to have access to the technology of the future? I firmly believe that we do all have that right — the alternative is to end up like Pavlov's dogs, when we may all be forced to perform at the will of a new kind of master.

Time and again I have asked to be given just one good moral reason why the data known on UFOs should not be published. So far no reason has been forthcoming, and I believe that none exists. Investigations of a private nature such as I have undertaken will be carried on. I believe firmly that others, with more intelligence and greater technical ability than I have, will continue this work.

To look more closely at the aerial network in and around the city of Auckland: the picture is a complicated one, but a prolonged study of the system reveals many connections with the geometric harmonics associated with anti-gravity and UFO phenomena. It shows without doubt that some technicians at least have direct communication with UFOs that have been active on the positions indicated on the Auckland section of the UFO grid. Who is actually in control of the UFOs? This we cannot as yet determine — but there are several possible answers, including the following:

1. The UFOs are controlled by extraterrestrials who are greatly advanced in science. These aliens are instructing our scientists in new technological fields.
2. Earth scientists have uncovered the secrets of anti-gravity and have managed to construct a small number of UFO-type vehicles. These anti-gravity machines are now being used to further research and to improve their scientific techniques.
3. The UFOs are under the control of extraterrestrials, and their activity is aimed at hindering earth scientists in their research.
4. An alien group of people from space have lived among us secretly throughout history and now control the world. They are in charge of all advanced scientific experimentation. (This, we feel, is the least likely answer.)
5. Other possibilities which we are as yet unaware of.

We do not know, any more than you do, which answer is the true one. But it may not be too long before we find out.

MAP 4

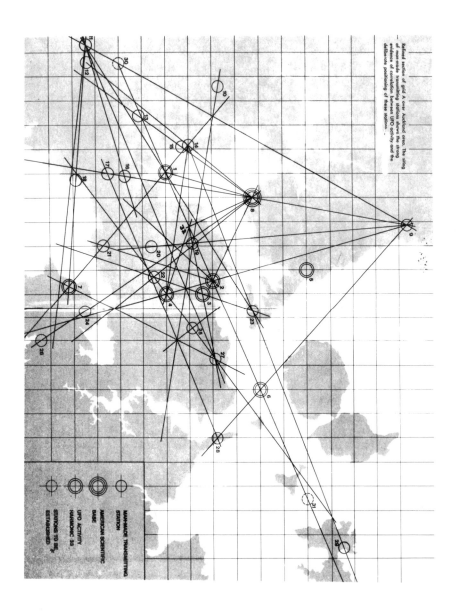

I was told by a foreigner holding a high position with one of the government ministries that I would be stopped from publishing this book by those in charge of "the experiment." "The group," I was told, "is all-powerful, and you can't possibly beat them." My answer was that I was fully aware of the power weilded by the "group," as well as of my own relative insignificance.

History shows that in other ages "insignificant" men have succeeded in upsetting the plans of power groups, and with perseverance and luck I may be able to do the same — because I am convinced that the "group," closely guarding secrets that should be freely available to all, is morally evil.

A study of the Auckland map will show that it is an exact reproduction of the grid map published in my previous book. The grid lattice covers areas of one minute of arc square.

Positions 1 through 6 are those of UFO activity previously plotted. These are, in more detail:

1. Rosebank Road factory demolished by an unexplained explosion. A UFO was reported over the scene before the explosion occurred.
2. Unexplained explosion at the corner of Rutland Street, Auckland city.
3. UFO observed hovering near the Museum, Auckland Domain.
4. UFO observed hovering behind a house in Inverary Road, Epsom, in suburban Auckland.
5. Lake Pupuke, North Shore, over which point a UFO has been observed.
6. Object was seen entering the water from the air at this point.
7. I was informed by the head of a government department in Auckland that a UFO had been seen hovering over this point.
8. This is the position of a base staffed by personnel from one of the most powerful nations on earth. This fact was first drawn to my attention during a visit to Victoria University, Wellington, in 1969. I had presented a lecture to students. After the lecture, which covered aspects of the UFO grid system, I was showing a copy of the Auckland grid map to the American air attaché, who had asked to be present incognito, and the editor of *Salient*, the university's student newspaper.

The student asked me what I knew about the American base on the North Shore, at Kauri Point.

Surprised, I asked: "What base?" He replied: "You must know what base I mean; you have plotted it on your map."

I told him, quite truthfully, that I had no knowledge of any such base. The point on the grid map to which he was referring was where I had plotted co-ordinates crossing at Kauri Point; he insisted that I must have known of the base in order to have plotted it so accurately. I explained that I was completely unaware of the significance of the position, and had only been aware that certain lines connecting other stations crossed at this point. I had left it to a future time to study the position further.

Reflecting on this conversation some days later, it occured to me that I had probably been "set up" in some way by the invitation to lecture at Victoria University; however, this conclusion may have been unkind to the students who were involved. In any case the visit was well worth the time and effort, since at least I had gained a hint about a base established on Auckland's north shore.

Since then I have found that the base does indeed exist — and that very few people in this city of more than half a million are aware of it. A New Zealand electronics technician contacted me, for example, and he turned out to be one person who had access to the base.

He was very interested in what I was doing and what I knew. "Don't you know what happens to people who know too much?" he warned me. Somewhat taken aback I went to some pains to explain to him that in the event of anything untoward happening to me, I had taken the precaution of making, and putting into safe keeping, several copies of a long list of names of people involved with the "experiment," and that they might be embarrassed at the inevitable questions that would follow a mishap to me. His question gave me some anxiety, but I felt fairly certain that the "group" would realise that putting me out of action would only draw attention to themselves.

I put a circle around the position of the Kauri Point base on the map and later, out of curiosity, measured the distance in minutes of arc (nautical miles) to another mysterious establishment staffed by Americans — at Woodbourne RNZAF base, near Blenheim, in the South Island.

The plotted distance was just on 288 minutes of arc, relative to the accuracy of the map I had access to at the time. It appeared that the two bases were positioned in this way for the purposes of setting up a harmonic geometric relating to twice the speed of light. My interest was immediately focused and I have believed from that time that there is a definite geometric connection between the two stations which allows electronic experimentation.

Recently I carried out a more accurate series of calculations, by computer, in relation to these two points and found much more persuasive evidence regarding a geometric connection.

I had more mathematical data to work with, collected over many years, and had discovered that the seemingly obvious did not always turn out to be the right answer.

One of the interesting facts I had discovered was that I could shift the harmonic values up, or down, the scale by multiplying or dividing by 6, or 60. We normally use degrees, minutes, or seconds in arc measure, relative to the Earth's surface, but equivalent geometric wave-lengths can be increased, or decreased, below or above these normal values. In fact the ones above can be decreased in length an infinite number of times for the creation of very high frequency transmissions.

I applied this exercise to the computed distance between the two stations, as follows:

Distance between stations:

Distance — 284.9006 minutes of arc (nautical miles).

Multiplied by 6 : nine times.

$$2.87114^9$$

The square root of the 2871l40 harmonic is equal to:

1694444 harmonic.

The latitudinal displacement between the two stations was computed to be:

4.706666 degrees.

which equals

16944 seconds of arc. (harmonic).

The longitude of Kauri Point is equal to:

$174^0\ 42'$

If we subtract 90^0 from this value to ascertain the position of Kauri Point within the appropriate 90^0 sector, we have:

$84^0\ 42'$

Which equals:

84.7^0

Which is a half harmonic of:

169.4 (harmonic)

I am not sure how accurate this value has to be, for practical application, but it has been found that this particular harmonic (169444) has a direct connection with communication; particularly space communication. See the last chapter; Wake Up Earth.

The circumference of the latitude which passes through the Woodbourne position is 269.53 degrees, relative to the equator, which could be associated with the harmonic values derived from the unified equations.

All the evidence suggests a use of very accurately computed geometric positions for the purpose of extremely advanced scientific experimentaion. If so, New Zealand is very strategically placed on the Earth's surface.

A further interesting factor was that the geometric co-ordinates connecting the Kauri Point station to the points at which massive explosions had occurred (Rosebank Road and Rutland Street, 1 and 2 respectively on the map) were equal. A line between the two explosion points, in other words, was the base-line of an isosceles triangle, the apex of which was the Kauri Point position.

I checked the length of the base-line and found that the distance between the two explosions was 288 seconds of arc, or twice the speed of light harmonic, subject to the accuracy of the plot.

Further, if the isosceles triangle so formed were to be bisected (which is shown by line 8 — 32 on the map), then the co-ordinate 8 — 32 was equal to co-ordinate 32 — 4. Position 4 is that of a UFO sighted hovering behind a house in Inverary Road, Epsom (a verified sighting). Could this be yet another coincidence? I could hardly believe so. The angle formed by 1 — 8 and 2, is equal to 288,000 seconds of arc, subject to the accuracy of the plot, which is also a harmonic of twice the speed of light.

I have recently studied this pattern again, at some length, and again, subject to the accuracy of the plot. I believe the following geometric co-ordinates are built into the system.

A radius with the centre at position 8, and passing through positions 1 and 2 would have a length of 231.48147 seconds of arc. If we multiply this value by 6 to shift the harmonic up the scale, then we produce the harmonic 13888.888. This is twice the harmonic of 6944.444, which is the reciprocal of the speed of light.

The circumference of a circle formed by this radius would be 1454.441 seconds of arc (relative). If we multiply this value by 6x6x6 then we produce the value 314159.27, which is the direct harmonic of Pi., or 3.1415927. Quite remarkable.

9. This is where we discovered the first aerial of the network, as described in Chapter 3. It was from this point that the whole aerial investigation started. The first geometric line-up we found was 9-2-4, 2 and 4 being two UFO positions previously

MAP 5

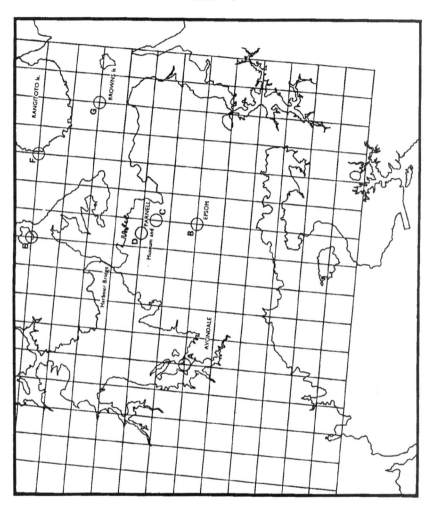

Shows refined section of grid A over the city of Auckland, New Zealand. Circles show positions of UFO activity. See grid map showing positions of man-made transmitting stations. (Original map published in Harmonic 33)

plotted. Other co-ordinates from 9 are: 9-30-11, 9-8-16-17, and 9-6-28. It would appear that these line-ups, then, are not just accidental.

Positions 10, and from 13 through 29, are all man-made transmitter stations which have sophisticated aerial systems attached to them. Photographs have been taken of each, and copies are filed away in a variety of safe places. The geometric patterns produced by connecting all the stations show definite evidence of linkage. The harmonics involved are complex, and I shall leave their solution for mathematically-inclined readers. The various angles formed by intersecting lines also have harmonic association.

Positions 11 and 12 appear to be two major stations. They fall within the area of the Waitakere Mountains, to the west of Auckland, and the aerial masts can be seen from some miles distant. It may be argued that it is purely coincidental that the stations are in geometric alignment with others on the map — but if coincidence is the answer, I dare say no one will have any objection to my having free access to the buildings in order to photograph and study the electronic equipment installed within. One of the buildings, by the way, is constructed like a fortress.

Finally, on the map I have plotted positions 30 and 31, which I believe to be sites where some type of transmitting equipment will be set up in the future. The distance between these points is equivalent to eight times the speed of light harmonic of 1439, or 8C. The square root of this value is 3.3927. The harmonic of 3927 is incorporated in this group of figures. I had earlier found that a harmonic of 3393 was one of many used in the detonation of an atomic bomb.[1] Activity of an odd variety has already been observed around these two positions, and a close watch will be kept to see what eventuates.

Aerials are still appearing, but we shall not complicate the map any further. We, and the many people who have aided us in our investigations, believe that there is more than sufficient evidence here already to support our demand for a full and open investigation into the whole system which of course is not confined to Auckland but is spread throughout New Zealand.

Who is in charge of the "experiment?" Where do the necessary funds come from? What is the intention of those in control of the system, when the work is complete and all the answers are in? Will they then tell us the full story about the UFOs?

Frankly, I doubt it.

---

[1] 3393 is the term 33927 corrected to four-figure accuracy

7> MATHEMATICAL VALUES OF INTEREST

IN MY EARLIER WORK I SHOWED THE VARIOUS STEPS I went through in my research which eventually led me to a unified equation based on the harmonic of the speed of light, and the Einstein equation $E = MC^2$. The equation indicated to me that all the physical substances in the universe were formed from the harmonic frequencies of light in various interlocking geometric forms. All matter, be it a star, a planet, or the structure of the atom, is formed by the harmonic resonance of light.

A very rough analogy of how light is individualised into a physical substance from the universal matrix, would be to liken the universe to a vast ocean. If a vortex or whirlpool is created in the ocean, then a small portion of it has been transformed into something quite different from the main mass. The area enclosed by the vortex operates under a different set of geometric laws. The change in state is caused by a spiraling motion being imparted by the influence of other forces.

I believe that the forces which cause a vortex to form in the universe matrix are manifested by the interaction between the universe and anti-universe. In other words the interaction, or pulsation, between matter and antimatter causes the creation, or dissolution, of substance. This idea conforms with the "steady state" theory of the universe. Many scientists believe that matter is being continuously created and destroyed, maintaining a constant supply of material in the physical universe.

Is it possible that light reciprocal harmonics from the anti-universe interact with the pure light harmonics of our physical universe to form resonances which create matter? If this is so then we must look for the reciprocal light harmonic of 6944 within the geometric structure of spherical mass formation in all parts of the universe. If this applies to the largest planet, or star, then it must also apply to the spherical structure of the atom.

The geometric or universal value by which we can measure spherical bodies, regardless of size, is angular measurement. The constant factor for the circumference in all cases is 360 degrees, or 21,600 minutes of arc. In respect to the earth we call the surface distance of one minute of arc one nautical mile, but the actual physical distance would naturally vary with the size of the body.

If we consider the diameter of all spherical bodies to be also measured in units of arc values, equal to those of the surface then we find that the constant value for diameter is 6875.493542. This could be termed the harmonic diameter for all spherical bodies. To bring this body into being from the universal matrix, vortexual action must be initiated and the body built up from fundamental particles. We would expect some sort of rarefied gaseous stage at the periphery of the body graduating to a more dense atomic structure, until a solid body manifests which gets much more dense towards its centre.

From this we see that in our hunt for the light reciprocal harmonic which actually creates the spherical body, we must not only consider the solid body itself but also the rarified gaseous or atomic particle, envelope around it, as this also has mass.

If we take the earth as an example we find that many different layers extend outward from the surface, getting increasingly rarefied with altitude. First of all the troposphere, where three quarters of the bulk of the whole envelope is concentrated. This consists of 78 per cent nitrogen, 21 per cent oxygen, 0.9 percent argon, 0.3 per cent carbon dioxide, with traces of several other gases plus copious quantities of water vapour. Next is the stratosphere and the mesosphere, which extend up to about 50 miles. The stratosphere consists in part of ozone or heavy oxygen formed by electrical discharges, or strong ultra-violet rays, passing through ordinary oxygen. At about 50 miles, up to between 350-600 miles, is the ionosphere, where X-rays and ultra-violet rays from the sun ionise the rarefied air. This produces electrically charged atoms and molecules, together with unattached electrons. This area contains only 0.001 per cent, by weight, of the atmosphere. The outermost layer is the exosphere, where sub-atomic particles are found, plus a 900-mile layer of thinly dispersed helium surrounded by a layer of hydrogen that extends 4000 miles into space. The atoms are so far apart in this area that they very seldom collide, which gives some idea of the density.

As can be seen from this, if my theory is correct, hydrogen is the first type of material to be manifested from the universal substance; then the heavier gases close to the earth's surface; and finally the solid matter of the earth itself.

The geometric harmonic diameter of the earth could then be extended to encompass the main mass of the surrounding atmospheric envelope to see if the harmonic reciprocal of light is evident.

If we add the harmonic equivalent of 6875.493542, namely 68.75493542, to the diameter to encompass the atmosphere we get

$$
\begin{array}{r}
6875.493542 \\
\underline{68.75493542} \\
6944.24847742
\end{array}
$$

As 6944 is the harmonic reciprocal of the speed of light in free space, it appears possible that spherical bodies are in fact formed by some sort of vortexual resonance which causes precipitation of matter. In the initial stages of formation are the rarefied gases; then, as the harmonic vibration intensifies to the point that it matches that of the light reciprocal, the more dense substances are built up. Finally at certain harmonic values solid substances occur.

If this is so then, in my theory, every spatial body must have some sort of gaseous, or ionic, envelope surrounding it. I should imagine that in the case of the planets, the type of gaseous envelope would depend on the orbital radius from the central sun or star. The orbital values would set up secondary harmonics which would modify the geometric makeup of the surrounding atmosphere.

It follows that all planets in the universe that have similar size and orbital radius to earth would have the same type of atmosphere and other characteristics. Accordingly there must be millions of planets which could be habitable for man. The ratio of the diameter of a planet to the height of the main bulk of its atmosphere would be 200:1.

Shortly after I published my second book I had a visit from an Australian who passed some information to me in regards to straight and curved line geometry. He was a most intense sort of chap and I still don't know the reason behind the visit, or the connections he has in his own country, but the information was most interesting. He left me quite a few notes, saying that I could make use of them as I saw fit. Possibly I can use the data in some future research but a small portion I will quote here:

Straight and curved line geometry; the globe and the disc. By choosing a single universal measurement unit we are able to convert directly from units of length to angles of geometry and back again. Taking the earth as a globe we see it has a circumference of 21,600 minutes of arc (or nautical miles) and a diameter of 6875.493

DIAGRAM 5

Showing that all spherical bodies have a harmonic affinity with the harmonic reciprocal of the speed of light.

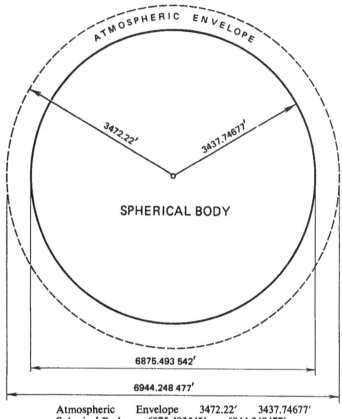

Atmospheric	Envelope	3472.22′	3437.74677′
Spherical Body	6875.493542′	6944.248477′	

Harmonic of the speed of light = 144/harmonic reciprocal = 6944. In geometric measurement the circumference of all spherical bodies is 360 degrees, or 21,600 minutes of arc. The diameter of all spherical bodies, in the same minute of arc units, can be expressed as a constant of 6875.493542 minutes of arc. If this value is then considered as a harmonic, and extended by the equivalent harmonic of 68.75493542, the resultant value becomes 6944.248477; the light reciprocal.

The application of this harmonic diameter to all planetary bodies in space would account for the mass of the planet and the surrounding atmosphere. The constant of 6875.493542 minutes of arc for the diameter, and a constant of 34.377468 minutes of arc for the height of the atmosphere above surface level. (Roughly 39.5 statute miles. This would extend to the mesosphere if applied to the atmosphere of the earth. Above this level would be the ionosphere and the exosphere.)

minutes of arc. It is stated in this theory that every globe has an equivalent disc which is equal to it. The best way to imagine this equivalent disc is to liken it to a globe which has been put into a giant press and squashed flat at the equator.

What we are interested in is the ratio of the dimensions of the globe; radius, diameter, circumference etc., to those of its equivalent disc. It is found that the diameter of the disc is equal to one half the circumference of the globe, and the circumference of the disc is one half of pi times that of the circumference of the globe.

As a globe the circumference = 21,600 nautical miles
As a disc the diameter   = 10800 nautical miles
As a disc the circumference = 33929.2 nautical miles

The circumference as a disc is 1.5707963 times the circumference as a globe, or half of *pi* (π).

This is a very interesting fact because my visitor is saying that the earth grid, as I discovered it, seems to be based on the possibility of one geometry switching over to another geometry. The idea of gravity being a force appears to be a fallacy. In reality it seems to be simply a state of tension, or a ratio between the two geometries. I found in my earlier research that this geometric harmonic of 33929.2 was one of the factors in the positioning and detonation of an atomic device.

Next let us look at measurement itself. We are led to believe that all systems of measurement, as used today, are purely arbitrary values set up by man himself and therefore a fairly haphazard way of finding quantities or dimensions of things. British measurement for example was purported to be a jumble of bits and pieces related to man's own dimensions. The inch was an eighteenth of a cubit, or the breadth of a thumb. The cubit was measured from the point of the elbow to the outstretched tip of the middle finger. The foot was about two-thirds of a cubit, four palms, twelve thumbs, or sixteen digits. The digit was the width of the middle of the middle finger. The meridian mile was 4000 cubits. I'm not sure where all these ideas originated, but I believe them to be pretty ridiculous, even though they are taught in our schools today. How many human beings, taken at random, would conform to these particular dimensions? We would have some peculiar-looking buildings around our cities if we standardised the construction measurements on the thin, fat, short or tall citizens who lived within them.

I consider that there is evidence which suggests British measurement was originally based on geometric concepts. If this can be proved then it follows that this method of measurement could be used in a universal sense, to harmonise structures to natural law. The first indications of this can be seen in the design factors of the Great Pyramid.

A pyramid, or geodetic inch, is equal to 1.0011 British inches. Could it be that in ancient times a pyramid inch and the British inch were equal to each other and some how derived from a geometric value associated with the light harmonic of 144? If so, then our ancestors were scientifically advanced to a much greater degree than we give them credit for.

In 1635 the author of *Sea-Man's Practice,* Richard Norwood, using a sextant of more than five feet in radius, made observations of the sun at two points which were 9149 chains apart and found a value of 69.5 statute miles for one degree of latitude. In 1671 the French astronomer Jean Picard, by means of trigonometry, was able to obtain a fairly accurate value of 69.1 statute miles. Newton made use of this value to complete his general theory of gravitation.

The figure generally taken for the circumference of the earth at the equator is 25,000 statute miles. If we divide this by 360 to find the number of miles in one degree the answer is 69.444. Taking everything else into consideration I'm sure this is not just coincidence. The value of 69444 is obviously the reciprocal of the speed of light harmonic.

A serious study of the origins of British standards of measurements could be of extreme interest and possibly many of our history books would have to be rewritten as a result.

The measure of one geodetic foot, equal to one six-thousandth part of a terrestrial minute of arc, which is equal to one grid foot, was proposed in early 1700 by Cassini. If this had been the standard accepted it would have been equal to the ancient Greek foot, which was five-sixth of a remen. The Parthenon was laid out to this unit.

The French metre could be taken as a fairly close scientific method of measuring. The standard was taken as one ten-millionth part of the length of a quadrant of the meridian measured through Paris. This was established reasonably accurately in 1798 and is the equivalent of 39.37 British inches. As British measurement itself appears to be based on a geodetic equivalent, this value of 39.37 could be close to a harmonic equivalent of the resultant earth magnetic field. Some work in this direction might prove to be worth while. The

British and metric systems could probably be complementary to each other.

Another ancient measurement of interest is the megalithic yard of 2.72 British feet, discovered by A. Thom. The unit is considered to be of Egyptian origin as it is found in the geometrical canon of Egyptian measures. John Mitchell in his book *The City of Revelation* brings out another point in connection with this unit: "All over the world the traditional units of length, area, weight and capacity are related to each other and derive from ONE ORIGINAL CANON OF COSMOLOGY. Two such are the English mile and the unit which now only survives in the East as the "pu" of Indo-China, its value given on page 358 of L. D'A. Jackson's *Modern Metrology* as 2.72727 miles, the fraction recurring. Without previous knowledge of this unit its former existence in Britain was deduced by Mr. J. F. Neal from his analysis of the intervals between ancient sacred sites, who called it the 'megalithic mile' on account of its ratio to the mile being virtually the same as that of the megalithic yard to the foot. There are 14,400 feet in one megalithic mile.

He points out also that the ratio between the dimensions of the earth and the moon is 10:2.72727. The key point here is that one megalithic mile is equal to 14,400 British feet. Again we have the harmonic of the speed of light, 1440, connected with British measure. There are also mathematical indications that the unit could be connected in some way with the exponential function "e" which is taken as 2.7182818. The mathematicians could delve into this area with possibly interesting results. If it can be proved that English measure was the only form of calculation that was harmonically associated with the structure of the universe and geodetic measure, then a crime of great magnitude would be committed if this system were lost to the world. Right now the pressure is on to force the metric system on all countries and if this is finally accomplished the true system of measure will be hidden away, and only be made use of by the initiates.

I believe a new system could be devised by the combination of geodetic and metric measure. The standard geodetic inch and foot could be retained and incorporated into a measuring system which has a base of 10. A basic unit could be 120 geodetic feet, which would accommodate the harmonics of ten and twelve. The unit would be 1440 inches long which, would give the direct harmonic of light. Another way would be to use a basic unit of 1.2 geodetic inches, ten of which would equal one geodetic foot.

A geometric figure which also indicates a remarkable relationship between the harmonic of light, the circle, and a system based on multiples of 10, is the decagon (see diagram). If a decagon, or ten-sided figure, is inscribed within a circle then the subtended angles are equivalent to 144^0 (the light harmonic). The angles between the side and the radius of the circle at each intersection are all 72^0, or half the light harmonic.

Another curious fact gleaned from my geometry books is that if the side A of a regular decagon, inscribed within a circle of radius R is laid off along that radius, the latter will be divided into the golden section (a ratio of 1:1.618, found to be incorporated into the structure of many ancient buildings). Our ancestors must have known something!

The next interesting figure to have a look at is the spiral. When we really think about it there is no such thing as true circular motion at any point of the universe. This is due to the relative motion of all physical bodies in space. Although we may describe a perfect circle relative to our position on earth, the instrument used to describe such a circle in actual fact would carry out a spiraling path in relation to the universe as a whole. When we think of all the different movements we are subject to we realise that it is virtually impossible to calculate the path taken by a physical body when it moves from one spatial position to another. For instance, we would have to take into account the actual movement in relation to the earth, the spin of the earth, the movement of the earth around the sun, the sun's movement within our galaxy, galactic movement and so on.

From all the research I have done so far I have come to the conclusion that during the formation of matter the wave-forms from which physical substance is manifest move through spiraling paths of 371.2766^0 cycles. These cycles set up a resonating pulse which creates a harmonic reciprocal reaction to the unified equations governing our reality. The value for *pi* in relationship to the radius of the spiraling motion is difficult to calculate due to the multi-dimensional movement. But I believe the value to be 3.24; the value of two *pi*, which could allow for the double cycle of matter and antimatter, would then be 6.48. The square root of this figure is 2.545584412, which is harmonically equivalent to the value built into the polar square section of the world grid system.

The world grid system itself is set up in harmony with the natural spiraling motion of the wave-forms in physical substance. The

DIAGRAM 6

THE HARMONICS OF A DECAGON

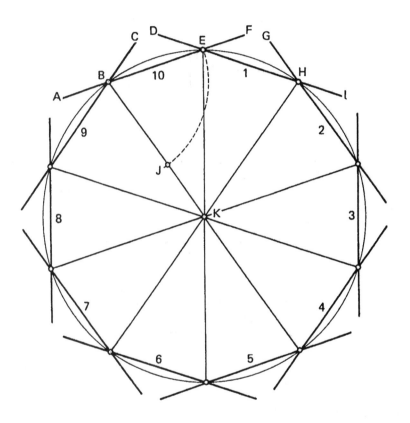

The decagon, or ten-sided figure, indicates a direct relationship between light, the circle, the harmonic power of 10, and the golden-section ratio of 1.618.

The subtended angles A–B–C, D–E–F, G–H–I, etc. each are equal to 144°, giving a direct relationship with the harmonic of the speed of light. Each inner angle K–B–E, K–E–B, K–E–H, K–H–E, etc. is equal to 72°, or half the speed of light harmonic.

If the side of a regular decagon inscribed within a circle is laid off along the radius, the radius will be divided into golden section. This is shown in the diagram by laying off the side B–E along the radius B–K. The radius is then divided into the ratio of 1:1.618.

main poles of the two interlocking grid systems on the earth's surface are placed at intervals on the natural spiral which coincide with the harmonics of the reciprocal of light.

The north and south poles of one grid are displaced 694.4 minutes of arc from the north and south geographic poles. The second interlocking grid has poles which are displaced 1054.4 minutes of arc from the geographic poles: the difference in latitude being 360 minutes, or six degrees. The two grid pole positions, north and south, fall on a spiraling curve which commences at the north and terminates at the south geographic pole. This is probably very hard to visualise without the appropriate demonstration models, but suffice it to say that the harmonic points on the natural spiral cause sympathetic resonances to be set up which combine with those of light, gravity and mass.

In *Harmonic 33* I demonstrated the relationship of the position of Wolf Creek crater in north-western Australia to the world grid system. Wolf Creek crater is a massive so-called "meteor crater" similar to the Arizona crater in the United States. Although many scientists believe that these craters, and many others like them round the world, were gouged out by giant meteors striking the earth, to date no large meteor fragments have been discovered. A fairly good scattering of a certain type of iron has been found in the vicinity of some of the holes, but the combined mass of the fragments would be only an infinitesimal fraction of the bulk required to blast out holes of such size. The presence of this pure iron could point to other interesting possibilities which will be discussed in a later chapter.

I indicated in my earlier work that I believed the craters were formed by explosions from below the surface. This would have been caused by the instability of spiral geometrics within the grid system. This could have been brought about by interference with the system in the ancient past, based on advanced scientific knowledge. All the evidence being compiled in modern times indicates that at some time round eleven to twelve thousand years ago a major catastrophe occurred which caused worldwide devastation. Some of this evidence indicates most strongly that atomic-type explosions occurred at various positions on the earth's surface. An ancient war perhaps? Or were the scientists of the day overreaching themselves and carrying out experiments with the structure of matter, without being in complete control of the resulting effects?

I said in my first work that "the force fields of the grid were naturally distorted when this happened and stresses were set up in various parts of the system. As the earth moved through space, various points in these areas of strain have lined up geometrically in relation to the solar system as a whole; the MC^2 section of the grid formula has possibly been fulfilled and a resulting explosion has taken place, with the known devastating results."

8> THE EARTH'S MAGNETIC FIELD

THE FIRST BOOK THAT I EVER READ ON THE subject of unidentified flying objects was called *Behind The Flying Saucers* by Frank Scully, an American reporter. This was in the early 1950s and the factual information contained in it impressed me very much. Some years ago, I lent my prized copy to someone and never received it back—the fate of many books in the early years of my research. Last week I was lucky enough to obtain a small paper back copy from a very good friend in the United States and on second reading I came across some information which makes sense now that I have had a number of years of research with which to correlate the data.

According to Scully, a group of American scientists carried out a crash programme during the second world war years to study magnetism and all the allied branches of science. Most of the knowledge gained has never been made public, and it appears that this comparatively small group is now so far advanced in the field of electro-magnetism that they could well apply the knowledge in the construction of antigravity-type vehicles. Scully also states that the destructive forces of electro-magnetism have been mastered in the field of weaponry.

It was his comments on the magnetic fields of the earth that interested me most. Evidently a device call a magnetron was invented by a physicist by the name of Albert Wallace Hull, who was born in April 1880. This invention was brought to the fore in 1928 when it was discovered that magnetrons with split anodes can generate very high frequencies.

Quoting Scully:

> Since then the magnetron has had many important applications. It depends on the fact that electrons can be ordered in their path by a magnet. In ordinary electron tubes the flow of electrons from the filaments to the plate is regulated by the charge on the grid. In the magnetron there is no grid, but the tube is in a magnetic field. As the intensity of the field increases there comes a stage at which the electrons are curled back into the filament, and never

reach the plate. At this critical point a slight change in the field produces a large change in the current carried by the tube.

The magnetron is especially valuable for producing high frequency oscillations used for generating ultra-short waves. The magnetron is a diode or thermionic tube having a strange axial cathode surrounded by a cylindrical anode. Its use as a magnetic prospecting instrument derives from the fact that in the presence of a magnetic field the electrons do not travel regularly from the cathode to the anode; instead they spiral around the cathode in circular paths, and after a critical magnetic field intensity is reached, the electrons will return to the cathode without reaching the anode. At this field strength the plate current will drop abruptly. The procedure in operating the instrument consists in decreasing the plate voltage on the diode until the voltage is reached at which the current falls off rapidly. The plate voltage at which this occurs is related to the critical field strength H by the relation H - 6/7200 V/R, where "R" is the radius of the anode.

(This equation is interesting when related to my own research because the value of 6/7200 is equal to .000833333. The square of this number is .000000694444, or the harmonic of the reciprocal of the speed of light.)

In practice a compensation procedure is used wherein the field to be measured is nullified by a known field produced by a coil arrangement. The magnetron is affected by the component of the earth's field which is parallel to its axis. The instrument theoretically may be used to measure any components of the earth's field by suitable orientation.

The sensitivity of the tube may be increased through regeneration by passing the plate current through an additional solenoid. Interesting experimental results have been obtained by using magnetic alloy field pieces to increase the affected magnetic field.

The earth being simply a huge magnet, a dynamo, wound with magnetic lines of force as its coils, tenescopically counted to be 1257 TO THE SQUARE CENTIMETRE IN ONE

DIRECTION AND 1850 TO THE SQUARE CENTIMETRE IN THE OTHER DIRECTION (EDDY CURRENTS), indicates that natural law has placed these lines as close together as the hairs on one's head. And yet they never touch or cross each other if let alone. If done so, by accident, the catastrophe would spread like a searchlight and destroy everything in its path.

(I agree with this statement up to a point, as I believe that matter is actually produced by the crossing of these lines of force.)

An original error of say a foot, at its source would burn everything in its path up to 20 miles and a mile and a half wide in ten thousandths of a second. If left to encircle the world the original flash would have banded the globe ten times in one second. FORTUNATELY AS A WEAPON OF DEFENCE THIS DESTRUCTIVE FORCE HAS BEEN MASTERED.

The spectroscope shows that there is an enormous magnetic field around the sun, and it is the present conclusion of the best minds that magnetic lines of force from the sun envelop this earth and extend to the moon, and THAT EVERYTHING, NO MATTER WHAT ITS FORM ON THIS PLANET, EXISTS BY REASON OF MAGNETIC LINES OF FORCE.

This I agree with, according to my own research. We are taught in our schools and universities that the magnetic field passes through one magnetic pole, then through the body, and out the other magnetic pole. I disagree with this explanation. I believe that the magnetic lines of force enter the body at the poles, then carry out a looped path through the body before passing out the opposite poles. As pointed out by Scully, the lines of force move in both directions. The flow is not in one pole and out the other, but in both poles, and out both poles, although the field intensity both ways is unbalanced.

If we can visualise one line of force so that we can trace out its path we can form an analogy by imagining it to be similar to a piece of string. First of all we make a loop in the piece of string. Now imagine it being fed through a fixed position with the loop remaining stationary relative to a fixed point. With the length of string as the axis we can now make the loop revolve in a path which is at 90⁰ to the movement of the string. The loop in fact would trace out a spherical-shaped form in space.

The lines of force of the magnetic field would form a lattice or grid pattern, due to the spin of the planetary body. A good analogy would be an ordinary machine-wound ball of string. The length of string has taken on the form of a ball, and at the same time has formed a crisscross pattern. If we again visualise this as a physical body being formed in space then we can now imagine a small vortex being created at all the trillions of points where the lines of force cross each other in the lattice pattern. Each vortex would manifest as an atomic structure and create within itself what we term a gravitational field. The gravitational field in other words is nothing more than the effect of relative motion in space. Matter is drawn towards a gravitational field, just as a piece of wood floating on water is drawn towards a whirlpool. The gravitational fields created by the vortexual action of every atom would combine to form the field of the completed planetary body.

The world grid that I speak of is the natural grid that is formed by the lattice pattern of the interlocking lines of force.

The density of the earth's magnetic field is the most important piece of information in Scully's book. The unbalanced field of 1257 lines of force per square centimetre in one direction and 1850 in the other does not tell us very much in itself. But we use the information to calculate the field strength over an area which has a harmonic relationship with the unified fields of space, and if the basic information is correct, we should find some mathematical values of great importance.

At the time of my earlier publications I was not aware of the extreme importance of the values at that stage of accuracy. I was close enough to see how they fitted into the equations, but a further fine tuning was necessary to reveal the knowledge locked within these two simple numbers.

The basic unit for harmonic calculation is the geodetic inch, or one seventy-two thousandth of a minute of arc; one minute of arc being 6000 geodetic feet. If we take the values 1257 and 1850 lines of force per square centimetre and calculate the field strengths for one square geodetic inch, the field density is 8326.71764 and 12255.08864 lines of force respectively. The fields being in opposition to each other. The combined field density is equal to 20581.80628.

Allowing for very slight variations in the conversion factors the difference in field strengths (12255.08864 minus 8326.71764) is equal to 3928.371. We could say that the resultant field density one way is equivalent to field "A" minus field "B," or 3928.371 lines of force. This value I found to be the harmonic reciprocal of the grid coordinate 2545.584412.

The combined field strength of 20581.80628 lines of force can be associated with the communication harmonic 169444 as follows.

Allowing for the matter-anti-matter cycle, we double the value:

(20581.80628 X 2) equals 41163.612
41163.612 squared equals 169444 harmonic.

The harmonic 41163612 also has a direct relationship with the geometric construction of the Great Pyramid in Egypt. The Kings Chamber in particular is built according to this value. It appears that the chamber could act in some way as a cavity resonator. Perhaps for communication? This is discussed in later works.

9> PYTHAGORAS AND THE GRID

AFTER PUBLISHING MY DISCOVERY OF THE WORLD grid system I soon came up against opposition from the academic world of the universities. Much derisive comment was made at various meetings, and the main objection appeared to be that I had used angular measurement of degrees and minutes of arc upon which to base my values of universal measurement. It was also argued that a harmonic value to base 10 was not valid as a universal multiple, as any other number, such as 12, could be employed just as effectively if my theories were correct.

At the time I could only counter these attacks on my work by pointing out the fact that I had endeavoured to make use of other values in my calculations for this very reason. I had found through trial and error that only angular measure in degrees and minutes of arc, in multiples to base 10, could be utilised to set up a system of universal harmonics. I found that this method was the only possible way to measure the harmonic relationship between light and matter regardless of the size of the body in question, be it an atom or a mass the size of Jupiter.

I also suggested that the critics should set up a system such as mine by using other basic values and harmonic equivalents if they were so sure of their ground, and to my knowledge this has never been accomplished with any success. The academics maintained that the division of a circle into degrees and minutes of arc was a random decision made by mathematicians in historical times and was therefore a purely arbitrary method of measure. The division, according to them, could just as well have been into any number of equal parts, depending on the whim of the mathematical body which set the standard. This naturally would make all my work completely valueless.

I continued to maintain that the division of the circle *must* have been made due to considerations of a geometric nature, coupled with that of natural law. All the work I had done to date indicated to me that the mathematicians of old had a knowledge of the universe which we are only once again beginning to understand.

The final solution to this argument could be overcome only by the discovery of a geometric connection between the harmonics of light and the harmonics inherent in the division of a circle. As I had based my light values on minute of arc measure there must be some type of geometric arrangement which would tie them together.

This was always in the back of my mind during the reading of many research books and finally I came across something which I believe will answer the critics. The friend who came to my rescue was none other than Pythagoras himself, a man of great stature and forceful personality who lived in the sixth century BC. He travelled extensively to enlarge his mathematical knowledge and was said to have gained much information from the priests of Zoroaster, who had in their possession the mathematical lore of the Mesopotamians. He founded a semi-religious, or mystical, cult based on mathematics, round about 540 BC in the township of Crotona, in southern Italy. He taught his disciples to worship numbers, the main idea being that number is the essence of all things, and is the metaphysical principle of rational order in the universe.

He discovered the mathematical relationships of the musical scale and the connection of musical harmony and whole numbers. He firmly believed that all harmony and things of nature can be expressed in whole-number relationships. Even the planets in their orbits, according to him, moved in harmonious relationship, one to the other, producing the so-called "music of the spheres".

The Pythagoreans explained the elements as built up of geometrical figures. One of the most interesting of these was the dodecahedron. That particular figure has locked within it a great deal of information on the geometrical nature of the universe. My first introduction to Pythagoras however was in the discovery that the humble right-angled triangle, with sides to the ratio of 3, 4 and 5, was the key to the relationship of the speed of light, to the circle.

The clue to this was found on page 62 in John Mitchell's book *The City of Revelation*. He was discussing sacred numbers and referring to the problem of squaring the circle. The suggestion was that the relative dimensions of the earth and the moon indicated an answer and that the same source provided the sacred numbers of the canon.

He demonstrated that if the circles of the earth and the moon are placed tangentially to each other and produced in their correct proportions, then each framed within a square, the geometric figure thus produced successfully squares the circle. With an earth diameter of 7920 miles and that of the moon 2160 miles, the perimeters of the two squares are respectively 31680 miles and 8640 miles. The radii of the earth (3690) and the moon (1080) in combination amount to 5040 miles. This, according to Plato, is a mystical number. It turns out that the circumference of a circle struck from the centre of the earth and passing through the centre of the moon would very closely measure 31,680 miles which is also equivalent to the perimeter of the square containing the earth.

Mitchell then went on to state that if the outer corner of the square containing the moon is joined to the corresponding corner of the square containing the earth, the triangle thus formed has sides of 2160, 2880, and 3600 miles. If divided by their highest common factor, 720, these numbers become 3, 4 and 5. He follows on to say that "confronted with facts such as these, it is scarcely possible to avoid the conclusion, orthodox in every age but the present, that the cosmic canon, inherent in the solar system as in every other department of nature, *was revealed to men not invented by them.*"

It was obvious to me that from these facts another extremely interesting conclusion could be arrived at. The various geometric relationships of the 3, 4, 5 triangle are many and varied, as can be seen by a glance through any standard geometry book. But the most important of all cannot be found in any ordinary publication.

As demonstrated in other sections of my work, the pure harmonic of the speed of light is 144. If we divide this by two, to find the harmonic of one half-cycle, or half-wave, the answer is 72. If we now apply this to the Pythagoras right-angled 3,4,5 triangle and extend each side in this ratio, then the figure will now have sides of 216, 288, and 360 units.

The harmonic proportions thus derived are equal to:

$$216 = 21600 = \text{minutes of arc in a circle}$$
$$360 = 360 = \text{degrees in a circle}$$
$$288 = 144 \times 2 = 2C, \text{ where } C = \text{speed of light.}$$

It appears from this that the harmonic of light has a very definite relationship with the geometry of a circle, and that the early mathematicians were fully aware of the fact.

If a triangle in this proportion is laid out in minutes of arc upon the surface of a sphere, then the combined angles formed by the corners of the triangle and the centre of the sphere are:

```
216
360 }minutes
288
864  minutes = 14.4 degrees
```

This again creates a harmonic in sympathetic resonance with the light factor of 144.

Can the critics still deny that the geometry of matter is directly related to the harmonic interweaving of light itself? There is no substance, in the absolute sense. We live in a reality of un-reality; all is an illusion and the stuff that dreams are made of. Our physical world is nothing more than a resonating ball of light and shade.

10> THE MAPS OF THE ANCIENTS

WHO WERE THE ANCIENTS WHO MAPPED THE coastline of Antarctica, long buried under massive layers of ice and hidden from the eyes of modern man? It is only in recent years that our scientists have probed beneath the ice with electronic instruments, and found the contour of the coastline deep down below the surface. It has been said that either the cartographers of old had the same scientific means of doing the job as we have, or that the coast was then free of ice and the contours mapped from a high altitude. This would mean that our ancestors had some means of air travel. We shall not venture too far into that, though much has been written on the subject. The maps themselves are of the greatest interest to us, from a scientific and mathematical point of view.

Charles H. Hapgood, a professor at Keene State College of the University of New Hampshire, in the United States, has provided a complete scientific analysis of one of these maps which indicates a very advanced level of mathematics as the basis for construction.

The chart used for the project was a copy of an old parchment now known as the Piri Re'is map. It was discovered in 1929 in the Imperial Palace in Constantinople and, according to the date inscribed, was produced in 1513. The signature found on it was that of Piri Ibn Hati Mammed, known as Piri Re'is, at that time an admiral in the Turkish navy.

What caused a special interest in this map was the fact that it showed South America and Africa in their correct relative longitudes. As there was no means of calculating longitude in the 16th century, this caused much puzzlement amongst the scientists.

In 1956, attention was again centered on the map when a copy was presented to the United States Navy Hydrographic office by a Turkish naval officer. A member of the staff referred the map to a friend, Captain Arlington H. Mallery, who had made a study of the ancient Viking maps of North America and Greenland. It was Mallery who suggested that the original map was made before the coast of Antarctica was covered in ice. He said it was his opinion that the southern part of the map traced out the inlets and islands of the Antarctic coast which are now buried under millions of tons of ice.

Many other scientists conceded that Mallery may be right, and subsequently Charles Hapgood decided to investigate the map in a thoroughly scientific way at Keene State College. He was helped to a great extent in the venture by a number of his students.

Their first step was to acquaint themselves with as much information as possible in regard to mediaeval maps. They concentrated mainly on the old sea charts or "Portolan" maps which guided the sailors of old from port to port.

It was found that the old charts appeared to have been copied from a more ancient master-map. What pointed to this was the fact that no major change had been made in the maps for over 200 years, dating from the 14th century. The original map had been so accurately constructed that no one in that period had the knowledge to improve on it. Mr. Hapgood states in his book that "the evidence pointed to their origin in a culture with a higher level of technology than was attained in mediaeval or ancient times."

It was a difficult task to determine the method of construction of the chart, but it was finally decided that the only possible way would have been to work from some central point. From this the mapmaker would select a radius of sufficient length to cover the area he wished to reproduce and then draw a circle. This circle would then be divided up into 16 equal triangular segments, each of which subtended an angle of 22 1/2 degrees at the centre. If the points of intersection of the various radii and the periphery of the circle were then joined, four different squares could be drawn to form the basis of a grid. By choosing one of the squares and drawing a series of lines parallel to the sides of the square and at right angles to each other, the map lattice would be completed. The details of the map could then be plotted in.

If the grid line which passed through the centre of the circle was orientated towards the north, then the map lattice would be much the same as that used in modern-day construction.

The difficult part was to find out where the centre for the Piri Re'is chart had been placed, as only a small fragment of the map remained. It could be seen that its centre would have been in a position a long way to the east.

A number of different projections were calculated over a period of three years, and each time it was found that errors in either latitude or longitude resulted. By gradually lengthening and shortening the radius and shifting the central point, it was eventually discovered that the most probable position for the centre was at 23.5

degrees north, 30.0 degrees east. The radius which was finally calculated to give the best results proved to be 69.5 degrees long.

Here again we have a very strong indication that our ancestors had an extensive knowledge of science and mathematics. The value of 69.5 degrees for the radius is very close to the natural earth harmonic geometric of 6944 (see Chapter 12) and the reciprocal of the pure harmonic of light. The mapmakers of that time apparently used a method of map projection which was based on universal mathematical constants, which afforded them great accuracy in plotting the surface features of the earth.

DIAGRAM 7

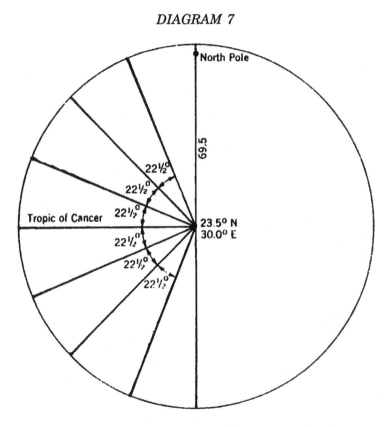

The diagram shows the most probable position for the centre of the map projection

11> RUSSIANS AND GERMANS DISCOVER A WORLD GRID SYSTEM

PYTHAGORAS TAUGHT THAT ALL THE ELEMENTS contained in the physical universe were built up from geometrical figures. The most interesting of these was the pentadodecahedron, which was identified as the "sphere of the universe", or the "hull of the sphere". The construction of the world was likened to the building of a ship, by the use of geometrical shapes. Plato also referred to this in the Phaedo where we see a statement that the "true earth", if looked at from above, is "many-coloured like the balls that are made of many pieces of leather".

Out of the regular solids, the dodecahedron is the one that most closely approaches that of a sphere. It is a solid that is bounded by twelve surfaces, and in the case of the pentagon-dodecahedron, twelve regular pentagons. If a ball were made up of twelve pieces of leather, the pieces would be in the shape of a regular pentagon. If the pieces were not flexible, but rigid, the geometric body would be a dodecahedron instead of a sphere. The ancient philosophers regarded this geometric figure as the building-block of the universe, and the knowledge was so secret that anyone revealing it was immediately put to death. It is possible for this reason that the schools of mysticism adopted the pentagram, or pantalpha, as their symbol. There was considered to be much magic power in the five-sided figure and the Pythagoreans regarded it as the symbol of health.

Is the earth some sort of gigantic crystal with a rigid skeletal-like structure beneath the surface? The Russians ran a story to this effect in 1973 in the *Komsomolskaya Pravda*, the official newspaper for the younger generation of the Soviet Union.

The globe was not just the simple spheroid that we imagined. The suggestion was that it first started out as a large crystal with angular dimensions and that after millions of years wearing-down processes, the crystal finally rounded itself into a ball. According to Soviet scientists, the angular edges of the primary crystal now lie beneath the surface of the earth. In some areas, the edges of the crystal protrude imperceptibly through the surface, giving us a slight clue to the overall pattern beneath.

Knowing nothing of these theories, a Russian historian by the name of Nikolai Goncharov had a hunch that there might be a pattern to all the centres of earliest human culture and accordingly began to mark them out on a globe. Later, collaboration with a construction engineer, Vyacheslav Morozov, and an electronics specialist, Valery Makarov, led to a complete hypothesis concerning the geometric nature of the earth. After working together for several years they published an article in the science journal *Chemistry and Life* issued by the USSR Academy of Sciences. The article was headed "Is The Earth A Large Crystal?"

The article was based on studies covering widely separated fields such as archaeology, geochemistry, ornithology and meteorology. They theorised that the earth projects from within itself a dual geometrically regularised grid. The initial form of the grid being twelve pentagonal slabs over the surface of the sphere gave evidence to the fact that the first shape of the earth was a dodecahedron. The second part of the grid is formed by twenty equilateral triangles making up an icosahedron. They maintain that by superimposing the two grids over the surface of the earth a pattern of the earth's energy structure can be perceived.

A careful study of the Russian system showed that the lines tracing out their dual grid on the earth's surface coincided with zones of active risings and depressions on the ocean floors, core faults and mid-oceanic ridges. One of the vertices of the triangles falls just east of Florida, near the centre of the infamous "Devil's Bermuda Triangle", known worldwide as an area of mysterious disappearances of numerous ships and aircraft. It is now known that there are twelve of these areas.

It was also noted that at various positions on the edges of the polygons, scientists have discovered regions of seismic and volcanic activity. Magnetic anomalies are likewise found at the vertices of the polygons. The nodes of the grid are centres of great changes in atmospheric pressure and hurricanes form in these areas, veering off to follow the paths of intersection formed by the interlocking patterns. Prevailing winds and ocean currents also fit into the network.

An extremely interesting point of the system is in the African republic of Gabon. According to the scientists, a "natural atomic reactor" was recently discovered there, which was active 1.7 billion years ago. This caused a mass of uranium 235 to reach a level of chain reaction. Oddly enough, this piece of evidence backs up the information published in my first two books regarding the geometric nature of atomic reactions. Certain modern-day atomic stations must be constructed on geometric locations in order to function efficiently-breeder stations in particular. An atomic bomb is a geometric device which necessitates geometric positioning for detonation.

Large mother lodes of mineral ore and vast oil deposits can be found where lines of the system cross each other. A whole new science is beginning to unfold from research into the geometric makeup of the world beneath our feet.

Satellite photographs have been correlated with the grid. The Ural Fold extends along one of the lines and a gigantic fault from Morocco to Pakistan coincides with one of the ribs. Large circular geological structures show up on intersections in Morocco, California and Florida. Even soil is apparently affected according to its locations on the grid: at different intersections the very elements making up the soil are mixed in different proportions.

Man himself, the authors say, has not escaped the influences of the energy emitted by the grid lattice. Many of the ancient cultures seem to have flourished on intersections of the system. The mind of man is evidently tapped into the very circuitry of the ball of energy that constitutes the world that provides his home.

Most startling of all is the revelation in their article that to line the system up on the surface of the globe so that all these different factors could be correlated, the point they located as position one was that of the Great Pyramid of Giza, in Egypt. The "measure of light" is the key.

It is obvious from these reports that the Russians are working along the same lines as I have been. I too had found similar manifestations in geometric locations round the world, by the study of two interlocking grid patterns. The Russian grid was shaped differently to mine but the same facts were becoming evident from the related research efforts. This hinted at the probability that the same mathematical concepts could be applied to either system.

The Russians are certainly on to something and a much more extensive in-depth study will have to be made of the network they have uncovered in order to "wrinkle out" all the secrets inherent within it. Suffice it to say that enough is known at this stage to guarantee a goldmine of scientific truths.

The Germans are not to be left out in the exploration of the energy fields within the earth. They are known to be far-reaching in the realms of science and not afraid to explore, or put into practice, concepts which to most other western scientists appear fantastic. The "buzz bombs", V2 rockets and jet aircraft developed during World War Two are direct proof of this.

A book written by Siegfried Wittman was published in Innsbruck, Austria, in 1952. It was titled *Die Welt Der Geheimen Machte*, or *The World Of The Secret Forces*.

An unusual number of people were involved in the research that went into the subject-matter of the book. The group formed a very impressive mixture of professional minds to be focussed upon one project: Dr. Willi Schlosser; Prof. Hellmut Wolff;Hans-Wilhelm Smollk; Heinrich Reblitz; Theodor Weiman; Herbert A Lohlein; Ferdinand Reich; Univ. Prof. Dr. Hubert J. Urban; Dir. Prof. Dr. K. Saller; Prof. Dr. George Anschutz; Prof. Dr. Theol; and Adolf Koberle.

After extensive research they came to the conclusion that the earth has upon its surface a grid system, in a checkerboard pattern consisting of positive and negative poles.

The squared pattern, according to them, has a centre pole surrounded by eight smaller poles within each section. The squares vary in size from the equator, getting smaller in the direction of the earth's poles. The main pole concentrates energy. Experiments conducted at north latitude 48⁰ indicated that the centre pole has a diameter of 2.45 metres. The eight smaller poles have a diameter of 60 cm. Four of the eight outer poles send energy up toward the sky in alternate pulses. The other four send energy outward horizontally to the north, south, east and west.

The squares at 48⁰ north latitude are 15.9 metres diagonally from centre to centre poles. A border field is mingled together in the north-west and south-east directions, and in the south-west and north-east directions. These four corners of the squares seem to connect the fields of two of the negative smaller poles, and two of the positive smaller poles. The side length measurements at the equator are 32 metres long. The main centre pole of each positive square shows a direction of energy from above to below the earth's surface. The created pulse forms a vortex. The negative poles work in the opposite sense.

Not much more is known to me of the German research effort at this stage as I have only sighted extracts from the book. One thing does stand out however from the scanty bits of information that I do have: the Germans carried out many of their experiments on latitude 48 degrees. What made them select this particular latitude in

DIAGRAM 8

North Pole

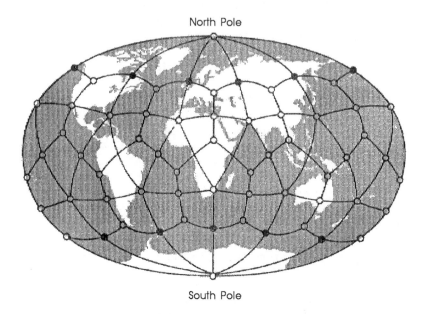

South Pole

World grid system discovered by the Russians

preference to any other? Could it be that 48 degrees happens to be 2880 minutes of arc? Have they also discovered that the harmonic of twice the speed of light is 288? The unified equation derived from this harmonic cannot be a particularly well-kept secret. This band of learned men appears to be aware of a grid complex similar to the one I described in my earlier writings. I would be most interested to be advised of their complete findings-particularly if they are now in possession of the knowledge to make use of the energy being radiated by the system.

I have a feeling that there are many people, or small groups of people, in the world that know the secrets of tapping free energy from the earth grid and that the knowledge has always been available to the select few. As far back as 1919, at least one man demonstrated that he could run electric motors and lighting systems without having to pay the power companies one cent for the power he used.

A young nineteen-year-old inventive genius by the name of Alfred Hubbard startled his contemporaries by powering an eighteen-foot boat around Portage Bay, not far from Seattle, by use of a free energy device.

The boat was driven by a 35hp motor without the aid of batteries. The electrical energy was supplied from a transducer within the boat. This device was in exact electrical resonance with his free energy transformer, which had been constructed on a small area of land. The transformer was supplied by energy collected from an array of ground aerials. Wires were run underground north, south, east and west for a distance of 1200 feet. At the outer end of each wire was attached a hollow tube, 18 inches long, filled with mercury. (From other information I have, I would assume that the tubes were made from pure iron. The reason for the iron-mercury combination will be discussed in another section.) The mercury-filled tube combination apparently created an electrical one-way gate system which directed the energy flow to the central primary coil.

The information I have states that Hubbard made use of what the Chinese call the "cosmic flower". This was, according to them, the source of all power. The electrical energy which was directed into the central coil of the system caused a resonating pulse tuned to the natural earth frequency. This caused an electrical current to flow through the secondary coil of the apparatus due to induction.

The coils were said to be round-shaped in both the primary and the secondary. The secondary coil in one instance was wound in a diamond configuration — or wound like a basket. I have a sneaking suspicion that the two superimposed coils had a similar configuration to the Russian grid pattern (pentagonal and triangular), but this will have to wait until experiments can be carried out. (Any further factual information from readers will be most welcome.)

A small outlay of capital and a series of experiments could, with a bit of luck, demonstrate one of the methods of extracting free energy from the earth. If the secret can be broken it should be possible to run several homes from such a device. I leave this open to those of you who have a streak of inventive genius.

12> TESLA — THE FORGOTTEN GENIUS

Some day I will harness Niagra Falls. — Tesla

THIS WAS THE STATEMENT MADE BY THE greatest electrical genius that ever lived, to one of his fellow students, in Budapest, in 1882. Nicola Tesla, born 9 July 1856, was then aged twenty-five and about to commence a lifetime career in the advancement of electrical knowledge which was to transform the world. If it were not for this one man, almost all modern-day electrical devices would not exist. It therefore seems strange that Tesla's name is known to so very few students in our universities. Many times I have mentioned Tesla to groups of students, during discussions, and have been met with a blank stare, and the question — "Who is Tesla?"

His birthplace was a small village called Smiijan in the country now called Yugoslavia. His father was a minister in the local church. His mother was illiterate, but was known in the village as one who had a clever and inventive mind. It is said that she invented a considerable number of labour saving devices, which could be used in the home. In later years Tesla stated that he inherited his inventive genius from his mother.

In one stupendous lifetime he gave us the whole foundation upon which to build the industrial empires of the world. It was he who invented the alternating-current motors that power every factory and production centre. He that designed the transmission systems that enabled power to be sent out over vast areas of countryside from a central generating source; the mass production systems and robot control that freed man from the slavery of labour; the basis for radio and radar, and remote control by wireless; modern lighting systems by use of high-frequency currents. The list is endless. No limit has been found to the electronic marvels which can be produced from the basic discoveries which issued from this one fertile mind. The whole world owes Tesla its future — and he has been forgotten, because he was a man who lived before his time.

Tesla was one of five children and even at an early age showed signs of a lively mind. He found that in many things he could surpass other boys of his own age, and this tended to isolate him from his contemporaries. He found it hard to find others to share in his interests and his intellectual attainments were often in advance of his years. Nevertheless, it seems that he still got up to all the other foolish escapades that young boys find to fill in their time — myself included.

One of the more dangerous ones was trying to emulate a bird. He discovered that when he breathed deeply he began to feel very light and buoyant. He considered that this discovery, plus the application of daring and an old umbrella, should suffice to free him from the pull of gravity and allow him to sail through the air with a certain amount of grace and dignity. He climbed up on the roof of a local barn with the trusty old umbrella, breathed a few deep breaths and jumped off into space. The umbrella, not being aerodynamically designed, folded inside out and Tesla carried out a very undignified plummet to the ground. This cost him six weeks in bed, and much embarrassment.

His next accomplishment was the invention of a special frog-catching hook which was immediately copied by all his friends and helped to ensure the demise of most of the frogs in the village pond. Then followed a series of gadgets attractive to small boys, which included very efficient blowguns and popguns the size of small howitzers. Damage to local property caused the sudden end to the production of such warlike weapons, and punishment administered to the end of Tesla. At the advanced age of nine years he constructed his first motor. The prime mover of this wondrous machine was a formation of sixteen may-bugs. I suppose in a way they could have been termed galley bugs, as they had to perform in much the same way as the galley slaves of old to produce forward movement to the parts of Tesla's machine. The design was quite ingenious. He glued two long thin bits of wood together to form a cross, much like the arms of a windmill. Another thin spindle was attached to this with a very small pulley glued to it. This was connected by a belt made from cotton to a larger pulley on another thin spindle. The engines (or maybugs) were then glued four abreast, facing forward, on each of the four arms. The poor bugs, no doubt dismayed at such cavalier treatment, beat their wings at panic speed and turned the windmill at a surprising rate. It was Tesla's intention to add more bugs, and thus more power to this truly remarkable machine, but a young friend decided to eat his jarful of spare bugs. This nearly caused Tesla to throw up, and he ended up destroying his invention in disgust.

The first stage of his schooling ended in 1870, when he was fourteen. The college he attended was called the Real Gymnasium, at Gospic. Already he was showing that he was well above the average in his abilities. He continued his studies at the higher Real Gymnasium, completing the full four-year course in three years. It was at this time that he became fascinated with physics and electrical experimentation and made the decision to devote his life to electricity. His father was anxious for him to enter the ministry and make a career of the church, but finally relented and promised Nicola that he would not prevent him from having his wish. The boy had overworked himself so much with his studies that he had weakened his body and been attacked, first by malaria then a severe bout of cholera. When nearly at death's door he whispered to his father, "I will get well again if you will let me study electrical engineering." He was promised by his father that he would attend the most advanced engineering school in the world. Tesla was nineteen when he began his studies in electrical engineering at the Polytechnic Institute at Gratz, Austria.

It was at the Institute that particular insights into the mysteries of electricity by Tesla first began to show themselves. A Professor Poeschl was demonstrating a gramme machine that could be used as either a dynamo or a motor. It was run by direct current and suffered a great loss of efficiency due to sparking at the commutator. (The commutator was necessary in all direct current machines to change the flow of electricity at the correct instant to obtain rotary motion.)

An argument developed between the professor and Tesla as to the design of the machine and the necessity to use direct current. Why cannot alternating current be used, suggested Tesla? This would eliminate the need for commutators and thus increase efficiency. The alternating current produced by the dynamos could be fed direct to the motors without the use of the reversing mechanisms.

The professor set up a special set of experiments to prove to Tesla that his idea was completely impractical and made the statement: "Mr. Tesla will accomplish great things, but he certainly will never do this. It would be equivalent to converting a steady pulling force like gravity into rotary effort. It is a perpetual motion scheme, an impossible idea."

Tesla had no answer to this at the time,. but instinct told him he was right and that some day in the future he would create such a machine. He continued his studies at the University of Prague concentrating on mathematics and physics. Always in the back of his mind was the idea of the alternating-current motor, and in his imagination he contemplated many different methods of building such a device, each time to fail.

On leaving the university Tesla obtained a position with the central telegraph office in Budapest. His genius for invention was not long in being noticed and in 1881 he was placed in charge of the new telephone exchange. It was while working for this company that he had the first flash of inspiration that was to rocket him to short-lived fame.

He was walking with a friend late in the afternoon in the city park of Budapest. It was February 1882, and a glorious day. Tesla was in a particularly happy frame of mind and gave vent to his joy by prancing about, and reciting poetry. Suddenly, he stopped in his tracks and exclaimed, "Watch me! Watch me reverse it." He appeared to be in some kind of a trance and his friend got quite alarmed at his antics, believing him to be ill. When Tesla finally calmed down he said, "No, you do not understand. I have solved the problem of my alternating-current motor." He then explained how he could see the whole concept in front of him, as if in a vision.

A rotating magnetic field which would clutch the armature of a motor with invisible fingers and cause it to rotate in harmony with it. A concept sublime in its simplicity. There and then, he drew a diagram of his motor in the snow to show his friend the technical aspects of his invention. This moment was the beginning of man's leap forward in the industrialisation of the world.

It was soon after this that Tesla was offered a position with the Continental Edison Company and spent much of his time improving the designs of the Edison direct-current motors. He also invented a system for automatically regulating the dynamos. He had been promised a substantial fee for all the new innovations he had produced for the company, and when this was not forthcoming on demand, he immediately resigned. If the payment had been made at the time, Tesla would possibly have remained with the company and they would have benefited immensely from his genius.

It was suggested by a member of the company that Tesla should emigrate to the United States and work with Edison himself. There were not many opportunities left open to him in Europe, so in 1884 the young Tesla arrived in New York with four cents in his pocket and a mind bursting with new ideas. At this stage he had already worked out the whole alternating-current electrical system in his mind. This included step-up and step-down transformers for the most economical transmission of electric power, alternators, and alternating-current motors to supply mechanical power.

When he finally met the famous Edison, he gave him an enthusiastic description of his alternating current system, only to be told that he was "wasting his time messing around with such things." Edison was committed to the direct-current system and would not be swayed by the arguments put forth by Tesla. The whole of the Edison empire was built on the premise that direct current was superior to alternating current.

He spent almost a year working for Edison, again improving and inventing new techniques for the production of the Edison dynamos. Promises had been made to him, for the second time to repay him adequately for his services. It is said that Edison had undertaken to pay $50,000 to Tesla when all the improvements were completed and the machines ready for production. When the time came for settlement, Edison treated the whole thing as a joke, so the disillusioned Tesla once again resigned.

It was now 1885. The fortune he was seeking in the promised land was not to come easily. He spent a year taking any menial job he could find just to keep himself alive. At one stage he even resorted to digging ditches. The foreman on the ditch-digging project was fascinated by the visionary descriptions of the new electrical innovations that Tesla related to him, and introduced him to an executive of the company named A. K. Brown. This man had enough faith to finance an experimental laboratory at 33-35 South Fifth Avenue, New York.

Tesla set to work and in a short time had a complete demonstration of his system ready for assessment. Included were alternating-current generators, motors, transformers, transmission lines and lights. After examination by Professor W. A. Anthony of Cornell University, it was announced that the Tesla system was equal in efficiency to any of the best direct-current machines then in production.

In 1887 Tesla applied for full patent rights for all of his electrical inventions. This was not approved by the patent office as they considered a single patent to cover such a great array of ideas was too unwieldy. They insisted that each important section be covered by a separate patent. Within the next six months seven USA patents were granted, and in 1888 twenty-two more were to follow.

The Institute of Electrical Engineers were now aware of this genius among them and invited Tesla to give a demonstration lecture on his alternating-current system in New York. This was a tremendous success. It was now recognised by the engineers of the world that there need be no limit to the transmission of power over long distances. The way was now open to develop the whole industry beyond men's wildest dreams.

Tesla was thirty-two when he was approached by George Westinghouse, who offered him one million dollars for all his alternating current patents, plus certain royalties. Tesla agreed, on the proviso that the royalty was to be one dollar per horsepower. Although this royalty was later withdrawn because of financial difficulties in the Westinghouse empire, a bond of mutual trust remained between these two great men for the rest of their lives. Tesla, at last, was being given the credit he deserved. America was his to conquer.

The General Electric Company, founded by the Edison interests, saw the writing on the wall and for their very survival had to negotiate a licence from Westinghouse to compete in the rapidly expanding electrical industry being built on the concepts of alternating current. No future remained for those who thought in terms of direct current only.

In 1890 the scientist Lord Kelvin was appointed chairman of the International Niagara Commission set up to determine the most efficient way of using the force of Niagara Falls to generate electricity. In 1892 Westinghouse won the contract for the Installation of the 5000-horsepower hydro-electric generators.

The transmission system was contracted to the General Electric Company. The whole complex was designed according to the ideas of Tesla. The massive alternators with external revolving fields and internal stationary armatures were personally designed by him; the transmission line including the step-up and step-down transformers was constructed to Tesla's two-phase concept. His childhood dream had been fulfilled — he had harnessed the power of Niagra Falls.

Now in his early thirties Tesla was a wealthy man and felt free to devote more of his time to pure research. Throughout his life he gave no indication of any type of business sense. The mere making of money was never a primary object with him, and as long as he had the necessary funds to buy all the equipment he needed for his experiments he was happy. His whole makeup was that of the discoverer. He was at one with the environment itself and had a compelling, restless urge to pry all the secrets from nature and harness them, in order to help his fellow man progress towards a higher level of being. He had a vision of the cosmos as consisting of myriad octaves of electrical vibration. It was his desire to be able to understand the interplay of harmonic oscillations that formed the basis of the universe. The lower octaves he had already explored with his 60 cycle per second alternating current. He was now ready to reach into the unknown and probe into the regions of ultra high frequency of light and beyond.

For these experiments he constructed a great range of electrical oscillators to produce high-frequency currents, and coils tuned to set frequencies or wavelengths in order to discover the characteristics of each energy level and the particular uses to which each could be applied. He found that the interlocking harmonics were similar to the musical scale and that his coils responded not only to the trans-missions of the original waveforms, but resonated at harmonic inter-vals above and below the original frequency. He had discovered the harmonic nature of matter.

He felt ready to take the next step in the practical application of his theoretical discoveries. During an interview in 1894 he said:

> You will think me a dreamer and very far gone if I should tell you what I really hope for. But I can tell you that I look forward with absolute confidence to sending messages through the earth without any wires. I have also great hopes of transmitting electrical force in the same way without waste. Concerning the transmission of messages through the earth I have no hesitation in pre-dicting success: I must first ascertain exactly how many vibrations to the second are caused by disturbing the mass of electricity which the earth contains. My machine for transmitting must vibrate as often to put itself in accord with the electricity in the earth.

He had previously addressed a meeting of the National Electric Light Association and had said, in part:

> I am becoming more and more convinced of the scheme, and though I know full well that the great majority of scientific men will not believe that such results can be practically and immediately realised, yet I think that all consider the developments in recent years by a number of

workers to have been such as to encourage thought and experiment in this direction. My conviction has grown so strong that I no longer look upon the plan of energy or intelligence transmission as a mere theoretical possibility, but as a serious problem to electrical engineering, which must be carried out some day...

We now know that electrical vibrations may be transmitted through a single conductor. Why then not try to avail ourselves of the earth for this purpose? We need not be frightened of the idea of distance. To the weary wanderer counting the mile posts, the earth may appear very large; but to the happiest of all men, the astronomer, who gazes at the heavens, and by their standards judges the magnitude of our globe, it appears very small. And so I think it must seem to the electrician; for when he considers the speed with which an electrical disturbance is propagated through the earth, all his ideas of distance must completely vanish.

A point of great importance would be first to know what is the capacity of the earth, and what charge does it contain if electrified. Though we have no evidence of a charged body existing in space without other oppositely electrified bodies being near, there is a fair probability that the earth is such a body, for whatever process it was separated — and this is the accepted view of its origin — it must have retained a charge, as occurs in all processes of mechanical separation.

If we can ever ascertain at what period the earth's charge, when disturbed, oscillates, with respect to an oppositely charged system, or known circuit, we shall know a fact possible of the greatest importance to the welfare of the human race. I propose to seek the period by means of an electrical oscillator, or a source of alternating currents.

One of the terminals of this source would be connected to the earth, as, for instance, the city water mains, the other to an insulated body of large surface. It is possible that the outer conducting air strata, or free space, contain an opposite charge, and that, together with the earth, they form a condenser of large capacity. In such case the period of vibration may be very low and an alternating dynamo machine might serve for the purpose of the experiment. I would then transform the current to a potential as high as it would be found possible, and connect the ends of the high tension secondary coil to the ground and to the insulated body. By varying the frequency of the currents and carefully observing the potential of the insulated body, and watching for the disturbance at various neighbouring points of the earth's surface, resonance might be detected.

For the experiments, Tesla chose a site on the outskirts of the town of Colorado Springs, Colorado. To the present day it has been thought that he selected this particular area just out of pure convenience. It was said that he was attracted by the dryness of the air which made it an excellent position for electrical experiment (violent electrical storms were common in the mountainous terrain around Colorado Springs and nearby Pikes Peak). But I believe this was not his prime reason, as will be demonstrated.

A large barn-shaped structure was built on the site to Tesla's specifications. It was just on 100 feet square, with sides twenty-five feet high. The roof then sloped upward to a high peak in the centre. A pyramid-shaped tower extended upward from the centre peak for a height of about eighty feet through which a mast was supported, reaching to a height of around 200 feet. On top of the mast was a copper ball three feet in diameter. A heavy duty wire was run from this copper ball down the mast, then connected to the large secondary coil of the electrical apparatus in the shed.

Power, which was supplied by a generator from the Colorado Springs Electric Power Company a few miles away, was fed into a transformer system and stepped up to around 30,000 volts. This was then fed into a condenser. When the condenser reached capacity it discharged into a coil. This provided a continually oscillating high-frequency current. The primary coil was constructed of heavy wire on a circular fence like arrangement about seventy-five feet in diameter. At the centre, the secondary coil, about ten feet in diameter, was wound with approximately seventy-five turns on a frame ten feet high. This inner coil was attached to a copper plate buried deep in the ground at one end and the other end connected to the copper ball at the top of the mast. The two coils were tuned perfectly with each other and created electrical resonances in the order of 100 million volts.

The whole system acted as a gigantic electrical pump, and enabled Tesla to cause massive discharges of energy to oscillate between the earth and the surrounding atmosphere. During his experiments with this fantastic piece of equipment he caused huge bolts of lightning to issue forth from the copper ball into the air, and manmade thunder to scare the living daylights out of the populace for miles around. He finally succeeded in burning out the generating plant at Colorado Springs due to the electrical overload placed upon it. This did not, of course, make him too popular with the local council, and he had to carry out extensive repairs to the plant before he was able to continue with his work.

He discovered that a rate of 150,000 oscillations a second, which produced electrical pulsations with a wavelength of 2000 metres, was necessary to produce the effects he required in the transmission of usable power through the earth.

If we convert the wavelength of 2000 metres to a minute of arc, or nautical mile equivalent on the earth's surface the result is 1.0792237. The experimental value was therefore very close to 1.08 minutes of arc, or one twenty thousandth of the circumference of the earth. 21600 minutes divided by 1.08.

The exact number of cycles to obtain a 1.08 minute wavelength would be 149892.18 per second. This would tune the transmitter in harmony with the world grid system.

In the early stages of my work I wondered why I could not obtain pure harmonics from all my calculations when dealing with physical substance — that is, exactly 144 for the light harmonic etc. Tesla stated that it was not possible to obtain pure resonance or harmonic vibrations, because if this were so then matter itself would disintegrate. A certain amount of resistance must be allowed for to prevent complete destruction of physical substance.

He tested his theory of power transmission by lighting 200 incandescent lamps at a distance of twenty-six miles from the laboratory while the giant oscillator was operating — the energy being extracted directly from the earth. Each lamp required about 50 watts of power — a total of 13hp. The claimed efficiency was 95 percent.

The Century Magazine ran an article in the June edition of 1900 stating comments made by Tesla regarding his Colorado experiments: "However extraordinary the results shown may appear, they are but trifling compared with those obtainable by apparatus designed on these same principles. I have produced electrical discharges the actual path of which, from end to end, was probably more than 100 feet long; but it would not be difficult to reach lengths 100 times as great. I have produced electrical movements occurring at the rate of approximately 100,000 horsepower, but rates of one, five or ten million horsepower are easily practicable. In these experiments, effects were developed incomparably greater than ever produced by any human agencies and yet these results are but an embryo of what is to be."

Tesla now had all the information he required to set up a station to transmit power to any point in the world, but before we move on to discuss his later activities let us have a closer look at the site he chose in Colorado where he tested all his theories and found positive proof of the harmonic structure of nature. In one of his unpublished articles he had stated in part that: "Long ago he (man) recognised that all perceptible matter comes from a primary substance, of a tenuity beyond conception, filling all space, the Akasa or Luminiferous Ether, which is acted upon by the life-giving prana or creative force, calling into existence, in never-ending cycles, all things and phenomena. THE PRIMARY SUBSTANCE, THROWN INTO INFINITESIMAL WHIRLS OF PRODIGIOUS VELOCITY, BECOMES GROSS MATTER; THE FORCE SUBSIDING. THE MOTION CEASES AND MATTER DISAPPEARS, REVERTING TO THE PRIMARY SUBSTANCE."

His experiments had shown him (as I had found in my own bumbling way) that matter was nothing more than a complex matrix of wave-forms locked together by harmonic resonance. The energy inherent in matter could be tapped if the secret of the geometric structure of the wave-forms could be broken. It appears that, by calculation, he had found that to tune in, so to speak, to this energy ball we call earth, he had to set up his apparatus on a particular point on its surface to ensure that the waves he proposed to transmit were in step with the natural medium. Colorado Springs was one of the ideal positions which was accessible to him.

The position of Colorado Springs is given as 38 degrees 50 minutes North latitude and 104 degrees 50 minutes West longitude. Calculations which have been carried out recently for this area show that a theoretical position of 38^0 49' 31.629" North latitude and 104^0 52' 22" West longitude would be the ideal position to set up a Tesla type experiment.

The exact positions where Tesla built his transmitter is unknown to me, but I believe it was not too far from the theoretical one.

During my years of research I have discovered that some of the scientific establishments have been positioned in such a way that the latitude value sets up a harmonic due to the relative distance from the Equator and the North or South Pole. Also I have found that there are harmonic intervals above and below the normal units of degrees, minutes and seconds in circular measure. Division or multiplication is carried out by the harmonic value of 6.

So: for the theoretical latitude position we have:

Distance to the North Pole	=	51.174548 degrees
Distance from the equator	=	38.825453 degrees
Difference	=	12.349095 degrees
Divided by 6	=	2.0581825 units
Multiplied by 2	=	4.116365 units
Squared	=	16.9444 units

The harmnonic 169444 is related to MASS, GRAVITY and COMMUNICATION and is demonstrated many times in my later works. The method of calculation also follows a regular pattern. The great circle displacement between longitude 104⁰ 52' 22" west and 90⁰ 00' 00" west, at the same latitude, also sets up an important harmonic. The value: 694.44 minutes of arc. This is the reciprocal harmonic of the Grid speed of light, 144000 minutes of arc per Grid second, in free space.

Tesla must have been well aware of the importance of the position he chose, but kept the reasons a closely guarded secret.

It is interesting to note that in this same area the military have chosen to set up the greatest electrical complex in the world — the North American Defence Command, NORAD. I am not telling tales out of school here because other publications have already pointed this fact out. The caption on a photo of the command post, in a publication which I have, free to any of the public who wish to buy one, states: "The main battle staff position in the combat operations centre (COC) at headquarters North American Defence Command (NORAD), Colorado Springs, Colorado, fronts a display area which allows observers to see the positions of airborne objects thousands of miles away. NORAD (COC) is hooked to all of NORAD's subordinate units and to every major command post on the continent."

I am sure the Russians are also fully aware of the significance of this position and that they have similar military command posts set up on the Russian continent, so I am not releasing anything that could in the remotest sense be termed a military secret.

From a public point of view though, one of the reasons becomes clear why the work and discoveries of Tesla remain suppressed: *the military application of his discoveries has been considered far more important than the welfare of the ordinary citizen of the world.*

Tesla was now ready to build his world power system. With a cash grant of $150,000 donated by the banker J.P. Morgan he was able to commence construction of his world wireless power and broadcasting station.

The site he picked for this station was to be on a tract of land owned by James S. Warden, a lawyer and banker. This was at Shoreham, in Suffolk County, Long Island. Tesla's idea was to create a radio city from which information would be broadcast on all wavelengths. I find once more that far better than my own inadequate description of the system, the reported words of Tesla himself give more of an idea of the magnitude of the enterprise:

> The world system has resulted from a combination of several original discoveries made by the inventor in the course of long continued research and experimentation. It makes possible not only the instantaneous and precise wireless transmission of any kind of signals, messages or characters to all parts of the world, but also the interconnection of the exisiting telegraph, telephone and other signal stations without any change in their present equipment. By its means for instance, a telephone subscriber here may call up any other subscriber on the globe. An inexpensive receiver, not bigger than a watch, will enable him to listen anywhere on land or sea to a speech delivered, or music played, in some other place, however distant. These examples are cited merely to give an idea of the possibilities of this great scientific advance, which annihilates distance and makes that perfect conductor, the earth, available for all the innumerable purposes which human ingenuity has found for a line wire. One far-reaching result of this is that any device capable of being operated through one or more wires (at a distance obviously restricted) can like wise be activated, without artificial conductors, and with the same facility and accuracy, at distances to which there are no limits other than those imposed by the physical dimensions of the globe. Thus, not only will entirely new fields for commercial exploitation be opened up by this ideal method of transmission, but the old ones vastly extended.

The world system is based on the application of the following important inventions and discoveries.

1. The Tesla Transformer: This apparatus is in the production of electrical vibrations, as revolutionary as gunpowder was in warfare. Currents many times stronger than any ever generated in the usual ways, and sparks over 100 feet long, have been produced by the inventor with an instrument of this kind.

2. The Magnifying Transmitter: This is Tesla's best invention — a peculiar transformer specially adapted to excite the earth, which is, in the transmission of electrical energy, what the telescope is in astronomical observation. By the use of this marvellous device he has already set up electrical movements of greater intensity than those of lightning, and passed a current sufficient to light more than 200 incandescent lamps around the globe.

3. The Tesla Wireless System: This system comprises a number of improvements and is the only means known for transmitting, economically, electrical energy to a distance without wires. Careful test and measurements in connection with an experimental station of great activity, erected by the inventor in Colorado, have demonstrated that power in any desired amount can be conveyed clear across the globe if necessary, with a loss not exceeding a few per cent.

4. The Art of Individualisation: This invention of Tesla, is to primitive tuning what refined language is to inarticulated expression. It makes possible the transmission of signals or messages absolutely secret and exclusive both in active and passive aspect, that is, non-interfering as well as non-interferable. Each signal is like an individual of unmistakable identity and there is virtually no limit to the number of stations or instruments that can be simultaneously operated without the slightest mutual disturbance.

5. The Terrestrial Stationary Waves: This wonderful discovery, popularly explained, means that the earth is responsive to electrical vibrations of definite pitch, just as a tuning fork is to certain waves of sound. These particular electrical vibrations, capable of powerfully exciting the globe, lend themselves to innumerable uses of great importance commercially and in many other respects.

The first world system power plant can be put in operation in nine months. With this power plant it will be practical to attain electrical activities up to ten million horsepower and it is designed to serve for as many technical achievements as are possible without undue expense. Among these the following may be mentioned:

1. Interconnection of the existing telegraph exchanges or offices all over the world.
2. Establishment of a secret and non-interferable Government telegraph service.
3. Interconnection of all the present telephone exchanges or offices all over the globe.
4. Universal distribution of general news, by telegraph or telephone, in connection with the press.
5. The establishment of a world system of intelligence transmission for exclusive private use.
6. Interconnection and operation of all stock tickers of the world.
7. Establishment of a world system of musical distribution, etc.
8. Universal registration of time by cheap clocks indicating the time with astronomical precision and requiring no attention whatever.
9. Facsimile transmission of type or handwritten characters, letters, cheques etc.
10. Establishment of a universal marine service enabling navigators of all ships to steer perfectly without compass, to determine the exact location, hour and speed, to prevent collisions and disasters etc.
11. Inauguration of a system of world printing on land or sea.
12. Reproduction anywhere in the world of photographic pictures and all kinds of drawings or records.

The complex that Tesla planned to build on Long Island to bring all this to fruition was at that time like something out of some science-fiction drama. The tower for the transmitter was constructed on a wide circular base from strong wooden beams, with all the necessary metal fittings produced from copper. It tapered towards the top and rose to a height of 154 feet. Surmounted upon this was a colossal hemispherical structure to form the electrode. The skeleton of this was also formed from wood and was to be sheathed in copper.

Not far from the base of the tower was a large brick building designed to house all the intricate machinery necessary to generate the massive amount of power required to run the station. Most of the equipment was of special design and Tesla had a great deal of trouble in having some of it manufactured. By 1902 the tower and the control building were completed.

Soon after this everything started to go wrong for Tesla. He had trouble getting supplies of equipment he required and the financial backers, who up till then had been highly enthusiastic about the project, withdrew their support. The whole project crashed. A plan that Tesla had for creating a similar station at Niagara Falls for Canadian interests was also abandoned. He never fully recovered from this setback. He was never again to receive the money he needed to carry out large-scale experiments.

The reasons for this were, and still are, veiled in mystery, and in 1943 he died alone, in a hotel room in New York, a poor and almost forgotten man.

This small resume of the life of Nicola Tesla does not give anything like the coverage of his achievement that it deserves. A large volume would have to be written to do anything like justice to this electrical genius who spent his life trying to give his fellow men a basis for a new and wonderful world. Why was he stopped? Would his dreams of a universal power system have allowed the poorer nations to advance too quickly? Could it be that the large international companies would have found it difficult to control such a system? Many questions — but no answers. I only hope that the students of the future will take time to study the works of Nicola Tesla and one day endeavour to complete his dream.

The reason for the location of the transmitter of the world power system at Wardenclyffe, in the Shoreham area of Long Island, would also have been because of the geometrics involved. If the station were to operate at maximum efficiency, it had to be set up in a position that ensured the propagation of the electromagnetic-wave-forms was in perfect harmony with the atomic structure of the Earth. The electrons in every atom of every element had to be resonated in order to transmit the energy being imparted.

During the first world war the Wardencliffe Tower was dynamited for some obscure reason, and most traces of Tesla's activity in the area completely obliterated.

At the time of writing the initial draft for this chapter I was unable to find the exact location of the tower site, because of the scanty records left behind for public viewing.

I did publish a theoretical position in my earlier works which showed a series of harmonics but was never really satisfied with the results. One of my readers in England decided to help me with the problem and wrote to a friend of his who lives on Long Island asking if it were possible to pin-point the site. He sent the results of his query on to me and I quote a section of his letter:

"I mentioned to my friend that you were unable to locate the site of Tesla's Tower. Well this produced an unexpected reaction from my friend because it is just around the corner from where she lives in the grounds of the Peerless Company. In fact the road that runs on the other side of the boundary fence, 50 yards from the octagonal concrete base, is called Tesla Street.

Peerless replied that according to the highways department (presumably Suffolk County) the coordinates are as follows:

40^0 56' 50.3" north/ 72^0 53' 55.6" west."

At last a position was available for study, although I have not been able to check the accuracy. If any reader can supply more information, I would be most grateful.

Computer calculations indicated that Tesla was in possession of knowledge far in advance of his time. If the position of the transmitter was near correct then the geometric placement was directly related to the unified equations discovered in my work on the world grid system.

The great circle displacement from the transmitter to a point on longitude 180^0 00' 00" at the same latitude, was:

269375.57 seconds of arc.

This was extremely close to the energy harmonic derived from the unified equation in relation to the speed of light at the Earth's surface, found in my latest research.

269364.5 harmonic.

The difference of around eleven seconds of arc would give an error of about 800 feet, which is not too bad for normal map reference.

See Diagram.

The longitudinal placement indicated that Tesla had chosen a position harmonically tuned to the reciprocal of the Greenwich meridian.

An article published in the "Arizona Republic" on Sunday, September 2, 1984, regarding Tesla's experiments, contained some interesting information, which showed a relationship with grid harmonics.

Quote:

With a pocket sized vibrator, he told reporters, he could generate resonant tremors that could split the Earth in two. He gave its resonance frequency as one hour and 49 minutes. Whatever the plausibility of his Earth-splitting scheme, the rather precise estimate of the Earth's frequency turned out to be close to the mark, as was demonstrated during the great Chilean earthquake of 1960, when geophysicists were able to measure the time it took waves to travel back and forth through the Earth.

Unquote.

DIAGRAM 9

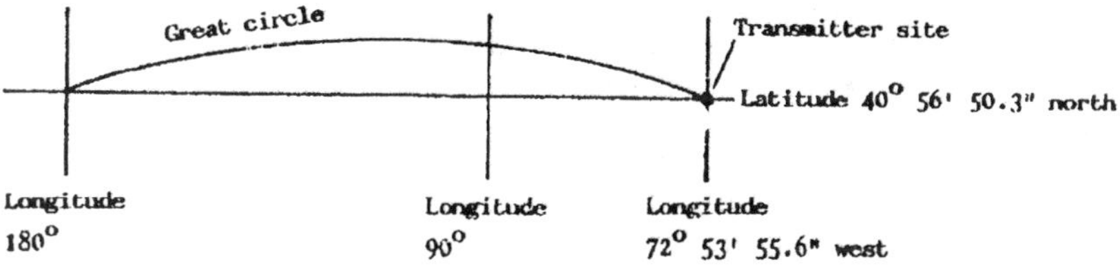

I wondered just what time base the Earth frequency was based on and after several calculations discovered that it was related directly with the yearly cycle of the Earth round the Sun of 365.25 days.

One Earth year	=	365.25 days
	=	8766 hours
One hour 49 minutes	=	1.8166 hour
8766 divided by 1.8166	=	4825.3211
Square root of 4825.32	=	69.464

In grid terms the reciprocal harmonic of the speed of light (144,000 minutes of arc per grid second, in free space, relative to the Earth's surface) is 69444444.

If we work backwards from this harmonic value, then:

69.444444 squared	=	4822.5308
8766 divided by 4822.5308	=	1.8177178
1.8177178 hours	=	One hour 49 minutes
		03.7842 seconds

The results are so close that I would venture to say that the resonant frequency of the Earth is directly related to the speed of light.

Another interesting point that I believe we should note is that Tesla insisted that 60 cycles a second would be the most efficient frequency to use in all the alternators and motors produced from his patents. There was much opposition to this from the manufactures and practical men in the field, but Tesla won his point and, to this day, 60 cycles a second is the frequency used in alternating-current transmission.

Why? It has been found that one of the basic natural frequencies of the Earth is six cycles per second. Tesla picked a harmonic of 6 which would be the most practical.

$$6 \text{ cycles a second} = 5.33333 \text{ cycles a grid second}$$
$$= 518400 \text{ cycles for one revolution}$$
of the earth, or 27 grid hours.
$$\sqrt{518400} = 720$$
$$= \frac{1440}{2}$$
$$= \frac{C}{2} \text{ harmonic}$$

116

13> SPACE COMMUNICATION

THE SCIENTISTS ARE NOW BEGINNING TO AGREE publicly that we are not alone in the universe. Millions of worlds similar to ours must exist and the odds are that on many of them life has developed in much the same way as it has on earth. Some civilisations will be just beginning, others will be far in advance of our achievements here, and possibly many of them have reached the stage of travelling freely across the vast reaches of space.

Our own progress has been fairly rapid in the last century, and it won't be long before we will be ready to try our first venture into deep space. If we do have neighbours, our first step will be to communicate by means of transmitted signals before we take the more difficult step of building vehicles to take us there. In fact, if we could communicate in some way, we might possibly gain vital information from a more advanced race that would enable us to carry out a probe into deep space much sooner.

The problem is, by what method, and with what type of transmission can this be accomplished most efficiently? Normal radio transmission is not the answer, as vast amounts of power and extremely expensive equipment are required to broadcast a signal for any distance. Even at the speed of light a time factor is involved if we hope to contact many of the nearest star systems. Communication is not a very practical prospect if we have to wait many years for a reply.

The best and most efficient method, as I see it, is to devise a system whereby the communication frequencies are tuned to the structure of matter and the harmonic wave-forms that permeate all space. With the correct aerial system, and frequency ratios to match, it may be possible to find a short cut to reach far-distant worlds which interest us.

Our planet is a resonating ball of wave-forms tuned to the unified fields of space, so what better antenna could we use to broadcast intelligent signals through the cosmos than the earth itself? If a method could be found to superimpose coded wave-forms within the natural grid of the earth, then they would permeate through space within the electromagnetic fields which join all the planetary bodies of the universe.

To do this, we would have to pick a geometric position on the earth's surface which would be harmonically associated with the structure of the atom. Then we would have to design an aerial system that would enable us to resonate the whole world. It would then become a spherical broadcasting antenna of immense potential, causing any signal imposed upon it to be spread throughout the galaxy.

It is possible that unbeknown to the United States Navy, they have solved the problem. With our present technology, and a few million dollars, the job can be done.

In the 16 August 1973 edition of the *New Scientist*, I found an article headed "New Home For America's Doomsday Radio".

Project Sanguine — the transmitters proposed for sending the retaliation signal to America's missile submarines following a nuclear attack — has quietly slipped back into gear, having been held up for four years by environmental protests. Two new sites have been selected for the aerials that spread over literally thousands of square miles and beam their submarine messages through the earth's crust.

Project Sanguine, as it is known, will if and when completed enable the President of the United States to activate his second strike missile submarine force lying hidden in deep canyons on the ocean bottom. It will provide the only remaining communications link between a continental America destroyed by a nuclear first strike and the deeply submerged submarine fleet which will then hurl retaliation against its aggressor.

Sanguine will use extraordinarily low frequencies — somewhere between 30 and 100 hertz, which have never before been used for communications purposes. Their great advantage is that they will propagate through the earth's crust, penetrating the ocean bed from below — providing radio communications with deeply submerged submarines for the first time.

Sanguine's buried aerials will have to cover an area of anything up to 100 miles square, and will have to carry currents so strong that in early experiments they rang telephone bells, interfered with TV reception, and electrified fences on the surface above. The navy has awarded contracts worth three million dollars for design proposals for a system and expects to place full-scale development contracts next year.

Sanguine's use of frequencies previously employed only on national electricity grids is only an extreme example of a long-term trend in radio communications with submarines. Conventional mf, hf and vhf waves are rapidly absorbed by sea-water and cannot be used. But even before the first world war it was realised that below about 40 kiloHertz attenuation rapidly falls off and communication becomes impossible. As the frequency is reduced from 40 to 10 kiloHertz, attenuation falls from 2.2 to 1.1 decibels per foot. All naval powers have long had stations operating in the lower part of this frequency band.

Unfortunately any radio aerial, if it is to be an efficient radiator, must have a length equal to at least one-quarter of the wavelength of the radio wave to be transmitted. At these frequencies the wavelengths are so enormous (say 20 miles) that this is physically not possible. Very low frequency (vlf) stations are all of great size and use very high power to compensate for the low efficiency of their aerials.

By 1969 several Project Sanguine research teams were in existence: RCA had a 4.3 million dollar contract to run a test facility; the US Navy had 20 million dollars put on one side for research in the following year; and there was talk of a final 1500 million dollar system.

The idea was to bury the aerial cables below the surface in a 22,000 square mile grid measuring 150 miles by 150 miles. The rectangles of the grid pattern would be eight miles by eight miles, and at each crossover point there would be a buried amplifier feeding current into the grid. Maximum current flow would be 300 amps and this would create a magnetic field of one gauss and an electro-magnetic field of 0.35 volt per metre.

The navy has selected two possible sites for the aerial grid. One is atop the so called Llano Uplift, a nonconducting rock formation 45 miles north-west of Austin, Texas. The other is in the Upper Michigan Peninsula where the bedrock is part of the Laurentian Shield. Total power will be of the order of 10 megawatts.

The information given indicates that the best area to build the grid antenna would depend on the type of rock strata below ground level. The right type of strata would act as a wave guide, it is suggested.

According to my research, the type of rock strata would have no effect on the transmission of the radio waves. The factor, as I see it, that would control the efficiency of the system would be the latitude and longitude of the position chosen. Because of this, I believe that the site suggested north-west of Austin, Texas, would be an ideal location for the job.

In my earlier books I had shown a position north west of Austin which would give a series of grid harmonics. Now, many years later, I have access to much more information which enables me to calculate a more accurate position, which is displaced only slightly from the original.

The diagram will show that the latitude sets up a harmonic geometric which is directly related to twice the speed of light — 288. The speed of light in free space being 144,000 minutes of arc per grid second, relative to the Earth's surface. The speed of light, according to grid theory, varies from 144,000 minutes of arc per grid second in free space, to 143,795.77 minutes of arc per grid second at the Earth's surface. (See my work, "The Bridge to Infinity".)

The great circle distance between the antenna position and longitude 180^0 west, at the same latitude, is 4116.36 minutes of arc. A study of all my works will show that the square of this number gives a harmonic value of 169444. Other sections of my published data will show that this harmonic is directly related to mass, gravity and communication wavelengths.

A further, most important, fact is that the great circle distance between the antenna position and grid pole "B" in the north is the harmonic of twice the speed of light at the Earth's surface or 2875.9 minutes of arc. Grid Pole "B" is displaced 694.44 minutes of arc from the north geographic pole, which is the reciprocal harmonic of the speed of light in free space.

The interaction of all these factors would ensure that all transmissions from the theoretical position would set up unified fields harmonized with the geometric structure of matter itself.

But this is not all. The dimensions of the aerials, the spacing and the area covered, are all vital requirements necessary to tune our world into the Cosmos.

The length of each side of the Grid Antenna is: 130.1691208 minutes of arc, (149.89171 statute miles). Therefore the area covered by the grid would be: 16944 square minutes of arc, (or square nautical miles). The harmonic of mass, gravity and communication.

The number of rectangular areas enclosed by the grid antenna, not including the centre square, would be 288, the harmonic of 2C, where "C" equals the speed of light.

Each small square section would have a side length of 6.944 minutes of arc, or nautical miles. This value is the harmonic reciprocal of the speed of light. 6.944 nautical miles is equal to 7.99612 statute miles (8 miles).

So it appears that if the aerials are spaced at 7.9912 statute miles and the sides of the square covered by the system are 149.928694 statute miles long, our aerial would be closely tuned to the structure of the Atom. Any signal transmitted by such a system should, in theory, travel a great distance into space.

Hello neighbour.

Since publication of this chapter the construction of the antenna system has become an environmental issue and the project has been postponed. Latest information suggests that the project may be shifted to a site near Crystal Falls in Wisconsin. The given aerial length and site position also indicate similar harmonic associations.

DIAGRAM 10

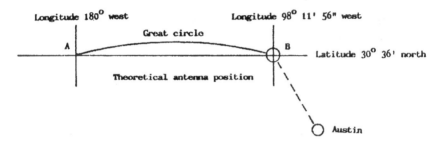

Showing the geometric relationship of the underground antenna to grid harmonics

Latitude displacement to north pole	=	59.4^0
Latitude displacement to equator	=	30.6^0
Difference	=	28.8^0

Relative displacement = 288 harmonic - 2C
Distance A - B   4116.36 minutes of arc.
This value squared = 169444 harmonic

The value 169444 has been found to have connections with the harmonics of mass, gravity and communications.

The number of rectangular areas enclosed by the grid antenna not including the centre square is 288, the harmonic of 2C, where C equals the speed of light. The number of amplifiers, shown by dots at each aerial intersection, is 324. This harmonic is shown in various ways throughout the book. 8 x 6.9444 = 55.555.

DIAGRAM 11

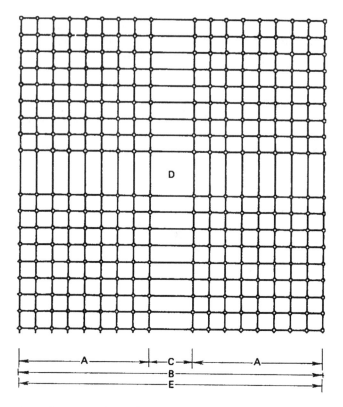

Showing theoretical grid structure of underground antenna for resonating the earth

Dimensions of grid antenna in minutes of arc:
(A)   55.555 (55.555 squared = 3086.358025, the reciprocal of 324)
(B)   130.1691208
(C)   18.489
(D)   Centre of grid aerial position
The square of 130.1691208 is equal to 16944

14> WHERE HAVE ALL THE FLYERS GONE?

FIVE DECEMBER, 1945. A FLIGHT OF FIVE AVENGER torpedo-bombers of the United States Navy took off from Fort Lauderdale, Florida, and flew out over a fairly calm sea. The weather conditions were clear. The time was exactly ten minutes past two when the leader roared down the run-way closely followed by the four other aircraft in the formation. Cruising off at 215 mph, the flight was slowly lost to view as the bombers winged their way out on an easterly course over the Atlantic.

The plan filed by the fight leader showed that the proposed course would take the formation 160 miles east towards the Bahamas, then north for 40 miles, and then finally back on to a direct course that would bring the five aircraft back to the naval air station. In less than two hours the flight would be completed, the planes back on the ground.

But those two hours were to drag on into a nightmare for the crews of the aircraft, and they were not to see their base again. That flight has gone down in the annals of Air Force history as the greatest air mystery of our time.

Word came from the formation at 3:45 p.m. when a strange radio message was received in the operations control tower at Fort Lauderdale. The flight leader spoke in a bewildered manner; he was obviously worried. He radioed: "We seem to be off course. I'm not sure of our position."

More calls were received over the next hour, and each time the leader seemed increasingly at a loss as to what was happening to his flight — and as to where it was.

Around 4 o'clock that strange afternoon a brief radio conversation was heard by the listeners in the control tower. The flight leader, by the sound of it, was beginning to panic; he had turned over the command to another pilot. The last message from the now overdue flight was received at 4:25 p.m.

"Our position still not certain," the message said. "Believe we are about 225 north-east of base."

With the receipt of this oblique message, a Martin Mariner flying boat equipped with rescue and survival equipment was hurriedly made ready and dispatched to the position estimated for the Avengers in order to guide them home. Meanwhile, the control tower was desperately trying to raise the flight commander, but no more was to be heard from him or from any of the other pilots. It was as though the flight had never taken place.

The anxious tower operators then tried to contact the Mariner that had been sent off to help the Avengers find their way home. There was no response. Communication with all six aircraft was lost.

By now the operations personnel were thoroughly alarmed. The coastguard at Miami were contacted, and almost immediately a coastguard rescue plane was sent off to follow the path of the other aircraft. After a thorough search of the last estimated position the coastguard pilot reported back that no sign of the six missing planes could be found.

Surface craft were sent out, and the area was searched throughout the night. By morning there were twenty vessels methodically scouring the sea, and soon they were joined in the air by 240 search aircraft, flying in a pattern from Florida to the Bahamas.

For two days an unceasing search was kept up. The area, scrutinised by sea and air as it had never been searched before, extended up to 300 miles from the coast over the Atlantic, and 200 miles into the Gulf of Mexico.

Not a single trace of the six missing planes was found. The search area was then shifted to the inshore areas and around the sinister Everglades in the faint hope that the aircraft had, for some inexplicable reason, flown inland. Before it was over the search operation covered some quarter of a million square miles, to become the most intensive air-sea search ever undertaken. But the results remained negative. The six aircraft had disappeared as though they had vanished from this earth, or into another dimension.

At last, with the search crews exhausted, the Navy reluctantly called a halt to the hunt. But search teams continued to rake through land areas, the beaches, and the Bahama Islands themselves. For weeks all debris cast up on the beaches, every item of flotsam, was minutely examined in the dying hope of finding some tiny clue, some tiny part of any one of the six missing planes. Nothing was found.

Months later a naval board of inquiry formally stated that no trace of the missing planes or their crews had been found, and that no adequate theory could be put forth to explain their disappearance.

An analysis made afterwards to try to determine the most probable position of the aircraft at the time they disappeared only helped to deepen the mystery further.

Had the flight of Avengers continued on a direct course to the east the air-crews would eventually have made contact with Great Asaco Island. If they had gone northeast they would have flown over Grand Bahamas Island, which is about twenty-five miles in length. Had they continued in a south-easterly direction, they would have sighted Andros Island, or any one of a great number of smaller islands scattered about that area. In fact, the only completely open areas were almost directly north or south, and it is most unlikely that either of these courses was followed by the missing six aircraft, since they were known to have flown off from the airfield in an easterly direction, in accordance with their flight plans.

At no time did any of the crew members indicate that land was within sight in the radio messages received. In other accounts of this incident it has always emerged that the crews were confused and apparently disorientated — almost as though they were flying in a void. They seemed not to know whether they were flying straight and level or upside down — sea and sky appeared to be as confused as if the crews had stumbled through a hidden doorway and had entered a topsy-turvy world with its own rules.

The only possible explanation seemed to be that for some unknown reason the formation had been flying along a circular course within the ring of the surrounding islands; otherwise, it was argued, at some stage they would surely have sighted land.

Since there were five aircraft in the missing formation, the chances of the navigation equipment in every one of them being faulty were so remote as to be an impossibility. All equipment had been thoroughly checked out and passed as fully servicable before the exercise. In the event of any disaster, of whatever nature, at least one of the five aircraft would have had time to send out a distress signal. All aircraft and crew were equipped with survival gear for use in the event of a crash landing or an enforced ditching in the sea. The same thing was true of the missing Martin Mariner. Moreover, this particular aircraft was bulging with survival equipment. If all six aircraft had crashed somewhere, or gone into the water, some trace, some item of wreckage, would eventually have been picked up. Yet nothing has ever turned up — not the tiniest trace.

The records of the incident are still open, and to this day no logical explanation has ever been put forward to account for the mysterious events of that December day.

In my earlier publication Harmonic 695, I had put forth the theory that the aircraft had flown into an area of space-time instability due to the partial destruction of the world grid, in ancient times. Now that I am aware that the grid system is a natural manifestation due to the formation of matter itself, I have checked the known facts once again and estimated the flight path by computer analysis.

At the time of my earlier findings I did not believe that our own scientists had the knowledge to set up any type of experiment which could have had any effect, what-so-ever, on the flight of the Avengers; so the disappearance was thought to be caused by forces beyond our control.

Now, many years later, the evidence at hand indicates, without much doubt, that the scientists did have a great deal of theoretical knowledge concerning the structure of space- time and that various experiments were being carried out in order to verify the unified nature of our reality.

The flight plan filed by the flight leader, on close analysis by computer, now reveals a strong possibility that the Avengers were part of an advanced scientific experiment, set up by our own scientists. If this were so, then the crews of the aircraft were probably not aware of it. If anything went wrong, or, if indeed the experiment was a success, they would, under the circumstances, be deemed expendable. The fact that the radio transmissions from the aircraft gave no indication that the crew members were aware of the cause of their predicament suggest that the experiment, if it took place, was known only to those who set it up.

The filed flight plan showed the following possibilities:

The proposed course would take the formation 160 miles east, towards Great Abaco Island, then north for 40 miles and then finally back onto a direct course that should take them to the Naval air station.

If we take these coordinates and transpose them into very close grid equivalents of minutes of arc, or nautical miles, then:

160 statute miles (flight plan) could be:
159.93256 Statute miles (grid)

Which converts to:

138.8888 nautical miles (minutes) grid

Which is equal to:

(69.4444 x 2) or twice the speed of light reciprocal harmonic (694444).

40 statute miles (flight plan)

Could be:

39.983139 statute miles (grid)

Which converts to:

34.7222 nautical miles (minutes) grid

Which is equal to:

(69.4444/2) or half the speed of light reciprocal harmonic   (347222).

The return, or third, leg of the journey would equal:

165.583 statute miles.

Which converts to:

143.79577 nautical miles (minutes) grid.

The speed of light at the Earth's surface (average) is: 143,795.77 minutes of arc per grid second.

A glance at diagram 12 will show that the filed flight plan closely fits the theoretical flight plan which allows direct association with the harmonics of the unified field.

In the diagram (A) represents the take-off point at Fort Lauderdale, (B) the turning point near Gorda Cay and (C) the turning point for home, near the Downer Cays. At the first turning point (B) the aircraft would be at a distance of 3229.8793 minutes of arc from north grid pole(B).

This converts to:

53.8313 degrees.

The Cosine of this angle equals:

0.59016475

The reciprocal of this value equals:

1.69444 (harmonic 169444)

This harmonic is associated with mass and gravity. If, at the time the aircraft reached these turning points, a pulsed harmonic transmission was broadcast from a strategically placed ground station, or stations, it is possible that a unified field effect could have been caused at these positions. It is also possible that advanced electronic equipment could have been placed in the aircraft without the knowledge of the crews.

Admittedly the theory is pure speculation but the flight plan fits and I have a feeling that this is more than just coincidence. As I said in my initial publication, I believe that all the aircraft were completely disintegrated, or moved through space-time.

Where, may we ask, have all the flyers gone? Do they still exist in some kind of space warp? Were our own people responsible?

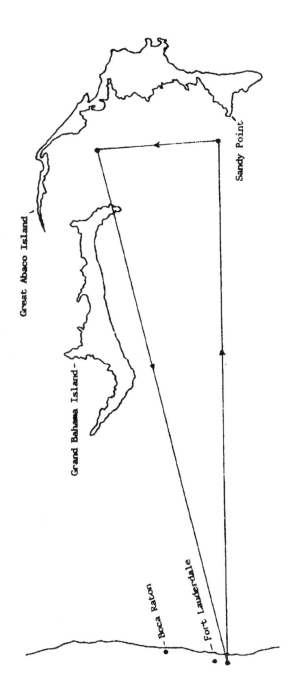

MAP 6

Map showing estimated, intended, flight path of five Avenger aircraft from Fort Lauderdale on December 5th, 1945

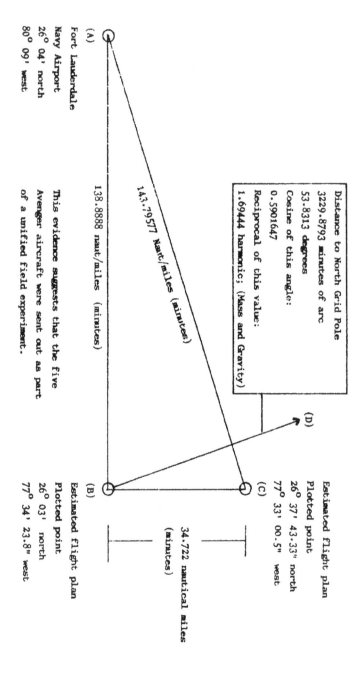

(A)

Fort Lauderdale
Navy Airport
26° 04' north
80° 09' west

Distance to North Grid Pole
3229.8793 minutes of arc
53.8313 degrees
Cosine of this angle:
0.5901647
Reciprocal of this value:
1.69444 harmonic; (Mass and Gravity)

This evidence suggests that the five
Avenger aircraft were sent out as part
of a unified field experiment.

138.8888 naut/miles (minutes)

143.7957 Naut/miles (minutes)

(D)

Estimated flight plan
Plotted point
26° 37' 43.33" north
77° 33' 00.5" west

(C)

(B)

Estimated flight plan
Plotted point
26° 03' north
77° 34' 23.8" west

34.722 nautical miles
(minutes)

DIAGRAM 12

Showing estimated flight of Avenger aircraft at the time
of disappearance. December 5th, 1945

15> PEOPLE WE WOULD LIKE TO KNOW MORE ABOUT

STARTLING THOUGH IT WAS TO HAVE FOUND A network of man-made aerials built into the UFO grid system, some of the subsequent events were bizarre.

Up to this time I had been aware of treading on the corns of a few faceless technicians and other parties who had some connection, scientifically or politically, with the UFO grid. It had to be only a matter of time before the corns were inflamed enough to bring their possessors out into the open. So far as I was aware, no direct action had been taken to prevent me from proceeding with investigations connected with my theories, or to try and stop my constant probing into the network.

Like all the best ordered secret societies, the group had given no positive indication that they even existed. So long as the public at large did not insist upon answers to controversial questions, the group's members, whoever and wherever they were, were apparently content to let matters quietly take their own course, no doubt hopeful that eventually I would be branded as just another crank, and that anything I had to put forward would automatically be discounted.

I was fully aware that there was a possibility that I would be written off as a crank, but I soon decided that this was a chance I would have to take anyway. Obviously I had to be fairly careful how I handled information I was now receiving. If I pushed too hard, I would almost certainly be regarded as a Grade A lunatic. On the other hand, if I kept all the information to myself I would lose any advantage I might have gained, and I would be placing myself in a position that could prove to be quite dangerous. Other investigators of UFO phenomena in the past have disappeared or have been victims of strange accidents as a result of probing too deeply into the so-called flying saucer enigma.

For these reasons I decided that my best course was to leak information out as it came into my hands, and also to filter out copies of all my notes through a loose-knit chain of contacts both within and outside New Zealand, so that it would be impossible to stop the truth from spreading. All the evidence so far gathered would be in the hands of certain newspapermen, so that it could be transmitted via the wire services immediately any move was made to stop my investigations.

I had no intention of becoming involved in some weird cloak and dagger game; certainly I have never regarded my investigations as either a game or a harmless hobby. I am also deeply aware of just how serious the "group" is about maintaining secrecy over their activities.

In fact, I took some pains to keep the "group" informed about the network I had set up to ensure that all information would quickly be disseminated in the event of some untoward accident coming my way. There were a few people whom I was certain had direct connections with the "group," if they were not members themselves. Through these people I let the word go out as to the precautions I had taken. One of them scornfully suggested that he could not believe any journalist would sit on such hot news when it might be possible for him to get a scoop on the news services of the world. My answer to him was: "Test the truth of what I have told you by trying to stop me in my investigations." So far the test has not been made; perhaps he realised that after all there are more honest and dedicated men in this world than we sometimes think.

At any rate the scheme appeared to be working very well; I found that the public, instead of labelling me as crazy, with first-class honours, actively encouraged my research into the UFO mystery. Letters came every day, from many parts of the world, after the publication of *Harmonic 33*. The majority of them enclosed useful information or offered further suggestions for lines of investigation. Only rarely did a letter turn up in my box that assassinated my character or intimated that I was off my trolley. It was clear that a large slice of the reading public knew that there had been something going on which they were not being properly informed about. On reflection I think it was this flood of encouragement that came through my post box, more than anything else, that drove me on with my investigations. By nature I have a strong streak of curiosity; but it helps a lot more than I can estimate to find that there are many other people around who are anxious to help in any way they can.

When we photographed the first radio transmitter which I found to have a connection with the UFO grid, though, our "opposition" must have blown their cool. We had made ten prints of the photos and these were in my possession when, a few days later, I was scheduled to carry out an airways flight to New Zealand's South Island. On the night of 16 March 1968, I was to stop over in the capital, Wellington, and on the next day, fly on to Invercargill, New Zealand's southernmost city, returning the following day (18 March) via various centres throughout the country. I was well aware of the significance of the photographs we had taken, and I considered it unsafe to leave them at my home while I was absent.

I had stowed them into my airways brief bag, and during my stay in Wellington I contacted the American Embassy's air attaché. I had told him the whole story, stressing that the photographs were in my possession. Until this time, in fact, I had passed a great deal of information to the Americans by way of the Embassy. There had been five personal discussions with the air attaché at his office in Wellington up to this time. At first I had thought that the Embassy's interest in my research was because I had found something new. As time went by I realised that this was not the case. On the contrary, it soon became clear to me that the scientists were well ahead of anything that I had been able to discover. So the Embassy's interest was more in order to keep tabs on what I might be finding — and to see if I did happen to come upon something that the scientists did not already know.

I was content to go along with this situation because I believed that everything I did, discovered or theorised should be kept in the open. If, on the other hand, the Americans or anyone else wanted to keep *their* findings a secret — well, that was their business. I felt that once it was known that I had acquired a certain level of knowledge they would have to admit something of the state of their own research, even if to do so was only in an attempt to dissuade me from continuing my own line of research.

The air attaché in fact turned out to be a valuable source of information, help and encouragement. It was he who assured me that my calculation of the UFO grid pattern for the global system was correct. Among other items he passed on to me: intensive UFO research was being carried out at Wright Patterson Airfield in the United States. The scientific laboratory there, set up for the purpose, was described as a complex of buildings covering a large area and staffed by many of the world's top scientists. Experimental work was carried out twenty-four hours a day, 365 days a year. At one stage the official asked me if I would consider a trip to America to visit this base. Naturally I said I would — any time they cared to put out an invitation. Perhaps the idea was vetoed in the States, for I heard no more of this. In retrospect it seems to me that although at that time I was in the very early stages of my UFO research, perhaps I had already stumbled on to something that was of deep interest to the American scientists. They must have realised that I was beginning to uncover information which they themselves had kept carefully hidden from the general public for many years.

The following night after this visit to Wellington, having taken pains to inform my Embassy contact that I had the photographs of a transmitter with me, I stayed at the Grand Hotel in Invercargill.

What took place there that night convinced me that there were other people in New Zealand besides myself who were keenly interested in our camera work. They are some of the people I would like to know more about.

After a leisurely dinner my co-pilot and I retired to the lounge for a chat and a cup of coffee. On this particular night there were two complete aircrews staying at the Grand. Members of the other crew were based in Wellington, and for some reason, which is still a mystery to me, the rostering section of the airline had switched the Wellington co-pilot on to my flight for the next day, while my Auckland co-pilot was to return with the Wellington crew on the early morning flight. We were not informed of this switch until after we had arrived in Invercargill earlier that afternoon. The co-pilot originally with me was most upset over this, as it interfered with some of his personal arrangements and also meant his getting up very early the following morning.

To verify the situation I telephoned Wellington and was told that the Wellington co-pilot was to crew the flight with me as far as the capital, while another Auckland co-pilot would carry on from there back to Auckland with me. I thought the whole thing rather odd; it meant that three crew members would be chopping and changing to do the work of two men. However, it was not really my concern, so I okayed the change and told my original co-pilot of his tough luck.

The Wellington co-pilot chatting with me over coffee in the Grand's lounge had been interested in my research, he said; so I brought out the photos of the aerial from the bag in my room to show him. Before he joined the airline as a pilot, this man had been associated with the DSIR (Department of Scientific and Industrial Research), and had carried out duties in the radio research division at Mc Murdo Sound, in the Antarctic. I though he might be able to tell me what range of frequencies the aerial arrangement in the photographs might be operating on.

We were soon deep into a discussion on this point. He tried to persuade me that the aerial was a completely mundane affair, in common use among ham operators for normal transmissions. Suddenly we were interrupted by a tall, conservatively dressed man who had wandered over from the company of two similarly attired gentlemen sitting around a table some distance away from us, at the centre of the lounge.

Just before the stranger came to a halt at our table I had slipped the photographs back into their large envelope, and this was now resting on my lap, so I'm sure he was unable, at any time, to see that the photographs were related to broadcasting equipment. Moreover, the table at which he had left his two friends was quite some distance away, and certainly he would have been out of earshot.

He asked me if we were talking about duck-shooting, and if we were interested in that sport? Somewhat non-plussed at this gambit, I told him we had no interest in ducks or any other kind of sporting birds, and that we were in Invercargill for reasons quite unconnected with shooting.

Then I asked him if he was staying in the hotel. He said that he was; he had, he said, a farm some miles distant from Invercargill, and he and his wife (of whom there was no sign) were in town to celebrate their wedding anniversary. This certainly seemed odd to me, and the sensation I was experiencing that this was no ordinary, casual hotel lounge encounter increased when the stranger drew up a chair and sat down with us, intent on carrying the conversation on for some time. I studied him more closely: he was aged between forty-five and fifty; over six feet tall and well built, although rather slim for his height. His features were on the rugged side, and his face roundish; a small fold of skin under the lower lip gave one an impression that at some time he might have been in a minor accident or suffered facial burns that required slight surgery. His hair was dark, slightly greyed, and thinning; his eyes light coloured and conveying an impression of considerable intelligence. His hands were long-fingered and strong, but not as rough as one would expect in a farmer. He wore a dark suit and black shoes. The suit was of conservative cut, well tailored though from a material I would describe as coarse, almost cheap. Perhaps this was one of the factors that made me feel he was odd.

After talking for a while about ducks he suddenly switched the conversation on to an entirely different channel. He asked if we were interested in ham radio or radio stations.

Trying not to show my surprise I told him we were not particularly interested; privately, I began to wonder how I could get rid of him without being obviously rude. He continued to insist that we must be interested in radio; he said he had a friend not far out of town who had a ham radio set-up, and if we were to go with him we would be very intrigued with the equipment. I tried to tell him that we were not very interested in radio, and that as it was now after nine o'clock we certainly did not feel like taking a trip out of town to see a ham operators gear. He then countered with the information that he knew someone in a local government radio station, and would we care to go with him to meet his friend there and discuss radio matters with him?

By this time my co-pilot was looking distinctly uneasy; suddenly he stood up and excused himself, disappearing into the TV lounge.

This left me alone with the stranger, wondering how best I could get rid of him without making a scene about it, and at the same time getting my envelope of precious photographs into a safe place. Finally I made it clear to him that I was not prepared to leave the hotel, for any reason. He at once asked me to write down the name of his friend at the government radio station on the envelope on my lap so that I could visit him next time I found myself in Invercargill with nothing better to do. It seemed to me that he wanted to put a name on the envelope so that he would be able to claim it as his, if somehow he could get possession of it. Needless to say I kept a firm hand on the envelope as he talked on.

From the conversation that followed I gathered that on the previous evening he had been aboard an American ship which was in the port at Bluff, and had had a few drinks with the captain in his cabin. He hinted that if I were interested I could go with him now to visit the ship. He did not explain how he had met the American captain, or how he had managed to get aboard the ship. This omission added to my suspicions, and I made up my mind to get rid of him.

I stood up rather abruptly and excused myself, saying that I had some urgent business to attend to, and made to walk away. He became apologetic, and did his best to keep me talking; he said he hoped he had not embarrassed me or my friend in any way. I left him then, and walked through the lounge past his two friends, who were still sitting at their table, downstairs to the main office. His two companions looked like businessmen; they had been keeping an eye on us all this time.

At the office downstairs I asked the receptionist for some Scotch tape and with it I firmly sealed the envelope, the photographs securely inside it, writing my name boldly on the front and back I had the receptionist place it in the hotel's safe, explaining that I would pick it up just before I left the following day.

The task completed, I went back upstairs and let myself into a public telephone box at the top of the stairs, just outside the entrance to the main lounge and the smaller TV room. I put through a toll call to Auckland and spoke to my wife. I told her some of the odd events of the night, and asked if she had been disturbed. She told me that some friends of ours were with her, and that nothing unusual had happened. Immediately after this brief conversation I went into the TV lounge to talk to my co-pilot. He told me that the three strangers had left a short time before by the stairway to the ground floor and the main entrance of the hotel.

Back down the stairs I went to ask the receptionist who the three men were who had just left, to ask whether they were staying in the hotel. All I got was a blank look. Who was I referring to? There were no men of that description staying in the hotel; she had been at the desk the whole time; no one had passed her office, no one had gone out of the main doors, in full view of her desk and less than ten feet away. Anyone leaving by the stairs from the first floor would have had to leave by those doors. There was no other exit. Doors leading into the bars at the back of the ground floor were locked at this time of night. The only other means of egress would be from the first floor upward, by means of the fire escapes.

I was beginning to feel as confused as the girl was looking. I went back up the stairs once more, and asked my co-pilot if he were quite certain that the men had left by the main stairs. From his seat he could see the top of the staircase quite clearly, and he confirmed that they must have left by the main entrance just a short time before.

How had they come into the hotel — and how did they leave? How did they pass in front of a receptionist without being seen? Who were they? And what were they after? I am positive that our darkly-clad friend was no more a local farmer than I am. I still wonder, frequently, what would have happened if I had left with them, and taken that offered trip to the radio station outside of the city.

A few days later I was again passing through Wellington. I contacted the United States Embassy and told the air attaché of the incident. I added that I was aware that I was being kept under observation, and that if any of the people who contacted me were overseas agents my advice to him was to see to it that they stopped bothering me. The New Zealand Government at this time was fully aware of my activities, and had given me written approval of my research. If anyone caused me trouble, I told him, I would immediately make known all the facts, the evidence, the theories — everything I had put together so far.

The attaché was sympathetic, and asked for more details about my encounter with the three strangers in Invercargill. Later on he confirmed that an American training ship had been at Bluff over the period I was there, but no more information than that was forthcoming.

The three men were not New Zealanders, I'm sure; wherever they were from, though, remains their secret.

During an operational flying period it is necessary each day to have a full crew on stand-by-duties at the airfield to allow for unforseen crew changes due to sickness or accidents. One morning in February, 1969, I was carrying out a four-hour stretch of one of these duties. Over morning tea with some other crew members in the upstairs cafeteria of the Mangere Airport, Auckland, terminal building, I was the victim of another odd occurrence.

Not far away from where we sat, at another table, was an unusual-looking couple busily examining an expensive camera, laughing over its mysteries like a pair of children. At first I gave them little more than a casual glance, and was half-turned away from them, talking to a captain having a quick coffee before flying an airliner south to Wellington.

After some moments of conversation I turned round, for some reason I have never been able to fathom, to look directly at the two who were still fussing over their camera. At the precise instant that I turned to face them the man raised the camera, aimed it at me, and took a photograph. Then, just as quickly, he continued to fumble with the instrument and turned it back to his companion as if the incident had never occurred — perhaps hoping that I had noticed nothing.

I was so surprised by this action that I was at a complete loss as to what I should do. After all, there was nothing particularly sinister about the event. He could have been a collector of photographs of airline pilots, for all I was to know. Somewhat embarrassed I turned back and resumed the conversation with the other skipper, at the same time wondering why a complete stranger would want to take my photograph.

They were certainly an uncommon-looking couple. He was a tall, gangling sort of individual, with thin, pipe-stem limbs. His most startling feature was his head: it was almost perfectly spherical, and it was as bare of hair as a billiard ball. The skin was a golden-tan colour, and very smooth; the colour was as I imagine that of an American Indian to be. I imagined that he would never have any need to shave. Not only was his head round, it was small in proportion to the rest of his body. He was dressed in light coloured slacks, and a bright reddish short-sleeved open neck shirt. In spite of his thin body he looked to me to be very fit and agile.

She was the exact antithesis of her friend; although slender, she was shorter than he; her features were long, almost aquiline. She wore her jet-black hair long, down over her shoulders in an old-fashioned style. Her eyes were very dark and large, and accentuated by a very pale, almost pallid, skin. She wore a dark, simple skirt and blouse. She was an unusual-looking person, but in her way attractive, although in a crowd she would certainly not attract as much attention as her companion.

I judged both of them to be in their early twenties. They looked friendly enough, one might even say jovial; whatever their business, I cannot say there was at any time anything suggestive of sinister intent about them.

But they worried me. And when I returned to the crewroom some five minutes later, leaving them still engrossed in animated conversation at their table, I couldn't stop wondering who they were.

After a few moments my curiosity got the better of me. I decided to go back upstairs and have another good look at them, and, if possible, talk to them. I went out of the Operation Room door, which is in a corner of the main foyer of the terminal building, and pushed my way into the crowd milling about the nearby ticket counters, heading for the flight of stairs some twenty yards away. I had only gone a short distance through the crowd when I nearly bumped into the tall stranger, who was striding in my direction. We gave each other a surprised look; and then, like a startled rabbit, he turned about and scuttled off through the crowd, to disappear into the far end of the building. This second encounter took only a few seconds, and I had no chance of catching up with him without causing some sort of disturbance. Besides, I had no real reason for pursuing him; he had done me no harm — at least, none that I knew of.

The next best thing to do, I decided, was to have another look upstairs to see if his companion was still sitting there. If she were, no doubt he would soon be rejoining her. However, upstairs there was no sign of her. Like her friend, she had disappeared. After waiting for a few minutes I went back to the crewroom.

It was on the face of it a quite trivial incident. Most people would have forgotten it within a few days. Yet even now, quite some time after, I find that the whole thing is still vividly etched on my mind. I'm intrigued by the questions they brought into my life: Who were they? What were they up to? Why did the man take my photograph? Why did he run off, looking so very startled, when we met in the crowd? And where were they from?

Until now I have found no real evidence to support the popular belief that aliens from another world are walking in out midst. Over the years there have been many stories and some striking accounts of contact between humans and non-humans. Logic tells us that with all the evidence that there now exists pointing to sustained contact by scientists of this planet with beings connected with the UFOs that visit our skies, there has to be direct communication between humans and aliens at some level. It follows that there is every likelihood for aliens to be among us.

If it turns out that there are indeed aliens here already, I would in no way be disconcerted to discover that the odd couple I encountered in the Mangere Airport cafeteria are among their representatives.

And if by some chance the round-headed gentleman who took a photograph of me, or his companion, should chance to read this, here is a message: I hope you will contact me and satisfy my curiosity. Why did you take my photograph? And what have you done with it?

16> THE SECRET OF LIFE (LAKHOVSKY) AND DELAND'S MAGNETIC CANOPY

IN MY EARLIER PUBLICATIONS, I DESCRIBED A TYPE of ground aerial system being used in many orchards in the United States. The apparatus has proved to be very successful in warding off frost damage to citrus fruit. A further effect has been the promoting of healthier trees and better general growth in the areas covered.

I gave dimensions for a similar aerial which would resonate at the frequencies of light and gravity. Since publication I have received more information on the American system and have been extremely interested in the actual dimensions used.

The aerial was designed by John Delrea Deland of Riverside, California, and has been in use since 1949. The units cover about one acre each and consist of a steel mast about 32 feet high, made of galvanised pipe in 12-foot lengths. The first is a two-inch pipe set into a three-foot-deep concrete base. Two other pipes of lesser diameter are screwed on to the bottom pipe to form a vertical mast 30-feet high. At the masthead, and also at the two pipe joints, a waterproof, three-quarter inch plywood disc is fitted. At the outer edge of the discs are seven drilled holes, evenly spaced and parallel to the mast. The holes are about 1/4 inch diameter, 51.42857^0 apart.

Ten hard copper wires are strung through each of the holes in the discs, parallel with the mast. At the top disc the wires are extended about eight inches parallel to the earth. This forms a wire cage around the mast. The wires pass through the outer edge of the concrete base then into trenches which are 18 inches deep and radiate from the mast centre at angles of 51.42857^0. One of the wires in the trench must be orientated with magnetic north.

The wires are run from the centre of the mast to a distance of 144 feet. They are then attached to a "magnetic pack" the design of which, according to the information I have, is a secret. The end of each wire is then brought above ground and pointed toward its corresponding end at the top of the mast. The trenches, which form the radius of a circle 288 feet in diameter, are then covered in.

The information sheet says that the device does not raise the air temperature of the grove. It is thought that a type of magnetic field of force is set up over the trees by the equipment, which creates within the trees themselves a condition which prevents freezing. Citrus fruit lying on the ground will freeze. Fruit still attached to the tree but touching the ground will also freeze in a short time. The fruit growing on the tree seem to be unaffected.

Protection has been given to trees with temperatures as low as 20^0 Fahrenheit. Besides preventing frost damage the trees appear to be healthier and to have a slightly higher production rate. No one seems to know how the apparatus works, and the write up says that there are apparently forces around us of which we know little.

The first thing I realised when reading this was that the radius of the circle encompassing the ground aerials was 144 feet or the harmonic of the speed of light; the diameter of course being 288 or double the light harmonic. With a mast height of 30 feet, the angles that the wire ends make with the ground at the periphery of the circle were calculated at 11^0 35', or 695 minutes of arc. The pure harmonic reciprocal of the speed of light is 694444, so 695 is near enough in a practical sense. See Diagram 22 for layout of the system.

Did Mr. Deland have access to secret knowledge when he constructed his aerials? Or has the method of construction been passed down through the ages without anyone really knowing how or why the system works?

I believe that as all physical substance is being manifested in alternate pulses of matter and antimatter, then such an aerial system would be subject to these pulses at the frequency of 144000 pulses a grid second. By induction, the tuned aerial would set up a secondary field which has a harmonic affinity with matter and life itself. This would increase the strength of the life forces and help to shield living things from any adverse influences.

One of my fellow-pilots, Mr. D. R. Offwood, became interested in the information I had on the aerial layout and proceeded to construct a similar system in a nursery in the South Island of New Zealand, to test the effects and carry out a series of experiments.

It was agreed that a quarter-size mast would be constructed, as according to radio theory a quarter-wave aerial should pick up a fairly strong signal. The aerial was set up and an investigation into electroculture was carried out between September 1972 and June 1973. A full report was written up and presented to me for

DIAGRAM 13

Showing dimensions of Ground Aerial.

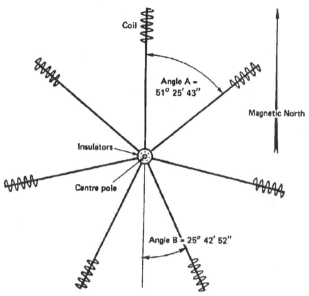

An aerial similar to the one described.The
measurements are in grid feet which are factored
by 6080/6000 to convert them to statute feet.
The height 29.515 grid feet multiplied by 2
gives a value of:59.03.The reciprocal of this
value is 1694: a harmonic which has connections
with gravity,mass and communication harmonics.

Separation angle of the ground aerials: 51.42857°
This is equal to 3085.714286 minutes of arc.
The reciprocal of this value equals 0.000324074
very close to the earth harmonic of 324 demonstrated
in other sections of the book.

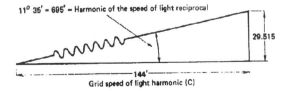

publication in 1974. The following is the main body of the report by Don Offwood, including tables of growth etc:

REPORT ON AN INVESTIGATION INTO ELECTRO-CULTURE AT CHRISTCHURCH BETWEEN SEPTEMBER 1972 AND JUNE 1973

This report is a record of two separate experiments I carried out during the spring and summer of 1972-73 in which I attempted to evaluate the reported effect the magnetic field has on plant growth.

This was done by growing plants inside an area of a wire aerial and comparing their rate of growth with that of other plants of the same species planted outside this area of influence. Such aerials are reported to be available commercially in California and are used to the exclusion of oil burning smoke-pots in orchards on frosty nights. It is suspected that the wires are of such arrangement that they are in harmony with the wavelength of light and the earth's magnetic field, and have the effect of concentrating or amplifying this energy source, which the plants are able to tap, it being the most natural of energy sources next to the sun.

The aerial was built to quarter-size of the dimensions shown in Diagram 22, because of the physical problems in building a full-size one, to the home handyman.

The vertical support was an old galvanised waterpipe, the insulators were made from commercial formica, the wire was number 10 galvanised, the seven wire coils having alnico bar magnets placed inside them, north pole uppermost. This arrangement was set up with one of the legs aligned along magnetic north.

This aerial was constructed on a nurseryman's land where the Waimakariri sandy loam soil had had no special treatment and was of a uniform nature. The nurseryman who kindly allowed me to use his land also supplied the lettuce plants, which were 2-3 inches in size, and uniform. He suggested lettuces for the test, as they are a quick-growing plant suitable for an experiment of this kind.

They were planted on 3 September 1972; beside the central pole; at 5 feet and 11 feet; and beside the coil at 30

144

feet, and at 50 feet out from the pole. This latter group were assumed to be clear of the influence, if any, of the aerial arrangement.

All the plants received water on planting and again that evening, to help them get established, but after this time the only water they received came from rainfall.

Readings of the average diameter across each plant were made five and eight weeks after planting and were as follows.

The dimensions are in inches:

TABLE 1

	11 October	5.5 datum	29 October	7 datum
50 feet out from pole	5.5, 5.6, 6.5	0.5	7, 7, 7.5, 8	0.5
30 feet out	6, 6	0.5	8.5, 9.5	2.0
11 feet out	7.3, died	1.8	10.0	3.0
5 feet out	8.3, 8.5	3.0	10.5, 10.5	3.5
Beside the pole	8.3, 8.3,		12.5, 13.5,	
	8.5, 8.8	3.0	(10.0, 10.0)	6.0

Using 5 1/2 inches as a datum for comparison of the measurements on 11 October, and 7 inches for those measurements taken on 29 October, the datum columns show the average plant size at each position, which displays the accelerated plant growth exhibited by plants closer to the centre of the aerial.

For example, the two by the pole finished up 6 inches greater in diameter than the examples which were clear of the area at the 50-feet station, and had well-developed hearts. The two plants which grew to 10 inches beside the pole were infected with aphids. As I had not expected the marked results shown they were unfortunately rather overcrowded, these two plants succumbing to the larger two.

The results obtained do show a marked improvement in the lettuce condition the closer they were to the centre of the arrangement. The two plants by the pole were 73 per cent larger than the plants outside the test area, although this figure is of course misleading on so few test examples. My conclusion is that the test plants exhibited accelerated growth rate and terminal plant size when planted within the arrangement of wires described, due to a cause not established or obvious to any conventional approach.

The reader may find it interesting to consider the following:

Angle of one segment	=	51.42857 degrees.
Half this angle	=	25.71428 degrees
	=	1542.857 minutes
Square root of this value	=	39.27922

Harmonic 3927922 is close to harmonic 3928371.
Harmonic 3928371 equals earth field A minus earth field B.

All of the ground aerials related to the north, south, east or west position exhibit this factor, or a value related to one half or quarter of it.

A further series of experiments was carried out by Mr. Offwood using a type of wire loop aerial which can be erected around a single plant or tree to promote growth. I came across this device quite by chance when browsing through a bookstore in Auckland. The book was call *The Secret of Life* by G. Lakhovsky, and was first printed in 1935, later reprinted in a revised edition by courtesy of Messrs Heinemann (Medical Books) Ltd — third edition 1963. Very few copies of the book were available locally so I felt lucky to acquire one for my ever-growing library.

To date, the work of Lakhovsky has been completely ignored by orthodox science, much I believe to the detriment of many thousands of ill people in the world today. His research and experiments were built on the fundamental basis that "every living being emits radiations." This had been backed up in recent times by John Pfeiffer, an American working in the field of radio astronomy. His book, called *The Changing Universe*, published in 1956, states in part: "each human being is an emitter of radio waves, a living broadcasting station of exceedingly low power. The stomach will send out not only infrared heat waves, but the entire spectrum of light, ultraviolet rays, X-rays, radio waves and so on. Of course all these radiations are fantastically weak and the radio waves are among the weakest. But the fifty-foot aerial of the naval research laboratory in Washington, the most accurately constructed aerial in existence, could pick up radio signals coming from your stomach more than four miles away."

The foreword to the book states that "Lakhovsky's original theories and amazing experimental results in human beings, animals and plants, as fully set forth in the revised edition, are destined to become a landmark in the history of radio biology, standing high above the ruins of orthodox misconceptions of the laws of nature."

What have we to learn from this remarkable man? He states that the living cell is an electromagnetic resonator capable of emitting and absorbing radiations of very high frequency. Life is dynamic equilibrium of all cells; the harmony of multiple radiations which react upon one another. Disease, on the other hand, is the oscillatory disequilibrium of cells originating from external causes.

Each living cell gives off radiations from its nucleus which has its own individual oscillating frequency. The geometric makeup of the cell causes it to act as an electric circuit which has self inductance and capacity. The natural oscillation of energy in the cell I believe to be due to the constant interaction of the matter and antimatter cycle discussed in other sections of this book. A pendulum-like pulsing occurs between the physical and non-physical substances. When stronger radiations are imposed upon the cell by outside influences, then the natural rhythm of the cell is affected and it begins to break down. If the radiation of the cell can be restored to its original rhythm then it will resume its healthy state.

Lakhovsky found that he could accomplish this restoration of natural rhythm by means of artificially induced oscillating fields. To do this he employed two different methods. The first, by the use of spiral loops of copper wire which would set up electro-magnetic fields harmonically tuned to the life forces. These loops of wire were placed around the plant or area to be treated, and the natural bionic rhythm would be intensified by the inductance of the wire loop. In one of his experiments he artificially inoculated a series of geranium plants with cancer cells and placed them in separate pots. He states: "A month later, when the tumours had developed, I took one of the plants at random, which I surrounded with a circular spiral consisting of copper and measuring 30 cm in diameter; its extremities not joined together, being fixed into an ebonite support. I then let the experiment follow its natural course during several weeks. After a fortnight I examined the plants. I was astonished to find that all my geraniums, or the stalks bearing the tumours were dead and dried up, with the exception of the geranium surrounded by the copper spiral. This had since grown to twice the height of other untreated healthy plants." (The tumour was eventually shed and only a scar on the stem of the plant was visible.)

When I read of these experiments by Lakhovsky I was sure that somehow, either by design or by chance, he had constructed his spiral coils to some geometric dimension which would set up a natural resonance with matter. Possibly any diameter coil would show some results, but one that was perfectly tuned would give him the remarkable results he had with the tumorous growths.

By calculation I discovered that a diameter of 30.02 cm was equal to a diameter of .972 geodetic feet, which gave a radius of .486 geodetic feet. The area of the encompassing circle would be .742 geodetic feet. In fact, the tuned spirals he used were within two hundredths of a centimetre (which is close enough practically, as this would be much less than the diameter of the wire used) to an exact dimension required to set up harmonic resonances tuned to time, and harmonics associated with the Great Pyramid. Any type of matter in such a field would be subject to sympathetic vibrations which would restore harmony to the natural rhythms.

The loop size decided on for the experiments carried out by Mr. Offwood was 12 geodetic inches, which we considered at the time to be a dimension which should give a reasonable result. Although we now know that ultimate efficiency would not be obtained with a loop of this dimension, the diameter of the wire used was such that a partial success would have been expected. As Mr. Offwood himself suggests, a metal hoop of any dimension would possibly have some effect on growth by concentrating the magnetic field in a small area, but the perfectly tuned aerial would give the maximum results. The following is his report:

> The purpose of this part of the experiment was to test a suggestion, that if an open loop of wire of one grid foot (approximately twelve and one eighth inches) diameter, was placed around a tree or plant, then the plant would grow faster than its counterparts. The suggestion was that these loops would have a similar effect to the main aerial's, that is, concentrate the magnetic energy within the area of its influence. The spiral effect created would extend from both ends of the wire loop to encompass the plant vertically.
>
> To test this idea I once again asked my nurseryman friend's indulgence and advice, and set up a series of wire loops on four varieties of plants, their unpronounceable botanical names being *Chamaecyparis lawsoniana*

(ellwoodii). Chamaecyparis lawsoniana (allumii). Phebalium squameum. Choisya ternata. The plants were all growing in rows. As the table shows, I varied the thread of the loops, the height of the loop above the soil, and the pitch of the thread, to see what pattern emerged, if any.

The loops were placed in position on 12 September, and all the plant heights recorded. Subsequent height

DIAGRAM 14

Wire Loop Aerial

measurements were taken on 5 January, 15 March, and finally on 11 May 1973, these measurements being subtracted from the original height to obtain the growth of the plant on each of these dates. I then averaged the height increase of all those plants with loops, those plants without loops, and compared them, showing the result as a percentage.

On 5 January the average height gain of the plants with a loop was 4.675 inches, while the average gain of those plants that did not have a loop was 4.640 inches. The difference between these is 0.035 inches, which is a 0.759per cent gain in favour of those plants with loops.

On 15 March the figures had changed to 10.300 inches for those with a loop, a 9.500 inches without, which gave an 8.42 per cent advantage to those plants with loops.

The 11 May readings showed that this advantage had increased slightly to 9.87 percent, as is displayed in table 4.

The reader will note that the three results were all positive, that is, the plants with loops grew taller than those without loops during the length of time the experiment was conducted, by the percentages shown. Another interesting point is that the growth tendency seemed to accelerate, as shown by the increasing percentage.

I am sure the reader will allow me to use three decimal points, as to reduce my results down to a more realistic single decimal point has a very marked effect on the end result.

TABLE 2

	5/1/73	15/3/73	11/5/73
Average height increase by plants with a loop.	4.675	10.300	11.400
Average height increase by plants without a loop	4.640	9.500	10.375
Difference shown as a percentage	+0.750	+8.420	+9.870

The results obtained from the other three test species follow with their associated tables.

As in Row A, all the test plants displayed positive results, that is, plants with a loop grew taller during the test period.

The tendency for this phenomenon to accelerate was evident in three of the rows, the exception being row B, which displayed a decrease from 9.190 to 9.010.

The small number of plants involved must also be considered as affecting the accuracy of these results and percentages, as misreading the ruler by a small amount has a magnified effect on the end percentage.

It will also be noted that I omitted to have some loops of a diameter other than a grid foot present, to test the possibility that mass of metal of any dimension would have a beneficial effect. Also the loops were made of galvanised wire, where I suspect copper might have been better.

I examined my results to compare left-hand to right-hand loops for any obvious advantage.

In Table 9, the plant growth for left-hand and right-hand loops for each row on the appropriate dates were averaged.

With two exceptions, if one set of plants started out growing well, they maintained their advantage. In row B the advantage changed from right-hand to left-hand, while in row C the change was left-hand to right-hand.

Overall, left-hand threads on the wire loops appeared to be favoured over right-hand by 10-2, but I am unable to offer any explanation, or draw any constructive conclusion from this, because of the small number of test plants involved.

I could detect no advantage between those plants having one end of the loop underground, as against those being clear of the ground; or between greater or lesser pitch; again this was due to the small number of test plants involved, and I was therefore unable to determine the optimum pitch.

In both experiments I showed to my own satisfaction that when plants are planted within an arrangement of wires as described they will exhibit a rate of growth superior to those plants not within the area of influence. I would suggest that under the above conditions, the energy of the magnetic field tends to amplify in such a way that any plant within the area is made healthier by this boost in its life-force, and will grow at an accelerated rate.

Work done by Justin Christofleau before 1914 and up to 1927 seems to show that this boost is of such a nature that it builds up over a period of time and may not take full effect for a year or more. He attributed his remarkable results to his equipment generating electricity, which accelerated his plant growth, while I suspect that the magnetic field will in time be found to be closer to the cause of this phenomenon.

Lettuces are relatively fast-growing plants, and I was therefore able to obtain results within a short period, but the aerial's effect on an orchard or a pine forest would be worth investigating.

Although of differing dimensions to the aerial described in *Harmonic 695*, this aerial did exhibit some of the same dimensions. I suspect that if an aerial or assembly of wires was arranged, involving several fundamental harmonics, then positive results would be available.

I have not attempted to write this report in a completely scientific manner as I am not a scientist. It is purely a record of my observations and comments on the results, so far as my limited knowledge of the subject allows.

Donald R. Offwood

February 1975

The results of Mr.Offwood's experiments show without doubt that a wire loop aerial does, in a most positive way, influence the growth rate and health of plants. The next step to take in further experiments is to make use of perfectly tuned aerials for maximum results and to try a series of loops constructed from wires of different metals. I believe that certain metals which have mass values close to the harmonic values of light, mass and gravity, could improve the radiation field produced within the coil. For instance aluminium, which consists of a combination of isotopes with mass numbers of 26 and 27, could be produced. If the compound consisted of measured proportions the average mass value could be made to match that of the harmonic energy equivalent derived from the unified equation: 26.944. The radiations from this type of wire should theoretically be more intense. It is interesting to note that wires made from aluminum are excellent electrical conductors and that transmission lines are now being made from this metal.

TABLE 3

ROW A Chamaecyparis lawsoniana ellwoodii

			Date 12/9/72	Date 5/1/73		Date 15/3/73		Date 11/5/73	
Thread	Base Height	Pitch	Height	Height	Growth	Height	Growth	Height	Growth
.	.	.	12½	16¾	4¼	21	8½	22	9½
.	.	.	15	20	5	26	11	27	12
.	.	.	14½	19¼	5	24	9½	25	10½
L.H.	5½	3¾	15½	20	4½	26	10½	27	11½
L.H.	5	3	14	19¼	5¼	25	11	26	12
.	.	.	15½	21½	6	27½	12	28½	13
L.H.	3¾	3¾	11	15½	4½	21	10	21½	10½
.	.	.	14½	20	5½	24	9½	25	10½
R.H.	7	4	14	18½	4½	23½	9½	24	10
.	.	.	12	16	4	21½	9½	22½	10½
R.H.	1	2	16½	22	5½	29	12½	30½	14
.	.	.	12	17½	5½	23½	11½	24	12
.	.	.	17	23	6	28¾	11¾	30	13
.	.	.	15½	20	4½	23½	8	24	8½
.	.	.	16½	20¾	4¼	24	7½	24	7½
R.H.	4	3	14	17½	3½	22½	8½	23	9
.	.	.	14	17¾	3¾	21½	7½	23	9
R.H.	5	2½	15	19	4	24	9	25	10
.	.	.	13½	17½	4	22	8½	23	9½
R.H.	3	2½	15½	20	4½	25	9½	26½	11
.	.	.	14	18½	4½	23½	9½	24	10
.	.	.	16½	21¼	4¾	26	9½	27	10½
L.H.	3½	3¼	13	17½	4½	22½	9½	24	11
L.H.	5	3	17	23	6	30	13	32	15
.	.	.	15¾	19¾	4	25	9¼	25¾	10
.	.	.	15¾	19½	3¾	25¾	9	25¾	10

TABLE 4

ROW B Chamaecyparis lawsoniana allumii

			Date 12/9/72	Date 5/1/73		Date 15/3/73		Date 11/5/73	
Thread	Base Height	Pitch	Height	Height	Growth	Height	Growth	Height	Growth
.	.	.	10¼	19	8¾	24	13¾	25	14¾
.	.	.	16	26	10	31¼	15¼	32	16
L.H.	0	3¾	13	23¼	10¼	30	17	31	18
.	.	.	13½	23½	10	30	16½	31	17½
R.H.	3	4	14	23½	9½	30½	16½	32	18
.	.	.	12½	21½	9	27½	15	27½	15
R.H.	5	8	13	23	10	30	17	29	16
R.H.	4	6¾	14½	23½	9¼	29½	15	31	16¾
L.H.	4	3	13½	22½	9	30	16½	31	17½
.	.	.	5	12¾	7¾	21½	16½	22	17
.	.	.	8½	17¼	8¾	24	15½	25	16½
.	.	.	10½	18½	8	23	12½	23	12½
.	.	.	13	24	11	31½	18½	32	19
L.H.	1¾	3	12¼	23	10¾	29¼	17	29	16¾
R.H.	9	3½	16	27	11	33	17	33	17
.	.	.	12½	23½	11	29¼	16¾	30	17½
R.H.	5½	3	14	25	11	29¼	15½	30½	16½
R.H.	4	3½	14½	24½	10	31	16½	32	17½
R.H.	6	3½	16	25¾	9¾	32	16	33	17
.	.	.	16	24¾	8¾	29	13	30	14
.	.	.	16	25½	9½	31	15	32	16
.	.	.	11½	19½	8	23½	12	24	12½

	5/1/73	15/3/73	11/5/73
Average height increase by plants with a loop.	10.050	16.400	17.100
Average height increase by plants without a loop.	9.208	15.020	15.678
Difference shown as a percentage.	+9.150	+9.190	+9.010

Three positive results again.

TABLE 5

ROW C Phebalium squameum

			Date 12/9/72	Date 5/1/73		Date 15/3/73		Date 11/5/73	
Thread	**Base Height**	**Pitch**	**Height**	**Height**	**Growth**	**Height**	**Growth**	**Height**	**Growth**
.	.	.	10	16	6	28	18	32	22
.	.	.	16	28	12	49	33	56	40
.	.	.	11	24	13	37	26	46	35
L.H.	3½	3½	16	26½	10½	47	31	50	34
R.H.	−1	2	14½	24	9½	41½	27	50	35½
.	.	.	13	26	13	49	36	58	45
R.H.	−1	3½	13	24	11	45½	32½	55	42
.	.	.	12	23¾	11¾	37	25	46	34
.	.	.	12	25¾	13¾	45½	33½	53	41
L.H.	4	4	13	26	13	48	35	55	42
.	.	.	15	26½	11½	46	31	55	40
L.H.	5½	3½	13½	28¼	14¾	47½	34	56	42½
.	.	.	15	24½	9½	43	28	48	33
R.H.	1	4	12½	27¼	14¾	45½	33	53	40½
R.H.	2	2	8½	24	15½	45	36½	56	47½
.	.	.	13	30¼	17¼	48½	35½	59	46
.	.	.	13½	26	12½	46	32½	Removed	
.	.	.	15	31½	16½	51	36	in error	
.	.	.	14	23½	9½	54½	40½	63	49

	5/1/73	15/3/73	11/5/73
Average height increase by plants with a loop.	12.710	32.710	40.570
Average height increase by plants without a loop.	12.180	31.250	38.500
Difference shown as a percentage.	+4.350	+4.670	+5.380

TABLE 6

ROW D Choisya ternata

		Date 12/9/72		Date 5/1/73		Date 15/3/73		Date 11/5/73	
Thread	Base Height	Pitch	Height	Height	Growth	Height	Growth	Height	Growth
.	.	.	8	15	7	20	12	21	13
.	.	.	9	17¼	8¼	22	13	23	14
R.H.	6	4	8	14¼	6¼	20	12	20	12
.	.	.	8½	14¾	6¼	18	9½	19	10½
R.H.	2	3	8	15	7	19½	11½	19	11
L.H.	3½	3½	8½	15½	7	20½	12	23	14½
L.H.	3½	3½	8½	15½	7	22½	14	22	13½
.	.	.	8½	16	7½	20½	12	21	12½
R.H.	−1	2½	8	16½	8½	21½	13½	24	16
.	.	.	8	15½	7½	22	14	22	14
.	.	.	8	15	7	17½	9½	19	11
.	.	.	8	16¼	8¼	22	14	25	17
.	.	.	8	14½	6½	22½	14½	24	16
L.H.	−1	3	8½	17½	9	22	13½	29	20½
.	.	.	7½	15	7½	20	12½	24	16½
L.H.	−1	3	9½	18½	9	23¾	14¼	24	14½
.	.	.	7½	Removed to allow extension of					
.	.	.	9	the sprinkler system.					
.	.	.	9						

	5/1/73	15/3/73	11/5/73
Average height increase by plants with a loop.	7.680	12.970	14.570
Average height increase by plants without a loop.	7.310	12.330	13.830
Difference shown as a percentage.	+5.060	+5.110	+5.350

TABLE 7

ROW A	Right-hand	Left-hand	
5/1/73	4.40%	4.95%	Favours left-hand
15/3/73	9.80%	10.80%	3–0
11/5/73	8.80%	12.00%	

ROW B			
5/1/73	10.07%	10.00%	Favours left-hand
15/3/73	16.21%	16.83%	2–1
11/5/73	16.96%	17.42%	

ROW C			
5/1/73	12.69%	12.75%	Favours left-hand
15/3/73	32.25%	33.33%	2–1
11/5/73	41.38%	37.17%	

ROW D			
5/1/73	7.25%	8.00%	Favours left-hand
15/3/73	12.33%	13.44%	3–0
11/5/73	13.00%	15.75%	

The fact that loops with a left-hand thread were the most efficient could possibly be due to the experiments being conducted in the southern hemisphere. The opposite would apply in the northern hemisphere. This would be similar to the vortexual action of weather systems, which is also electrical in nature.

Lakhovsky carried out extensive research into cell structure, and in 1923 he constructed a machine called a radio-cellulo-oscillator which he used in his experiments with plants. As his work progressed he came to the conclusion that the use of ultra-short waves alone was not the complete answer as the thermal effects were sometimes dangerous.

He conceived an idea for a new type of machine that would give "an oscillatory shock to all the cells in the body of a human being simultaneously." By use of damped electrostatic waves thermal effects were at a minimum and cell injury would not occur.

In 1931 Lakhovsky perfected what he called his multiple wave oscillator. This apparatus was capable of generating an electrostatic field covering all wavelengths from 10cm to 400 metres. Within such a field all cells could find their own frequency of vibration within a range of 750,000 to 3 milliards per second. Added to this, each circuit gave forth a series of harmonics extending far into the infrared and visible light regions.

This machine was eventually used in many hospitals in European countries for the treatment of numerous diseases. This included the treatment of cancer. No harmful effects have ever been reported, but many beneficial results were obtained.

A completely new branch of science was opened up, by this man, into the electrochemical structure of living matter. His research was obviously important to mankind. Is his work to be lost to us because he was ahead of his time?

Because of my own extreme interest in the structure of matter, I intend to build a multiple wave oscillator for my own private research. Who knows what other secrets may be prised from the limitless expanse of natural law?

17> THE HARMONICS OF HUMANS

THE UNIFIED EQUATIONS TELL US THAT THE WHOLE Universe is manifested by the harmonic geometric matrix of light itself. The whole of reality is light. Therefore, it follows, that we as human beings must consist of nothing more than a geometric collection of the harmonic wave-forms of light — guided by intelligence.

What we must look for is some proof of this in the evidence available to us. There are, in fact, several clues which indicate that the human form is in harmony with the Universe we live in.

The first clue is the gestation period of a human being. Nine months, or an average of 270 days. There is a great scattering of birth times which are either side of this 270 day average, but if we argue for perfect harmony then there must be an optimum time between conception and birth which would help to guarantee the production of a perfect human.

As each day forms a part of our geometric time cycle it seems reasonable to assume that perfection would be more likely to result from a gestation period of: 269.44 days.

This would tune the body directly with the harmonic value derived from the unified equation: 26944.

Note:

Slight variations of the unified value are manifested due to changes in the light speed as the distance from the Earth's centre increases. This is fully explained in my book, "The Bridge to Infinity". Values of 2695, 26944 and 2693645 have been calculated using the small variations in light speed. For this exercise I have used the average value of 26944.

The second clue is indicated by the temperature at which the human body functions most efficiently. Like any machine the human body will start to deteriorate physically if the temperature becomes too low or too high.

The Dictionary of Medicine (the Marshall Cavendish) states: "The average temperature of a human being is taken to be 98.4°F in Great Britain, but American doctors prefer to take it as 98.6°F. Readings between 97°F and 99°F are completely normal. Temperatures much below 97°F are usually only found either in under-activity of the thyroid, or after exposure to cold. Temperatures between 99⁰F and 100⁰F may not be of much importance, especially in children, but readings of over 100(0)F are almost invariably indicative of some infection (or sometimes some other form of inflammation)."

I would predict that the temperature at which the human body performs most efficiently, both physically and mentally, is 98.80412⁰F.

> 98.80412⁰ fahrenheit = 37.1134⁰ centrigrade - The harmonic reciprocal of 371134 = 269444.

If the unified harmonic is built into the body at birth then the temperature at which it functions appears to be at a level which would set up the harmonic reciprocal, causing a reaction, and life.

A third clue is evident in the nodal points in the human body where bio-energetic processes are most prevalent. These are the major points used in the science of acupuncture.

The following is an extract from the book, "The New Soviet Psychic Discoveries", by Henry Gris and William Dick. Page 418. (Sphere Books Ltd.)

At Alma-Ata, the Leningrad surgeon, Dr. M. K. Geykin, was experimenting with Kirlian photography. He had spent some time in China, where he worked on acupuncture. Fascinated by Kirlian's method, he decided to visit him in Krasnodar and induce him to build a gadget that could help physicians find the points of acupuncture on the human body. Kirlian listened to him with great interest. He had already discovered long before that the 695 points on the human body considered to be the points for acupuncture coincided with the points of intense luminosity brought out by Kirlian Photography.

"Kirlian was the first, with his photography, to come up with a machine to determine the points of acupuncture." It was a joint effort between Kirlian, Dr. Geykin, and electronics engineer I. V. Mikhalevsky. Later Soviet physicist Viktor Adamenko constructed his own instrument, which had a very original and stable electronic circuit. Adamenko's device not only determines the points of acupuncture but observes the bio-energetic processes in the human organism.

The number of acupuncture points: 695

The reciprocal harmonic of the speed of light at the Earth's surface. Again it appears that the body's bio-energy system is tuned to react to the harmonic of light.

The fourth clue was published in an Australian magazine called, "Simply Living" several years ago. The following is an extract from a long article regarding the mathematics of the world grid system.

THE FORMATION OF MATTER

Using three main harmonics, Cathie was able to initiate a basic equation. The harmonics he chose were:

1703 — The Earth Mass Harmonic
1439 — The Speed of Light Harmonic
264 — A harmonic that recurs within the polar squares.

Initially, these correlated as:

1439 + 264 = 1703

but extending the accuracy to five figure harmonics this became:

14389 + 2636 = 17025

This could be interpreted as:

Light + 2636 = Mass Formation

So, what does the harmonic **2636** represent? Surprisingly, this is the harmonic square root of 695, the reciprocal of the speed of light, which allows the incredible conclusion that:

Mass = Speed of Light + square root of the reciprocal of the Speed of Light.

i.e. $M = C + \sqrt{\dfrac{1}{C}}$ *

* In equations, the speed of light is referred to by the symbol, C.

Suddenly, we have an expression in terms of light energy for the value of Mass in Einstein's famous equation,

$E = MC^2$. Einstein, himself, stated that the answer to space travel would be found if we could replace the value for mass in his equation with a value in pure energy terms.

But let us return to the original equation

1439 + 264 = 1703

before we progress further with Einstein's equation. I imagine most readers are probably gasping for breath at this stage, so let us see if we can find any evidence to support Cathie's equation from outside his own research.

This equation seems to be attempting to relate the manifestation of mass from pure light energy, so it could be said that when the harmonic of **264** is applied to pure light energy, matter-formation is kicked into action.

Let us look at one of nature's most amazing processes, the DNA behaviour, so basic to the preservation of life on this planet and the building block of organic matter. Science knows how it happens but not really why. If we look at it geometrically we can see not only the key to the answer, but strong support for Cathie's Equation as well.

DIAGRAM 15

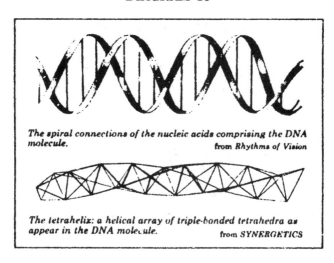

The spiral connections of the nucleic acids comprising the DNA molecule.   from *Rhythms of Vision*

The tetrahelix: a helical array of triple-bonded tetrahedra as appear in the DNA molecule.   from *SYNERGETICS*

The geometry of the DNA molecule

Buckminster Fuller's geometric analysis of the DNA molecule (which is basically in accord with the Watson-Crick model) found that helical columns of tetrahedra (tetrahelix) nestle together in local clusters of five tetrahedra (ten make a helix cycle) around a transverse axis in a tetrahelix nestling column.* But five tetrahedra, triple-bonded to one another around a common edge axis fall short of 360 degrees by 7 degrees, 20 minutes. This gap is called the *birth unzipping angle* of the DNA/RNA behaviours. The unzipping occurring as the birth dichotomy, the new life breaking off from the old pattern with the perfect imprint and repeating the other's growth pattern.

Can we assume that this angle is arbitrary within the geometry? If Cathie is right then harmonics should be clearly evident in this natural process.

7^0 20' = 26400 seconds of arc.

*Although Watson and Crick did not indentify the tetra helix columns themselves, the numbers of increments they measured are the same.

If it is shared by each of the faces then each angle becomes 44 minutes which equals 2640 seconds. We can therefore see that 264 has clearly emerged as a primary harmonic associated with the formation of organic matter.

I believe that the combination of all these factors shows without much doubt the human form is unique. We are at one with our environment.

There would be very few, if any, people on Earth who would have the perfect harmonic combination, but those with the factors which are closest to the ultimate would be, in theory, the healthiest and most intelligent of us all.

It would be interesting to check a small group of these people and see if they meet the criteria.

18> BUILDERS IN STONE

THERE ARE MEN AMONG US WHO UNDERSTAND THE mathematical secrets which govern the universe. Now they are frantically, but clandestinely, trying to find ways of putting them into practical use.

One cause for both the haste and the secrecy has been the inevitable realisation that we are not alone in the universe. There is ample evidence that intelligent beings visited this planet thousands of years ago: traces of long-past civilisations in many respects far more advanced than our own can be found in ancient structures. The evidence of superiority — in every sense — of the ancients has shaken those who have rediscovered their legacies; an analogy would be the sudden discovery by life-long inmates of a mental hospital that there was a world of "superior intelligence" just beyond their locked gates.

We have been visited and watched for possibly thousands of years. While our twentieth-century sciences have opened up the doors of space for us, it is also reasonable to assume that the ancients had knowledge far in advance of our own, and that space travel was to them a natural adjunct to their civilisation. Yet, in spite of their great intelligence and frightening control over sources of power and energy, they were unable to prevent whatever the catastrophes were that visited the planet and eradicated many signs of their life here. With the state of the world as it is at present, our modern scientists must speculate many times a day on our chances of survival.

Were there survivors of the ancient civilisations — and if so, what became of them?

Did they escape into space, to build still other, greater civilisations? Or were they people from space in the first place, who looked upon Earth only as a small colony in a galactic empire? Are we descendants of these people — or are we a new race carefully created and cultivated by the space people as organisms adapted to life here, to be custodian of the planet until they require it once more? Are we a prize herd, owned by someone Out There? Do they carefully watch us, even now, coaxing and guiding us, teaching and punishing us, moulding and remoulding our future according to our own progress and with regard to how we handle our own problems?

These are but a few of the many questions that have been put forward by nonconformist thinkers in recent decades. Whatever we choose to imagine, there is always the hard fact: in historical times there were races on this planet with an intelligence far superior to our own; there is evidence, literally, by the ton that says so. There is evidence too, I suggest, to show that there are similar "intelligences" among us today — and that their presence on our globe is a fact known to our own scientists.

The evidence of the ancient civilisations has been uncovered in many parts of the world in the form of stone ruins. After studying these massive stone edifices, archaeologists have usually produced profound theories as to their purpose, finally to class them as temples erected in honour of some sun god or other, built in order to house pagan rituals, or for even darker purposes — such as human sacrifice.

As we all know, a number of inexplicable stone ruins have been found as remnants of past cultures — including those of the Mayas, Incas, Aztecs, and Egyptians. In many cases the ruins indicate patterns that were originally geometric in their design. Reconstruction and measurements have proved beyond doubt that in many instances the buildings and structures had inherent in them mathematical concepts which had direct connection with light, gravity and mass. The buildings were not simple monuments or places of worship to dark gods; nor were they designed the way they were for purely aesthetic reasons. They had a definite scientific function.

The function, I believe, was connected with power production, communication, transportation, celestial computation, healing, and possibly many other purposes which may still be obscure to us.

I believe that there are unquestionable geometric links between the Great Pyramid in Egypt and Stonehenge, the fascinating arrangement of monoliths on Salisbury Plain, England. I have uncovered evidence to substantiate my claims, and I sincerely hope that Stonehenge experts will have the grace to take a closer look at some of their own conclusions.

Some readers have come to feel that I am always ready to condemn all scientists out of hand. I have no doubt at all that the majority of scientists are men and women of integrity who carry out honest research in their chosen fields; unfortunately, the society in which we live is such that many of these dedicated people are unable to inform the public at large of their findings. There is a communication gap, partly a result of the lack of a common vocabulary or terminology that might put the people on the same wavelength as the scientists, and partly deliberately imposed. Money rules the world; the boat of vested interests cannot readily be rocked. The number of scientists, dedicated or otherwise, who have dared to speak out of turn, in defiance of the monied establishment is very small indeed. The solution to this particular problem is education — the bridge that will close the gap between the laity and the scientists, the ecclesiastics of the 1980s. In time that bridge will be built. Meanwhile, I am sure, there are scientists who must be suffering the pains of hell for having placed the means for destroying great portions of humanity in the hands of politicians and military rulers.

I appeal to these intellectuals, if they have a shred of honesty left, to tell the truth about the atomic bomb, about the preparations for germ warfare, about all the scientific marvels that the world would enjoy today if a sane and reasonable control could be placed upon the knowledge which is theirs.

There are scientists who agree with me; I know this, for they have spoken to me about the problem. I can pry into their secrets and pass them on as I uncover them — because I am not one of them. Is it right that they should have a layman for their spokesman? It is a position which I fill uneasily. "It is not for the public to know these things; it is not good for them," one scientist assured me. I'll let you be the judge of that.

As I dug in closer to the truth of the UFOs and the power sources which they use, I was twice approached by a "middle-man" who was interested only in finding whether or not I would stop my research for a price. When he found that I was prepared to go on with my research and publish at all costs, I was warned that unspecified "strange things" would happen to me if I persisted. This is not a delusion of someone suffering from a persecution complex; it is perfectly true. A noted lawyer has the name, and a record of the veiled threat and who made it.

I was able to give the middle-man his answer during a television interview; I let it be known that I had taken a number of precautions — such as having a number of copies of manuscripts, charts, calculations, maps and other research data — placed in several safe spots, so that if anything untoward happened to me the work would be carried on and eventually published anyway. I said that I was not afraid.

A little later I was again approached, offered a position working with a small band of scientists with the hint of a very healthy salary. My answer was the same; and on this occasion I gave a full report to the New Zealand Government of the offer.

Power groups today all have this in common: they are unable to understand a person who refuses to be bought. Frankly, I would like nothing better than to be able to carry out full-time research on all the matters that interest me for the rest of my life; but I would also have to be completely free to disseminate whatever knowledge I might gain, whatever conclusions to which I might be drawn.

With that off my chest, I would like to quote from a newspaper story carried by the *Aukland Star* on 23 September 1969. It was filed from the London office of NZPA-Reuter, and it was headed:

STONE-AGE POWER STATION?

A group of amateur archaeologists has come up with a startling answer to one of the world's oldest and puzzling mysteries — the origin and purpose of stone-age monuments, such as Stonehenge.

Evidence assembled over seventeen years could alter current thinking on the mysterious circles of stone.

The suggestion is that the stones form a gigantic power network.

Mr. John Williams, Abergavenny, Monmouthshire, thinks all such monuments in Britain may be aligned in a single geometrical pattern.

Mr. Williams, a solicitor, has compared the positions on ordnance survey maps of more that 3000 prehistoric stone circles and single standing stones.

He says every one is aligned to neighbours up to twenty miles away at an angle of 23 1/2 degrees, or a multiple of that angle.

Over the years he has taken thousands of photographs of standing stones and believes he has found a significant clue to their use.

A surprising number of photographs appeared spoilt, as if "fogged."

"I thought nothing of it for years and put it down to bad camera work," Mr. Williams said today, "but in 1959 a friend and I photographed the same stone in Brecon together. Both pictures came out with a fogged band across them in the same place. My picture was taken in colour and the fog-band was dark blue. This led me to surmise that something in the stone was spoiling the pictures, a kind of ultra-violet light.

"Since then I've had many more examples of the same phenomenon," Mr. Williams continued. "Most, if not all, standing stones contain quartz, a crystal similar to that used with the cat's whisker in early wireless receivers. I believe most stones would show the fog effect if systematically photographed. I now think the stones form a gigantic power network, though I cannot guess for what purpose."

Mr. Williams offers two further clues. More than 200 of the stone sites are in north-south alignment and are named after King Arthur. "But Arthur," says Mr. Williams, "does not signify a Celtic warrior king. In Welsh the name means Great Bear, and this may be a clue that the power system was based on polar magnetism."

Said Mr. Williams: "Radio waves and X-rays have always been there, although modern man only recently discovered them. Is it possible that prehistoric man discovered something analogous which is still unknown to us?"

Dolmens, groups of stones with a roofing stone, often delicately balanced, are usually thought to be sepulchres. But Mr. Williams says human remains have been found on only 2 percent of such sites. He believes the roofing stones were placed as rocking stones to operate the power system.

Naturally I was very interested in this report, as it backed up a good deal of my own theories. The fact that the stones as described by Mr. Williams are lined up at angles of 23 1/2° or multiples of that figure is most significant, as this is the angle of inclination of the earth's axis. Mr. Williams undoubtedly was aware of this when he was interviewed, though the point is not brought out in the article.

It will be worth while to pay a quick visit to Stonehenge: it comprises two circles of upright stone blocks, with two other series of standing stones inside, each of which is in the shape of a horse-shoe. The outermost circle evidently contained originally thirty stones, each 13 1/2 feet high; the arrangement is known as the Sarsen Circle. The diameter of this circle is 97 feet, 4 inches, according to measurements published in the book *Stonehenge Decoded*, by American astronomer Gerald S. Hawkins. The author carried out a scientific survey of Stonehenge and of all known data and references to it, and then with the aid of a computer was able to show that the geometric arrangement of the massive stones formed a highly accurate astronomical clock. This study also demonstrated that the architects of that time had an extremely advanced knowledge of astronomy and mathematics. The measurements I give here are those published by Hawkins in his fascinating book.

Of the thirty stones which once stood in the Sarsen Circle, only twenty-four are today in their original positions. The thirty upright stones were once topped by thirty lintels, mortised at each end; only five of the lintels remain in place. The stones were not quarried locally, but were brought from a position near Newbury, some forty miles away.

Outside the Sarsen Circle there was yet another circle, the Aubrey Circle, named after its discoverer. What remains of this is a series of fifty-six evenly-spaced holes which vary in depth from two feet to four. The diameter of this fairly accurate circle was measured at 288 feet, with a distance of 16 feet from one hole to the next. While the circle was not a perfect one, the greatest error radial-wise was found to be 19 inches; and around the circumference, in the spacing of the holes, 21 inches.

Between the Aubrey holes and the Sarsen Circle two other circular patterns of holes — now named the Y holes and the Z holes — have been discovered. There are thirty holes in the Y series, forming a circle roughly 35 feet outside the Sarsen Circle, and in the Z series twenty-nine holes, from 5 to 15 feet beyond the Sarsen Circle. The holes are not regularly spaced. Excavation of each hole brought to light a single blue-stone fragment of the rhyolite variety.

Further descriptions and measurements of the Stonehenge complex would fill a volume; but the above information was of vital interest to me. Coupled with the discovery by Mr. Williams of what seemed to be a form of radiation issuing from the large stones, Hawkin's work helps one to form a clearer picture of the possible purpose of the geometric pattern of the quartz stones.

The diameter of the Aubrey circle is of significance. The average diameter is given as 288 feet. I feel sure that if a precise check were to be made, the true measurement would be found to be 287.8 grid feet; a grid foot being a fraction larger than a standard foot. As is shown elsewhere in this book, the value of 2878 is equal to 2C, that is twice the speed of light harmonic of 1439.

Next, we note that the Sarsen Circle had thirty standing stones; thirty is also the basic spacing of the UFO grid system. The diameter of the circle is given as 97 feet 4 inches. It is not indicated whether the measurement is taken from the edge or from the centre of the stone uprights. Again I have a hunch that if the measurement is again checked and translated into grid feet it will come to 96.6 feet, which would give a radius for the Sarsen Circle of 48.3 grid feet. As shown elsewhere, the square of the speed of light reciprocal harmonic of 695 is equal to 483.

It appears as though Stonehenge was constructed to the universal geometric harmonics of light itself. The radius of the Aubrey Circle is that of the speed of light; the radius of the Sarsen Circle corresponds to the square of the reciprocal of the speed of light.

And what of the fact that the large stones appear to be of a crystalline structure, and apparently emit a form of radiation, as shown by the fogging effect on the photographs taken by Williams? He himself suggests that the quartz crystal is similar to that used in the early crystal type of radio much revered by small boys in years gone by — myself included. I believe he is very close to the truth. The small chips of blue-stone found in the Y and Z holes could also have a crystalline structure and be caused to resonate to harmonic fields set up by the inner and outer circles based on the harmonics of the angular velocity of light itself.

Could Stonehenge have been designed as a gigantic crystal set? A massive geometric device constructed in ancient times to serve as a transmitter and receiver of signals from the heavens? This I believe to be a probability, not just a possibility.

There is still further evidence pointing towards this. When men build a modern radar station on a flat ground level site it is necessary to surround the central radar scanner with a circular earthen wall in order to create an artificial horizon. This low barrier cuts out all random clutter from the radar screen, and provides the operator with a positive horizon from which to calculate angular altitude.

Stonehenge, too, is surrounded by a similar wall although it is formed of the ubiquitous chalk that is found in abundance in this part of England. The chalk mound forms the rim of a circle some 320 feet in diameter. This white wall, when it was first built, must have been some 20 feet wide and 6 feet high, according to measurements of its remains.

The fifty-six Aubrey holes were also filled with chalk rubble, so perhaps there is some kind of electromagnetic affinity between the molecules of chalk and the quartz crystal in the stones of the Sarsen Circle, and the stone chips placed in the Y and Z holes.

Another type of modern electronic equipment is a navigation device used for aircraft, and known as VOR, standing for Very High Frequency Omni-directional Range Station. The equipment consists of a ground station, and special apparatus in an aircraft which analyses signals transmitted from the station. By constant variation of the phasing of the signals transmitted from the ground station, the equipment in the aircraft can lock on to individual, one-degree radials from the station. By this means an aircraft can either fly away from or towards the ground station on definite, set magnetic headings.

It is perfectly possible that Stonehenge was an ancient equivalent of the modern VOR station. The Sarsen Circle's thirty quartz upright stones may be likened to thirty radial high-frequency transmitters. The fifty-six Aubrey holes may have set up certain interference patterns, with signals being emitted from the tuned crystals in the Sarsen stones. Many permutations would result when the radiating patterns of the signals from the Aubrey holes and the thirty Sarsen stones were combined, which could have set up a very great number of electromagnetic radials for navigational purposes. Such signals would travel far out into space, as they would have been tuned to the harmonic of light itself.

Something else of great significance to me was revealed in the Hawkins book. He refers to a certain line-up of stones, revealed by computer analysis, at equinox sunset.

When positions designated by Hawkins at "94" and "C" are lined up with the sun, the displacement in azimuth clockwise from north, in degrees, is given as 269.5! Here we have the harmonic of 2695 showing up again: better still, it is the result of a computer programme. Could this be merely chance, as scientists insist? How many chances am I allowed before someone in authority will admit publicly that perhaps — even a qualified perhaps — I just may have discovered something — something that may turn out to be of immense value to mankind.

Stonehenge could have been both a cosmic clock and a navigational ground station. To produce the harmonic resonance required

171

to cause radiation from the stones, the geometric pattern must be aligned astronomically with certain key positions related to the sun and moon; thus a two-fold purpose can be attributed to the Stonehenge system.

More evidence of what I have suggested here is sure to come to light in the future, but I believe enough has already been presented to suggest that a closer examination of the inherent mathematics of Stonehenge will uncover a veritable goldmine of information. I admit the possibility that in fact scientists have already done exactly this; the fact that we, the public, have heard nothing from them would be nothing unusual.

Another line of research which would be equally rewarding would be a mathematical probing of the Great Pyramid, of course carried out using the harmonic measurements inherent in the UFO grid.

May I remind you that the word "pyramid" has the literal meaning "measure of light."

One day, hopefully in my own lifetime, an academy will be established of scientists whose only allegiance will be to the truth, and to the reporting of the truth to the public, and whose principal functions will be to undertake research on the ancient monuments whose secrets we have never been able to properly plumb.

Any true man of science would already have taken recognition of the facts and figures I have pointed out in this chapter. He would already have undertaken research along these exciting paths.

The monuments of ancient times bulk large; they stare us in the face; their secrets defy us.

The human response is to shrug them off.

"Merely temples and places of worship, erected by slave labour," is the "explanation" that we generally get.

Somewhere there may be surviving masters of the ancient world, enjoying a quiet chuckle at our obstinate blindness.

NOTE:

Since the publication of this book I have carried out a further probe into the mathematical structure of Stonehenge with the aid of a calculator. I have found that the values, as shown, although only to four-figure accuracy, are indeed built into the complex. A complete mathematical breakdown of the concentric circular patterns, the spacing of the standing stones and the Aubrey Holes, has been accomplished, and the findings show that the values are in accord with those demonstrated in the harmonic unified equations. There is now no doubt in my mind that this structure is of immense scientific importance, and that the understanding of the mathematical message, inherent within the geometric pattern of the stones will one day enable man to conquer the universe.

It is my intention to publish this data in a later book.

19> FROM ALPHA TO OMEGA

A LPHA CENTAURI, THAT CURIOUS STAR MILLIONS of light-years from earth which has excited scientists because of radio signals that apparently originate at its surface, may well be one of the goals of the space age. One of the scientific crutches that will help our first space travellers to limp to that destination may well be Omega.

For well over a year controversy raged in New Zealand as to whether the aerials of an Omega navigational station should be permitted to decorate one of the picturesque South Island valleys, like a gigantic web spun by some psychotic spider (see diagram).

Reports and comments have been thrown about, words have been distorted and quoted out of context to support one or another partisan cause, and evasions at Government level have done nothing to help clarify the Omega story. Mainly the controversy has centred around this point: would an Omega station assist Polaris submarines? If so, would not such a station become a primary target in the event of a major war, even if New Zealand were neutral?

Eight of these so-called navigational radio stations are to be positioned in various localities around the world; the South Island of New Zealand was selected as the location forone of them. Already there are four stations in operation — in Norway, Trinidad, Hawaii and near New York.

Supposedly, the full system of eight stations is to be set up for the sole purpose of providing a global navigational network for shipping, submarines and aircraft. No doubt the Omega stations will fulfil this purpose at maximum efficiency, as the concept is certainly far in advance of the wartime system known as LORAN, or long-range navigation.

Simultaneous readings from these or additional stations will give a position on any point of the earth's surface within a half-mile accuracy.

However, a very large number of New Zealanders, including scientists, university professors and the general public, have expressed a fear that the installation of such a station in New Zealand would immediately make this country vulnerable to nuclear attack in the event of World War III. The fear comes from the belief, erroneous

DIAGRAM 16

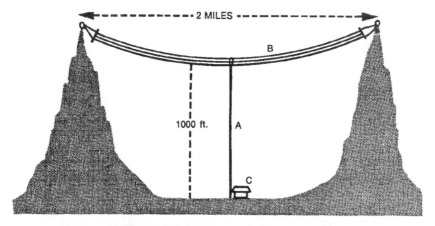

THE BASIC OMEGA TRANSMITTER

A The aerial transmitter 10 kw.
B Carrier wires improve efficiency of aerial A but do not transmit.
C Small control hut.

The wrist-thick wire aerial is the only part transmitting. If a station is built on flat land a 1000 ft. high aerial is set up with an umbrella-shaped web of supporting wires around it, and the cost is much more than that of the mountain-slung aerial shown.

or not, that the hidden purpose of Omega is to enable nuclear submarines to obtain accurate fixes of position while still submerged, in order to carry out an attack. If this were true, then any country with such a station would obviously become a priority — A target for the enemy.

But is this the real purpose of Omega, in fact?

Possibly, but not probably. Nuclear submarines do not need this type of system. Inertial navigation systems already in use are far more accurate and reliable, and cannot be tampered with by any hostile nation or its agents. The official voice on Omega is speaking accurately when it declares that Omega is not essential for military forces of any nation.

Then why should the Americans be so very anxious to establish Omega stations in other countries, and against the popular wishes of the people of those countries? There is certainly a widespread belief that something is being concealed about the Omega plan, and that all the facts are not being revealed. Already the press has informed us that persons involved with the operations of these stations will be covered by the Official Secrets Act (*New Zealand Herald*, 2 July 1968). Would this be reasonable if Omega were not of a military nature? I for one do not believe so. Then can there be some other reason besides the officially stated one for building a particular station at a particular position?

As might be expected, a rather large shoal of red herrings has confused the whole Omega issue even further — deliberately, I suspect. Three different "likely" sites for New Zealand's Omega were selected for assessment in the South Island, and a couple more were suggested for localities in South Australia for good measure. When the normally easy-going New Zealand public began to show signs of uneasiness about the project, inferences were given by way of the daily press that the Omega project would be handed over to Australia, with the station to be built in New South Wales or Tasmania.

This possible switch in plans may have been designed to have a psychological appeal to the New Zealand public; the implication was that New Zealand was being so difficult over the whole affair that this peaceful little dominion didn't jolly well deserve an Omega station, so Uncle Sam would give it to Australia instead.

If this indeed was the ruse, it was not altogether a howling success: the public tended to breathe a little more easily at the thought that after all their country would not become a potential target; but still there were loud demands that the Government should turn down any offer for Omega, even if the station were to be presented as a gift. Let the Aussies have it, by all means; who wants a wooden horse sitting in their back yard?

There were months of this argument and counter-argument. Everyone got into the act, including university students who paraded carrying anti-Omega placards. Eventually some decision had to be made. It was announced that a site close to Lake Pearson in New Zealand's South Island had been chosen for Omega. This locality happened to be the "cheapest" one "assessed" right from the beginning.

The decision came as no surprise. Back in 1968 I had been approached by a group of university students who asked me to plot the proposed positions assessed for the station, to see if there was any connection with the UFO grid which I had discovered, or if there were any other geometric evidence to explain Omega as anything other than a sophisticated civilian navigational system.

I informed the students that I was not particularly interested in their battle over the Omega issue, as I had more than enough evidence of my own to check into regarding UFO activity without getting mixed up in what had all the earmarks of becoming a political free-for-all.

All the same, I did make a rough check of the geometric positions of the sites that had been mentioned, and I found that the Lake Pearson area was the only one that showed any connection with grid harmonics. I left it at that, after telling the students that I had no further interest in the matter. If this was indeed the area which was eventually to be selected, then, at that time, I might become a little more interested.

In April 1969 the decision was announced: Lake Pearson was to be the site of the Omega station. The scientists had sifted through all the pros and cons for this site and that and, they said, Lake Pearson was the one — the most magnificent and suitable location upon which to place the box of tricks reverently called Omega.

So now I was most definitely interested. Out came my worn maps and log tables.

The latitude and longitude of the lake were checked once more, and a recalculation made of the harmonic probabilities of the area. I was convinced that the scientists were up to something that they had no intentions of revealing to the public at large.

I calculated a position just north-north-west of the lake which I thought to be a likely site for the station, and forwarded the information to the air attaché at the American Embassy in Wellington, in the hope of sparking some sort of comment from somebody in authority there. I was not sure what harmonic principle the station would be built to incorporate so I had to work by hunch alone. However, I was certain that when the exact sight was known a mathematical connection with the grid system would be evident. A direct answer was not forthcoming, but a few weeks later I met the air attaché by chance in Auckland and he told me that the calculations I had sent to Wellington were "not too bad." I felt that at least I was getting close.

Some months later I received further information and found that the position I had chosen was evidently an error. *Canta*, the newspaper published by the Students' Association of Canterbury University, published a lengthy article on the Omega issue, and their illustration of a rough map (see map) showed the actual position to be at the south-eastern end of the lake.

The area where the aerial was to be suspended was enclosed by four mountains. At the northern end, Purple Hill (5505 ft) and

MAP 7

LAKE PEARSON LOCALS NOT TOLD ABOUT OMEGA

Runholders in the Lake Pearson area did not know that their district had been chosen as a possible Omega transmitter site a "Canta" reporter discovered during a visit to the area two days after the Physics Department and "Canta" simultaneously exposed the military nature of Omega.

They had been aware of the presence of what they assumed were some sort of Government surveyors in the district, but did not see anything sinister in this as they were used to Government departments trespassing. "They seem to think they own the country, and never ask our permission," said one runholder.

One person, a bach owner who was also a radio ham, did meet the "surveyors" and learned that some sort of transmitter was planned.

Residents understand that the transmitter antenna is to be erected between Purple Hill and Constitution Hill, as shown in the map, across a valley running from the Flock Hill homestead towards Avoca railway station.

One end of the antenna would be on Flock Hill station and the other on Craigieburn station. Both properties are leased from the University of Canterbury (Educational Reserve 1577). About a mile away, on the edge of Lake Pearson there is 320 acres of Crown Land, originally set aside as a township reserve, and it is presumed that the Americans would build their base there, if Lake Pearson is the site selected.

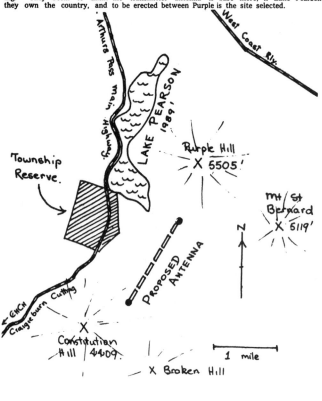

Mt. St. Bernard (5119 ft); and at the southern end, Constitution Hill (4409 ft) and Broken Hill.

Local residents believe that the two-mile aerial will be slung somewhere between Purple Hill and Constitution Hill. The properties at either end of the aerial were said to be leased from the University of Canterbury itself (Educational Reserve 1577). It seemed to me that it was quite a coincidence that the land to be used was university owned. In any event, the *Canta* report spelled out for me a very small area which I would easily be able to check in order to find any interesting mathematical harmonics.

My original calculations, as published in my earlier work, Harmonic 695, indicated that the most likely position of the aerial would be: 43° 08' 09.6" south / 171° 48' 43.9" east. The associated geometric harmonics were found to be closely related to reciprocal values of the speed of light and time, according to the accuracy of my work at that period.

I have extended my research considerably since then and now have access to computers which help to simplify the work and allow a wider coverage of all the geometric parameters discovered so far in the search for harmonic relationships. The best theoretical position, according to present knowledge, calculated by computer, would be:

43° 08' 37.61" south / 171° 48' 20.653" east.

Recent research has indicated that the latitudes of several scientific stations have been calculated in such a way that the relative displacements from the Equator and the North, or South Pole, will create a geometric harmonic.

So, the latitude of 43° 08' 37.61", or, 43.14378 degrees would have a displacement as follows:

Distance from the South Pole	=	46.85622 degrees
Distance from the Equator	=	43.14378 degrees
Difference	=	3.712440 degrees

The harmonic 371244 is the mathematical reciprocal of the geometric value derived from the Unified Equation: 2693645.

The position, because of the latitude, would allow a tuned electromagnetic wave transmission to resonate in harmony with the Unified Fields. (These values are explained more fully in my later book. "The Bridge to Infinity, Harmonic 371244".)

The longitude position also created an interesting harmonic. As all calculations are related to each section of 90 degrees we process the longitude as follows:

$$171.805737 \text{ degrees}$$
$$\text{minus} \quad \underline{90.000000} \text{ degrees}$$
$$\underline{81.805737} \text{ degrees}$$

The Tangent of this angle is :
6.94444

The harmonic 694444 is the reciprocal value of the speed of light in free space, 144,000 minutes of arc per grid second, relative to the Earth's surface.

A further harmonic is evident in the relationship of the transmitter to the North Grid Pole at:
78° 25' 33.33" north / 105° 00' 00" west.

The great circle distance between the two points (accurate to within 0.45 minutes on the computer) is 7844.6296 minutes of arc, or nautical miles.

If this value is multiplied by 6, three times, in order to raise the harmonic, a value of 1694440 is found. Recent research indicates a direct association of this harmonic with mass, gravity and communication.

The communication harmonic would also, in theory, be built into the aerial system itself and a further exercise on the computer suggests the following:

Height of aerial given as:
1,000 feet

A theoretical value of:
996.72393 feet would be equal to:
0.1639348 minutes of arc, relative.

Multiply by six twice to raise the harmonic:
5.9016548

Which is the reciprocal harmonic of:
0.169444 (communication).

During March 1971 it was announced in a New Zealand newspaper; that the Americans had finally decided that the Omega Station would not be established in New Zealand.

On Friday, August 11, 1978, an Australian Newspaper published an article which stated in part:

> "Federal Government will call tenders tomorrow for an Omega Navigation Station to be built at Darriman, in Gippsland————The building is expected to be ready in mid 1980 and the station is scheduled to be operational before the end of 1980.
> It will have a 427 metre high steel lattice tower to carry the antenna system.
> The antenna system comprises 16 cables supported from the top and extending to the ground about 730 metres from the base in an evenly spaced array".

I will leave my readers to hunt out the exact location of this one and calculate the appropriate harmonics. I would be interested in any results which look promising.

Once I had taken a good hard look at my theoretical calculations and felt some satisfaction with the results, I thought the next steps would be to put the station into my original grid map to see just how it fitted into the system.

The various positions I have calculated over the years have all been within a few hundred feet of each other so the relationship to the World Grid System remains the same on the large scale map.

It at once became obvious that the position was an ideal one. The station fitted on to the grid as though one had been tailor-made for the other (see map). I produced the grid map years before Omega was ever heard of, and I have no claims to being clairvoyant. It can be no accident that the site fits in so neatly with the grid system; I'm certain that the station was planned years ago by those in charge of the earth-bound project to explore the grid system.

From Alpha to Omega — from the beginning to the end; from earth to the stars.

There are some on this planet who already have possession of all the necessary knowledge to make citizens of space of us all.

When will they let us in on the secret?

MAP 8

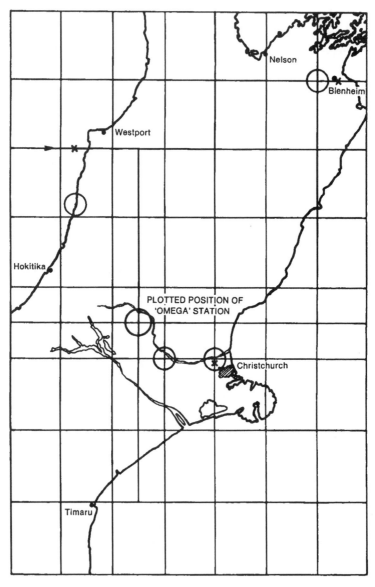

Section of original grid map published in *Harmonic 33* (1968).
Calculated position of Omega station plotted into map in August 1970 shows
possible correlation with UFO grid.

20> THERE IS SOMETHING IN THE AIR

ON SATURDAY 7 DECEMBER 1969, the Brammall family were settling in to watch their favourite TV programme, *High Chaparral.* Just before it was due to start, at around 8:25 p.m., all power in the district was suddenly cut off. A violent lightning storm was lighting up the sky to the south-east, with bright, long-drawn-out flashes following one another in a spectacular sequence.

Ted Brammall went outside to watch the storm and immediately saw a brilliant object which he later described as resembling a "large flourescent light." Jennifer Brammall came out of the house to join him, and they watched it for five minutes. When the power came on again, Ted telephoned to the Power Board, and was informed that the entire district had been blacked out, probably as a result of a violent electrical storm in the vicinity of Rotorua.

The object the Brammalls watched was large, and very bright. It hung in the air, with a backdrop of dark clouds; stars, showing through breaks in the clouds, which Ted glanced at from time to time, gave him an idea of its great size.

After hovering motionless the object moved "slowly and deliberately," tilting over so that cone-like projections on its bottom surface, covering a great deal of the area and looking like "oval dark areas," could be clearly seen. To the further astonishment of the watchers, the light emanating from the object pulsated to match the brilliance of the lightning flashes. Spine-like projections of coloured light — blue, green and red — radiated sideways and downwards. Apart from this single, slow-motion roll, the object remained stationary. Later, in a statement to an investigator (Sam Rix), the Brammalls declared that the object gave the impression that it was constructed, a machine of some kind. They later made independent drawings of what they had seen; their statement and their sketches are in my files — along with many other eye-witness reports and sketches from different parts of the country. Sightings like this are now a very frequent occurrence, but since officially UFOs don't exist, the news media are inclined to leave them alone.

But the Brammalls know they saw something — an object that conforms in all respects to typical descriptions of UFOs. At least they know that they are not alone. Here's another detailed report, again accompanied by sketches made soon after the sighting, and signed as a truthful record by Y. R. Plant, E. F. Plant, S. Plant, B. R. Plant, and M. C. Clapp, all of Auckland. The sighting took place at Te Kaha, East Coast.

At about 9:00 p.m. on the evening of 22 January 1969, we noticed a bright flashing light that appeared to be travelling behind the ridge of the hills opposite. It became stationary, and brilliant flashing continued as it appeared to revolve.

At the same time, at intervals of approximately two minutes, a lightning-like flash from a point slightly further south lit up the sky. It came from behind a small black cloud above the mountains, and the flashes were directed at the revolving light. A similar occasional flash was seen much further south.

There were five of us, my wife and I, my two teenage sons and their friend, watching this phenomenon for about an hour, when we realised that there was much activity going on in the sky. What appeared to be a small star would suddenly fall at exceptional speed, and then hover in the sky. At one time there were about six of these falling lights, one of which disappeared towards the south in a hopping motion.

In the eastern sky there was a large bright light with rays emanating from it, and below this a small "star" hovered up and down. As we watched, a long, dark cloud formed above the mountain range.

After observing this continual activity for three hours, two lights were seen to rise from behind the hills. One light was red and the other a bluish-green rotating light, and they gave the impression of being attached to one object, as they moved in conjunction with each other. This remained stationary for thirty minutes before moving slowly up behind the long cloud. At this time the flashing on the ground ceased. Twenty minutes later, five red lights, evenly spaced, rose above the mountain range, hovered for about five minutes then travelled back and forth above the hills. This was still occurring when we eventually retired, four and a half hours after first sighting the flashing light.

Group observations are obviously of much greater interest to any investigator than casual, individual sightings. Stories and data can be checked from one observer to the other, and greater faith can be placed in such reports when they are found to match in important aspects. New Zealand's most fascinating group sighting came in December 1968, when a number of primary school pupils at Te Muta School, Havelock North — the centre of a region which has yielded sighting after sighting in the past four years — reported seeing a flying saucer at close range. All six children agreed on the object's size and shape — and on having been "scared" by it. They reported that they saw both a hatch and an antenna as the saucer-shaped object hovered at low altitude over some poplar trees, that it made a clicking noise, and that it was about half the size of the school's swimming-pool — which they were attending at the time as a non-swimming class. They drew the attention of their teacher to the object; suddenly it shot upwards, and travelled off in the direction of the nearby town of Hastings, leaving a vapour trail behind.

A teacher reported that he watched the same object for about ten minutes as it moved backward and forward across Hastings. The nearby aerodrome and the Civil Aviation Department at Napier confirmed that there were no aircraft in the area at the time of the sighting.

Gavin King, aged ten, described it like this for the *Hawke's Bay Herald-Tribune*, which ran the story on 20 December: "It was round, with three things on top ... there were lights all round the bottom and there was a sort of hatch on the side ...It made a clicking noise, like a clock."[1]

Graham Hebden, aged ten: "At first the object looked like a bird, but it grew to the size of about half the school's swimming-pool as it finally hovered over the trees."

Peter Taylor, aged nine: "It had 'things' hanging from it. They had 'round things' attached to them."

Gavin King and other pupils later made sketches of what they had seen. Meanwhile, a Havelock North woman said she had seen something, evidently the same object, for about five minutes. Mrs. M. Berg, of Lipscombe Crescent, said she stood at her door and watched the object approach from the south-east. "It was the noise it made that caused me to look up," she said. 'It was a funny

---

[1]A similar clicking noise was associated with UFOs, as described in *Harmonic 33*.

noise — something different." She watched the object until it was straight above her house.

She said that the bottom of the object was like the bottom of a boat, and that it had square wings.

These reports were made just four months after some other odd occurrences nearby, at Taradale.

John Dow, aged 19, apprentice joiner, and his friend Paul Franklin, were out at the Taradale dump one September evening, looking for rats to shoot. It was around 9:30. Suddenly the two youths heard something they were later to describe as "sounding like thunder." The ground beneath their feet shook; looking up into the sky they saw some thirty moving lights, at intervals disappearing from view. They watched the spectacle for about half an hour, and finally, mystified and excited, they went home.

Lights had been seen in the sky over this area many times during the past few months: just one year before, verified sightings of UFOs were reported from the nearby Hastings area. At that time I plotted these on the grid map of New Zealand and found, not too much to my surprise, that the verified positions all fell neatly on parallel latitudinal lines of the grid.

So strange objects in the sky were not too unusual in this area. The following night the two boys returned to the dump; it was a Saturday, and they planned to keep a vigil. They saw nothing of interest and went home slightly deflated. On Sunday night they were driving in John Dow's car; Paul, looking back, spotted a bright white light, but there was nothing of particular note to record.

Two nights later they were driving near the Waiohiki golf course when they saw a green light in the sky; the colour changed to red, and soon they saw a "pencil of light" flash across the sky.

The following statements were given in evidence at the Napier Magistrate's Court, when John Dow, charged with dangerous driving, pleaded not guilty. In court he said: "As we were passing the Taradale motor camp, Paul, who was staring out the back, suddenly let out a scream that this (the pencil of light) was coming at us. I saw it in the mirror. Paul dived out of his side; his feet kicked mine."

Dow was pitched half out of the car: "I started to get up," he went on, "and Franklin said: 'For God's sake stay down! They are after us!'"

Now out of control the car plunged on for about two hundred yards along Taradale's Gloucester Street, and finally crashed through the plate glass window of a fruit shop. It was this sudden end to the chase that brought the two youngsters first to hospital, and later to the Magistrate's Court in Napier.

Prosecuting was Sergeant W. T. Pender. After Dow described the light which chased the car as being about two and a half feet across, Sergeant Pender asked him what he thought it was.

"A flying saucer," Dow answered.

The prosecutor asked whether the coloured lights could have originated from an explosion in the dump. No, Dow asserted, they had watched the lights in the sky for about half an hour.

Mr. W. K. I. Dougall dismissed the dangerous driving case against Dow. However, before sending Dow on his way, the magistrate had something to add.

"Most of these lights people see have a natural cause," he declared, "and the 'flying saucer in hot pursuit' might have been the lights of a car coming around the corner ...The sooner he (Dow) talks to a sensible adult about the matter, the better."

However, two pertinent facts remain: the story given by the two youths in explanation for their car crashing through a shop window was accepted by the police; the magistrate admitted that Dow had got into such a state of mind that he had acted involuntarily when "something had distracted him."

The second point is that the insurance company concerned with damages to the car also accepted Dow's story. This at least was something new in New Zealand. A statement I have on file from Paul Franklin shows that other people in the district, including at least two policemen, had witnessed the lights in the sky over Taradale.

There have been countless other sightings, not only of objects in the sky — but of evidence showing that strange objects have landed.

Pouarua South Road stretches for a mile across a gravel surface on the Hauraki Plains. It heads into an uninviting scrubland where manuka bushes predominate. Here a fifty-acre block of land is owned by a former dairy farmer, Bert O'Neil, who on 4 September 1969 made a startling discovery. Something, it appeared, had landed on his property leaving a bleached circle of manuka about fifty feet across; there were three V-shaped grooves of disturbed peat soil in the centre of the circle, each about two or three inches deep and spaced precisely nine feet apart. Nowhere had the manuka been crushed, leading Mr. O'Neil to theorise that "three legs had been slid into the ground and then splayed outward." A reporter for one of Auckland's weekend newspapers wrote: "The manuka, which is extremely healthy elsewhere, seems to have been bleached grey-white and dry by heat inside the clearly defined circle. The scrub has definitely not been burned."

The Ngatea circle caused considerable excitement — more than any previously reported UFO sighting in New Zealand, in fact, for here at least was something tangible. Hordes of people came by car for days after, trampling about the area in search of heaven knows what.

As usual, official investigators were among the late arrivals, and before long the explanations were coming at rapid-fire pace. The area had been hit by a "blight," thus the grey-white manuka; the marks in the ground had been made by pigs, rooting for feed; and so on. A fungus was found to be growing on the manuka, and this was acclaimed as the cause of the condition of the scrub — although no one was able to state why only a near-perfect circle had been attacked. Then it was found by scientific examination of the manuka, that the branches and trunks were dry of sap and had been "cooked" from the inside out — rather as if they had been exposed to extreme radiation.

A TV garden-show host, Reg Chibnall, made independent tests on the soils from inside the circle and from outside; he found that seed grew normally in the latter soils, but produced miserable, diseased-looking plants in pots containing soil from inside the circle. The then Minister of Science favoured the fungus-and-pigs version and dismissed the whole affair. Meanwhile, scientists at Auckland University concluded that dead spiders in the bleached manuka area had been killed from radiation. Mr Don Lockwood, of Waihi, made another interesting discovery: twenty-two feet out from the centre-line position of the ground marks, the manuka showed signs of where the radiation had ended and the rest of the tree had died. This point of demarcation was just above ground level, but increased in height up the trees the further to the south the checks were made.

Tree and other samples were collected by Mr. H.L. Cooke, of Tauranga, and these were examined by a horticulturist in the same city. Mr. Stuart-Menzies, who gave the following report: "The scrub is radioactive and has been cooked instantaneously from the inside outward. I know of no earthly source of energy which could produce this effect. The manuka was bleached dry but showed no visible signs of burning. Every ounce of moisture in the plant had been instantaneously vaporized, and it was bone-dry and brittle. This is most unusual in manuka, which normally takes a long time to dry out. Some kind of high-frequency radiation cooked the material from the inside outward. The energy received reduced the pith to black carbon, without the outside showing any sign of burning. The cells in the medullary rays were burnt by the sudden vaporisation of cell sap. A meteorite or lightning could not do this, and it was too sudden for combustion."

Mr. Stuart-Menzies added that the process appeared to have been similar to that employed in infra-red-cooking, "but on an enormous scale."

So the Ngatea circle remains a mystery. Mr. O'Neil wishes he had never found the area where something out of this world landed — he is tired of the neighbourly ribbing he has been exposed to ever since.

It is well known to me that radar operators at various airfields throughout New Zealand are constantly picking up unidentified objects in the sky on their screens. Official reports are filed, but these men seldom speak of what they have seen — more than ridicule, they fear losing their jobs; such is the official wall of silence. On numerous occasions airfield authorities have become so excited over radar blips of unknown flying objects that incoming aircraft have been diverted in order to allow control to have a close look at the intruders.

Other airfield workers frequently see objects in the sky that are certainly not aircraft — or birds, or marsh gas, or Venus in descent. In front of me now are two independent reports made by workers at Auckland International Airport concerning something that attracted their attention on 3 December 1967. To protect the two workers concerned, I shall not give their names; their signed reports are in my possession, and are available to *bona fide* investigators:

"While working at the airport, I saw two silvery-to-pale lemon lights cross the sky from south-south-west to a north-north-east direction. They were convex on both sides and on the upper side was a small dome. They flew together for a short time until the lower one began to make sharp alterations in its altitude, zig-zagging up and down. They were in sight for about four to seven seconds...They finally disappeared from sight in a bank of clouds to the north."

The second report is confirmatory:

"Two saucer-shaped objects, silver in colour, traversed the sky from SSW to NNE. They flew in formation for a little while; the lower saucer then moved jerkily about the other saucer until they both disappeared behind a big bank of clouds on the horizon to the north. Both objects travelled at an extremely high speed, in excess of a thousand miles an hour." Both reports include drawings of saucer shaped craft featuring a prominent dome.

So much for a mere sampling of sightings and more dramatic events close to home; in every other country of the world there have been reports of a similar nature — strange objects in the air, on the ground, in the sea; the sudden appearance of alien beings; the discovery of peculiar artifacts, constructions.

One of the most irritating kinds of report is the incompleted account. South American newspapers abound with half stories about UFOs — sudden appearances of saucers, their disappearance in the jungle, the setting forth of posses to track them down; and then — silence.

In October 1968, a group of climbers searched the Andes for a flying saucer base; they reported that they had found, but as a by-product so to speak, a "fortress" of a previously unknown civilisation. This was in a region of Chile known as Talca, 150 miles south of Santiago. There had been repeated accounts of UFOs in the area, cars stopping and starting without explanation, out-of-season flowers blooming. The "fortress" comprised two platforms, each about seven hundred square yards, and made from 233 blocks of volcanic rock, each block with an average weight of ten tons.

February, the following year: on the assumption that the Andes platform might in fact have been a kind of launching area for UFOs ("cosmodrome" was the word seized upon by the wire services), an expedition led by Humberto Sarnataro Bounaud, a thirty-two-year-old businessman and painter, prepared to explore the giant blocks, as well as a cave said to be located beneath the platform. Many peasants and villagers in the area claimed they had seen flying saucers apparently taking off and landing in the mountain near the platform.

Unhappily, the press has never informed us what became of Bounaud's expedition. Did it ever set off? What did they find? What was the secret of the cave?

Meanwhile, around the same time, doctors in Colombia were reported to be baffled by the case of a man who died from a mysterious sickness after he reported seeing a flying saucer. The man was Arcesi Bermudez, fifty, who became ill after he said he saw a blue and orange UFO with flashing lights in his back garden in Anolaima, southwest of Bogota. He claimed to have approached to within ten feet of the craft, and then turned back to get a flashlight. As he was returning the UFO flew off.

A week later Bermudez was dying, suffering from attacks of vomiting and diarrhoea; gastro-enteritis was the diagnosis, but Bermudez's low temperature puzzled the doctors. Until the moment of death he maintained his story of approaching close to a landed UFO. If there was an inquest, the findings were never published in the papers I read; the dead man's symptoms sound suspiciously like radiation poisoning.

Closer to home, on 28 December 1968, a man in Goulburn, New South Wales, saw and spoke to a being from Saturn; at least that was the story being investigated by the late Dr. Miran Lindtner, president of the Unidentified Flying Objects Investigation Centre in Sydney, and Dr. D. Herbison-Evans, an astronomer from the physics department of Sydney University.

The man had the encounter with the alien, he said, while on a hunting trip near Goulburn; ten years before he had a near-identical experience in exactly the same spot, while hunting for foxes.

According to Dr. Lindtner: "He says he shot at and hit something, which let out a terrific noise. Then there was a flash of light and something — we don't know what — burnt through the arm of his coat and left a small mark on his arm. The mark took a year to heal, but before it healed it grew in size and now measures three inches by two and a half inches. It is exactly the same shape as the planet Saturn — a globe with a ring around it."

On his more recent trip into the area, the man saw a craft of about forty feet in diameter and some ten feet in height. As he approached the craft, a being walked around from the other side of it — a humanoid, about five and a half feet tall, with long hair and youthful features; it wore silver-coloured shoes. There was a conversation — in English — for about three minutes, during which the being revealed that it was from Saturn. With that, the being hurried back to the craft, which rose fifteen feet above the ground, hovered, and then moved off. Before it disappeared from view, the man took four photographs of it.

The year 1969 was an eventful one for UFO researchers. An Argentine researcher, Dr. Pedro Romaniuk, when the private John Kennedy University opened its biopsycho-synthesis summer term of lectures at Buenos Aires, declared that both the Soviet Union and the United States possessed damaged flying saucers. The American prize, he said, had been taken when it fell at Alamogordo, New Mexico. According to Dr. Romaniuk, this fact had been brought to the notice of the US Air Intelligence Centre by the director of the North-Western Observatory, Dr. Silas Newton.

Quoting Dr. Newton, Romaniuk said that the extraterrestrial craft had small exit traps instead of doors, allowing the passage of small-sized beings only. Inside the seamless, hard metal craft were found six small dead bodies, said to be morphologically similar to man, and probably dead from atmospheric decomposition following the failure of one of the doors to work properly. According to Dr. Newton, the ship was propelled by cosmic energy; the bodies were covered by a metallic transparent blue suit, resistant to scissors and blow torches.

After *Harmonic 33* was published I began to receive correspondence from people in many parts of the world, anxious to pass on clippings, photographs, information, theories. Much of the material received in this way has been of doubtful value, and some of it has been far-out "crank" work; there is one letter that I keep coming back to, though, and I'd like to check its contents. I hope to for myself — some day. The letter is from a Scandinavian "new Australian," and it has, in my opinion, a ring of veracity. I hope to meet its writer in person one day — and hunt both the dingo and the UFO he mentions. Here is his story — in his own words:

> On my arrival in Australia in January 1958, I set out for the far north-west of Queensland and the Northern Territory in search of the dingo. It was during one of my first explorations into the nearly inaccessible wilderness that I found the canyon, with its "saucer."
>
> I had walked into the canyon for about four hours, and believe I had covered between ten and twelve miles, when I noticed "something" under an overhanging shelf, making the place partly a cave. I use the word "something" because it was rather hard to make out what it was exactly, due to its colouring.
>
> The object was kind of grey. It could be greyish-green, greyish-blue or greyish-red; one could easily walk past it from a distance without seeing it.

I watched it for some time before I continued into the canyon, which became deeper, and I never reached the end. On my return I looked for the object, but could not see it. Being a good bushman, I knew I was at the exact spot where I had seen it before, but there just wasn't anything there. I satisfied myself that it must have been something created by the light, but realised that the sun didn't reach down to the bottom of the canyon. To make sure, I picked up a pebble, and threw it to where I supposed the object to be. The result was the stone was stopped in mid-air, or when it hit the object. It then slid down to the ground, and on impact with the rocky ground the stone made a noise; although there had been no noise when it stopped in mid-air.

I decided that whatever it was, it must have a shell or be a solid mass, but soft enough not to make a noise when hit by a stone. I then decided that whatever the object was, it was still there, but not visible to the eye. I left it at that and returned to my camp deciding to take a closer look the next day.

The next day I returned and found the object was again visible. I had brought with me a long piece of fencing wire and my transistor radio. I started to yell and to make my presence known to whatever it was, and I admit I felt an idiot doing so, but nothing happened. Then I switched my transistor radio on, and when music came from it, the object started to react. I watched it closely. The object gradually faded away, but the process was so slow that it was hard to say exactly when it became invisible.

I had brought the fencing wire with me to find out if the object were an electric phenomenon. I tied this long wire to a stick and reached into the nothingness. Then with a match soaked in saliva and wiped, I touch the wire. Had the object been electrical, I should have felt a slight tingle in my fingers, but I did not. Gaining confidence I took hold of the wire with my hands, but still I could feel nothing. When I clamped my teeth on the end of the wire and touched it with my tongue, I could feel some rhythmical vibration coming through the wire.

The vibration seemed to change in rhythm when one yelled, played music or threw a stone towards the invisible object. But even without any noise, a vibration kept coming from it.

I've later seen the object change from visible to invisible, and again it was hard to follow the gradual changes from one state to the other.

I first encountered the object late in 1958, and during my stay in the area for about eight years I've visited the canyon approximately thirteen or fourteen times, and each time it has been there, either visible or invisible. At first I believed that my presence made it fade away, but since the first experience with it I've been able to yell, play music and throw stones at it without it fading away.

I've looked at it by night, and it doesn't give off any light, and it's only harder to see. I'm sure that whatever it is, it's harmless. I admit I tried not to interfere too much with it in case it was capable of retaliating. What I could see of it, it had no windows, doors, or any other parts such as holes, etc.

The underside of the overhanging shelf seemed to sweat; it is moist whereas the whole area including the canyon is bone dry.

There have been years between some of my visits, and at times only months, but it has always been there.

Whatever this object is, it's nothing like anything we've ever heard of originating from this planet. Could it be — a craft cunningly hidden in an isolated canyon, protected by a force field until its crew comes back to claim it? And where *are* the crew? Blending with the crowds on Bondi Beach, mingling with captains of industry in Sydney, staked out somewhere handy to the vast and top-secret American space research station in the Australian desert — a space station so secret that even Australia's prime minister has admitted he knows little of what is going on there?

One of the most recent records of a visit by an extraterrestrial space craft consists of the Alberton photographs. Ellis E. Matthews, of Alberton, South Australia, had some unused movie film left in his Paillard Bolex camera when he stepped on to the veranda of his home one evening in 1967. From where he stood he saw about one mile distant and between 15 and 20 degrees above the horizon a UFO. Using a 1.9 aperture and with full zoom, he shot off his remaining film, focused on the object — a total of some fifty frames.

It was some eight months later that he had the film developed — by Ilford Australia, Oakleigh, Victoria. Both Mr. Matthews and his wife have provided notarised statements as to what they saw in the sky.

The film was subsequently sent to me by Mr. Matthews, and with his permission I forwarded a section of it to International UFO Research and Analytic Network in New York for intensive analysis. After detailed microscopic study Major Colman Vonkeviczky, Project Director of ICUFON, forwarded a full report from which is quoted the following conclusions:

1. The object is unidentifiable as any earthly commercial or military vehicle. The self-illumination and light streaks cannot be identified as position lights as demanded by international aviation regulations.

2. A meteor or a satellite could not be stationary for 10/18 of a second, and could not present a clear-cut image of its form and shape.

3. The filmed aerial vehicle is in its form and type fully identifiable with what are popularly termed "flying saucers."

Mr. Matthew's film was shot in colour; the flying object on the crucial frames, when seen projected on a screen, shows a disc with a "cabin" beneath it. There are lights around the periphery of the disc, and there is light streaming out from what appears to be a "port" on the "cabin."

Most interesting of all: silhouetted in this "port" light is a figure, vaguely humanoid in shape. By comparing the first frames of the sequences with the last, it is observed that the figure is in movement.

This is one of the best UFO series of photographs ever made. Experts have declared it to be genuine, and Mr. Matthew's integrity has never been in question. He has never made any attempt to seek commercial gain from his remarkable film, and has sought no publicity whatsoever. What we have on this film strip is undoubtedly a genuine series of pictures of a UFO, complete with a being who might be its "pilot."

This chapter has been a melange of seemingly unrelated and unsolved mysteries; a flying object of small size pursues a pair of teenagers driving around a small country town — investigators follow up UFO reports in the Chilean countryside and discover a "cosmodrome" — something lands in the bleak outbacks of the Haurake Plains and leaves a wide circle of dying scrub, its woody parts cooked from the inside outward by radiation of an unknown kind — school-children, their teacher and an independent housewife see a UFO in the skies of Napier, the children observing it at sufficiently close quarters to be able to draw the object in detail — radar equipment at airfields pick up UFO blips as a matter of routine.

But stop! UFOs don't exist! The Condon reports says so. One is reminded of the story of the bumble-bee. This clumsy-looking creature, with its vast bulky body and its fragile wings, is patently, and according to all the laws and rules of aero-dynamics, incapable of flight.

But in its blissful ignorance of the situation, the bumble-bee flies anyway. Until it should develop a sound grasp of aero-dynamics, and then realises it is breaking the law, it will continue to fly.

UFOs don't exist. They couldn't possibly exist. They don't fit into any branch of earth knowledge. Therefore, they are not.

Meanwhile, as each month goes by, reports of UFOs all over the world continue to mount up. Thousands of people every year see them, approach them, are made nauseous by them; some even die from exposure to them.

Is the official denial of UFOs based on sincere disbelief? Or is there a vast snow-job, a monumental cover-up, in operation?

If Senor Bermudez of Bogota left a widow and bereaved children, they might be the ones to answer these questions.

21> OOPARTS AND OOPTHS

I N 1961 ARCHAEOLOGISTS DIGGING AT THE PALATINE
Hill, Rome, uncovered a previously unknown room. In a niche
of this room there was a painting, the subject of which was so
startling that no explanation satisfactory to all shades of belief has
yet been offered.

The painting?

In the centre ground stands what appears to be a modern spacecraft, a rocket in fact. It stands on a launching pad, and from it
runs cables or guys; in the background there is a tall wall — for all the
world resembling a counterblast wall. Asks Ivan T. Sanderson, former British naval intelligence officer and a distinguished biologist:
"What was it that the Roman artist painted? Was it imagination?
Reality? A forecast of the future?" A reproduction of the painting
appears in his book, *Uninvited Visitors*. It deserves careful scutiny.

Why a painting of a rocket ship should appear on the wall of a
hidden room dating from ancient times — *how* it could possibly be
there (yet it is!) — could be anyone's guess. Yet, curiously enough,
there may be many more links between places of worship and space
travel than one might first dare to think.

This is not intended as an irreverent statement; there need be no
offence taken by anything written in this chapter by readers of
devout Christian or other beliefs. But we would like to present
some facts and some theories that might tend to open up fascinating
lines of investigation for serious research work.

Consider, first of all, a typical place of worship in any country of
the world today; and reflect that religious architecture has virtually
followed a specific pattern from ages past. Mathematically speaking
architecture of the kind displayed by the great cathedrals of Europe,
for example, would present the greatest possible challenge to the
designers and the builders of the time, with the great naves, the
towering structures, the superb arches. Chartres, dating from the
twelfth century, said by some to represent the finest flowering of
religious architecture, is believed to have been designed on principles of Platonic mathematics, in which the harmonies of the entire
universe were to be expressed. Gaze upon the faces of the finely
sculptured kings and queens at Chartres, unidentified and unknown

representations; with expressions of supreme nobility they look down upon the thousands of tourists who come each year. Look at the twin spires of the mighty cathedral — and mentally compare their shape and proportions with those of Apollo 12.

Look at any Christian church with new eyes, and see the resemblance between the typical church spire and a typical rocket ship. Study pictures of Islamic mosques, oriental pagodas, Buddhist temples; places of worship in India, Thailand, the Middle East: see how their towers soar upward, towards where most people believe "heaven" to be located. Allowing for differences between Occident and Orient in the interpretation of detail, attempt to get a mental X-ray picture of the basic tower structures — and see how alike they really are beneath the superficial additions of various forms of buttresses, decorations of gargoyles or carved reliefs.

Moscow's Ivan the Great bell tower in the Kremlin, seen with newly-opened eyes, is a three-stage rocket topped with a semi-spherical capsule; the multi-stage rockets disguised as towers surrounding St. Sophia's, Constantinople, are suddenly obvious; the beautiful gothic arches inside Cologne Cathedral repeat the rocket shape; Chinese pagodas, Indian temples and stupas, Armenian bell towers, and simple country churches anywhere in the Christian world — all suddenly appear to have been built expressly in imitation of spaceships.

But granted the coincidence of shape — *why*?

That is a question that Vyacheslav Zaitsev, philologist at the Byelorrussian Academy of Sciences, has sought to answer in a number of works (*Cosmic Reminiscences in Written Relics of the Past; The Evolution of the Universe and Intelligent Beings*; plus many magazine articles, condensations of some of these appearing from time to time in the magazine *Sputnik*). But this field of research was not opened up by Zaitsev; he gives credit to Nikolai Rynin, a friend and pupil of Konstantin Tsiolkovsky, the Russian scientist who at the beginning of this century established principles for the building of space rockets.

More than forty years ago Rynin was drawing attention to the correspondences in the myths of various peoples in regard to earth visits by beings from other worlds. In 1959 another Russian scientist, Modest Agrest, considered that many events described in the Bible were in fact references to visits made to this planet by astronauts from other worlds. Three years later the American astrophysicist, Carl Sagan, published a similar hypothesis.

Let us be clear about this, there is no scientific backing for the theory that has been put forward and which we now draw attention to — that the resemblance between religious architecture and machines designed for space travel is no mere coincidence. For a recently published version and up-dated account of evidence drawn from ancient rock inscriptions, Biblical sources and other writings and artifacts, see Erich von Daniken's *Chariots of the Gods*. This Swiss archaeologist also puts forward the provocative theory that the origins of man are linked with visits to earth by beings from other planets in ancient times.

Returning to church architecture: where did the archetype come from — the archetype that has been perpetuated with slight variation from ancient times up to the present day? And what are the reasons for the particular form of that archetype?

When David ascended to heaven, the *Apocrypha* relates, the angels showed him the "church image" that was to become the archetype of the Temple of Jerusalem. Returning to earth David built a model of this from memory, and ordered his son Solomon to erect a House of the Lord along the same lines. So, it is believed, the Temple of Jerusalem, built in the tenth century BC, came to be conceived.

This is Zaitsev's question - it is, of course, a rhetorical one: "Perhaps the 'church image' was the image of a space-ship? Perhaps some human being was induced by the astronauts to go aboard the 'celestial machine,' where he saw the abode of God? Such an interpretation of this ancient Judaic legend about the origin of Solomon's Temple would appear still more believable in the light of other texts, notably the *Apocrypha*."

Hindus believed their temples were built in the image of those of other worlds, again the design being revealed by a deity. The classical work, *Ramayana*, tells of a "celestial chariot," a two-storeyed vehicle with "many rooms and windows" which "roared like a lion" at launching, "issued a single-toned sound" and "blazed like red flames" as it raced through the air until finally it looked like 'a comet in the sky'.[1]

Another source, the *Mahabharata*, says the vehicle was "activated by winged lightning." the Sanskrit work, *Samarangana Sutradhara*, contains a long description of the vehicle which in Veda works is referred to as *vimana*.

---

[1] Vyscheslav Zaitsev, "Temples and Spaceships", in *Sputnik*, Sept., 1968.

As Zaitsev points out: "Christian and Judaic, like Buddhist and Brahmanist, architecture go back to one source, a certain 'celestial temple,' the look of which on earth was best imitated by domed churches."

Supposing space-ships from other planets landed on earth long ago, to primitive man would not the effect have been closely similar to that of "cargo cults" by modern aircraft landing in such places as New Guinea and New Britain in recent times? In those latter cases the arrival of aircraft led to a worship of the creatures who arrived by the craft, and various religious practices were adopted as a means of trying to induce the aircraft and their magical cargoes to return.

A word or two about the "cargo cults," as anthropologists have dubbed them. Believed to have sprung up first in Fiji in the 1880s, the pattern has always been repeated; a prophet appears from among the people and proclaims the coming of salvation, possibly in the form of a ship or an aircraft loaded down with a host of goods — ranging from refrigerators to canned food. He orders certain rituals, and even such activities as the building of a storehouse, an imitation landing strip or a wharf. Basically all such cults are probably primitive attempts to set in motion the necessary social changes required for coping with a situation of cultural conflict — the impinging of the modern and the "civilised" upon the ancient and "barbaric" — all in the guise of a new religion.

In ancient times, one might conjecture, ships came to this planet from another world (other worlds?), bringing strange beings and strange — but vastly useful — goods. Perhaps the ships left, perhaps some remained; perhaps some remained in orbit, and some men of this planet, recognised for their superior intelligence or powers of leadership compared to others in their group, were ferried to the space vehicles and presented with gifts — and given instruction in simple technology, such as the invention of the wheel, irrigation canals, better techniques of working with stone or metal, and so on.

Certainly there is reason to believe that something of the sort may have happened, possibly some 15,000 years ago.

For it was about that time that man began a massive breakthrough in the handling of himself and his environment, a fact that has never been satisfactorily explained. In that long ago man suddenly, for no apparent reason, began to develop new techniques in such matters as splitting bones to create tools, although existing techniques had been in vogue for nearly a million years.

Man is a puzzle to biologists, so tremendously different from his nearest relatives, the giant apes, if we are to accept the Darwinian theory of evolution. Among the primates, recent studies have shown, man has 312 unique and exclusive characteristics that no other primate possesses. For some reason he has evolved at a pace which, compared with that of the evolution of other creatures on this planet, can only be described as fantastically rapid. The evolutionary process is known to be very slow, imperceptible over the course of even hundreds of generations. Man's greatest evolutionary achievement was to develop a brain which from a capacity of 400 cubic centimetres (established from very early skulls of ape-like men) evolved to a capacity of 1300 cc, in the space of a million years — a mere tick of the evolutionary clock. Yet it took some thirty million years, on the other hand, for primates to evolve a hand with an opposable thumb which, according to the evolutionists, is what gave man his advantage in the race.

Two American writers, Otto Binder and Max Flindt, have recently put forward a theory postulating that the answer can only lie with a visit to this planet in ancient times of another intelligence from another world, and a conscious effort on the part of the visitors to breed a race of men on earth, either from motives of altruism or in a spirit of biological experimentation. If the spacemen were here, did they ever really leave? Did their presence give rise to the almost universal myth of racial origin, a descent by superior beings from "the stars" or "the sky?" And did those feet in ancient times walk upon England's mountains green?

The question of biological experiments we leave to the biologists. But dig into evidence for yourselves — and start an avalanche. We suggest the following areas for fruitful investigation:

Myths and legends.

The ancient classical religious works from all countries inhabited since long, long ago — particularly India, China, Sumeria, Babylon, Egypt.

A fresh examination of "secret" systems of knowledge, religious and scientific, including works on alchemy, astronomy, the secret books of the Masonic orders and the Rosicrucians, and the system taught in modern times by Gurdjieff.

Religious architecture.

The "inexplicable" presence of what Ivan Sanderson calls OOPARTS (for Out Of Place Artifacts) and OOPTHS (Out Of Place Things).

For the remainder of this chapter let's have a look at some of the more outstanding "out-of-place objects:"

In 1965 a Chinese archaeologist published a report which speculated that space beings may have visited this planet some 12,000 years ago. His principal items of evidence came from caves in the Bayan-Kara-Ula Mountains, on the China-Tibet border. Here have been found some 700 stone discs covered with mysterious designs and writings. Each disc has a hole in the centre, from which spirals a double groove out to the circumference. The caves are inhabited to this day by people of the Ham and Dropa tribes — frail people, only some four feet in height; they defy ethnic classification. The discs have been dated to several thousand years ago.

When finally deciphered, one of the hieroglyphs, possibly set down by an ancient member of the Ham tribe, reads: "The Dropas came down from the clouds in their gliders. Our men, women and children hid in the caves ten times before the sunrise. When at last they understood the sign language of the Dropas, they realised that the newcomers had peaceful intentions..."

The discs were scraped free of adhering rock particles and sent to Moscow for study. There scientists made two startling discoveries: the discs contained a large amount of cobalt and other metals; and they were found to vibrate in an odd rhythm, as though they carried an electric charge or were part of an electric circuit.

Primitive art — cave drawings, clay figurines — provide an abundance of material for the serious researcher into the possibility of space visitors having been here long ago. A rock picture found near the town of Fergana, Uzbekistan, is of what looks like an astronaut; an artist in the Swiss Alps 4000 years ago drew a picture of a man in a space helmet; the wall painting of a rocket ship in a niche of a secret room beneath an old Roman church has already been mentioned: a fresco in the Dechany Monastery, Yugoslavia, depicts angels flying inside machines that closely resemble present-day spacecraft; something very like a spaceship is seen on a seventeenth-century icon. The Resurrection of our Lord Jesus Christ, in the Moscow Theological Academy, as representing the House of the Lord.

Japanese archaeologists have found at several excavations *dogu* — clay figurines — of humanoids clad in peculiar spacesuits, with helmets entirely covering their heads. On the helmets are representations of something akin to slit-type glasses, breath-filters, antennae, hearing aids and even night-sight devices.

Rock pictures of "spacemen" have been found in the Sahara, in Australia, in Soviet Central Asia and in other parts of the Old and New Worlds. There are so many known drawings and carvings of this kind, in fact, that they have become known as "the visiting cards of space travellers."

When we come to look at OOPARTS, as opposed to representations on rock walls and in figurines, the former are "undeniably manufactured or artificial objects said to have been found *inside* solid, undisturbed rock strata, just as fossil animals and plants are found."[1] Some of the more startling OOPARTS that have come to light include flat-headed steel nails discovered deep in a sandstone quarry in Scotland; fine gold threads inside a large quarried block of limestone from northern England; a bell-shaped, metallic vessel blasted from rock in Dorchester, England, the metal containing a large proportion of silver; and a variety of objects found inside lumps of coal (which would date them back to at least twelve million years ago), including a beautiful gold chain of intricate workmanship, a prize for a Mrs. Culp of Illinois who found it when a lump of coal she was putting into her stove, in 1891, broke in two. An object in the Salzburg Museum, Austria, is another mystery — a perfect cube of meteoritic nickel-iron, about two inches square, which is encircled by a precisely turned deep groove, understood to have been *machined*, found in a block of coal that would have to have been between twelve and twenty-six million years old. A German engineer, engaged to construct sewers for the city of Baghdad, discovered on a dusty shelf in the local museum among objects labelled as "ritual objects" some "stones" dating back a thousand years. Only one thing was known for certain about these "stones" — they came from the Sassanid period. The engineer added another piece of knowledge: the "stones" were in fact batteries.

Other out-of-place items include a remarkable model of the solar system dating from olden times and recovered from a sea-bed, in which the movements of both planets and their satellites around the sun are accurately effected by the turning of a crank; the workmanship and materials preclude the construction of this incredible device in recent times. Where did the detailed astronomical knowledge come from? And where did the technology for the making of the model come from?

---

[1]Ivan T. Sanderson, *Uninvited Visitors*, Cowles, 1967.

22> SPACESHIP OR SURVEY PEG?

I N 1908 AN EXPLOSION OF CATASTROPHIC
proportions in Tunguska left a surface scar, flattened 400 square
miles of forest, and destroyed 80 million trees. Local inhabitants
described an enormous ball of fire in the sky that looked like a
comet. This was immediately before the explosion. Afterwards,
scientists examined the crater, but no meteoric mass was found,
only small bits of metal scattered around, and some reports hint at
traces of metallic alloy. In recent years, Russian scientists have
again investigated this spot and reported traces of radio-activity.
Had Nature gone crazy again? I don't think so. That UFO was one
that didn't get away.

Many years later, the following news item was released from
Moscow:

> A 50-year-old mystery has caused major dissension among
> Russia's leading space scientists. They cannot agree about
> a theory that the "Great Siberian Meteorite" which fell in
> the remote forests on 30 June 1908 was, in fact, a space
> ship from another planet.
>
> An expedition from Moscow is now working in the area,
> taking radiation measurements.
>
> Three Soviet scientists, Professors Korkarkin, Krinov
> and Fesenkov, believe the object was "probably" a meteor-
> ite — but they prefer the cautious word "phenomenon."
> Professors Alexander Kasentsev and B. Lepunov insist
> that it must have been a rocket or ship from Mars.
>
> Kasentsev has released some details of his spaceship
> theory after years of accumulating evidence.
>
> The known facts are that on that June day, inhabi-
> tants of Siberia's Jenisaci area, saw a gigantic ball of fire.
> Then a colossal explosion devastated nearly 400 square
> miles of forest. The shock waves were registered as far
> away as England.
>
> Scientists looking in vain for a crater, or traces of a
> meteorite, found that in the centre of the blast area only
> the tops of the trees were snapped off. But the meteorite

theory persisted until the explosion of the Hiroshima atomic bomb.

Just after the war, Kasentsev pointed to the similarity between the Hiroshima devastation and that in Siberia, and suggested that the "meteorite" was an atomic explosion at a height of one and a half miles.

In 1951, Kasentsev and Lepunov developed the theory of an atomic power-propelled vehicle which exploded while trying to land.

Expeditions to the area still fail to find any meteorite evidence, and the controversy has flared up again.

Russian aerodynamics expert, Manotskov, has joined the ranks of the "spaceship" theorists. He declares the Siberian "fireball" was breaking as it approached the Earth, so that its final speed was about two kilometres (1.24 miles) a second, compared with a meteorite's usual speed of 30 to 60 kilometres (18-37 miles) per second.

1. The great circle distance between point (G) and point (H) is equal to 347.2 nautical miles, or minutes of arc. The harmonic reciprocal of this value is 288, or twice the speed of light. If we double the value then we get 6944 (695), the speed of light reciprocal.

2. The great circle distance between point (C) and point (H) is equal to 411.635 nautical miles, or minutes of arc. This value squared is equal to 16944 (1695). Later research proved this value to be associated with the gravity acceleration factors, and mass.

MATHEMATICAL KEY TO DIAGRAM SHOWING RELATIONSHIP OF TUNGUSKA EXPLOSION TO UFO GRID

A, B, C, D, = Polar section of UFO grid as published in *Harmonic 33*. Each of these points is a major aerial position of the grid system.

E = Pole of UFO grid.

F = North geographic pole.

G = Intersection of grid longitude 90^0 of Tunguska explosion 60^0 55.8'.

H = Position of Tunguska explosion. Latitude 60^0 55.8' / Longitude 101^0 57' East.

C = Position of major aerial on longitude 90^0 / 65^0 8.88'.

MAP 9

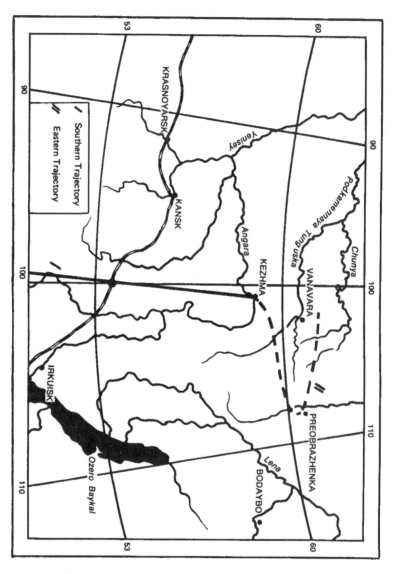

A map tracking the movement of the space visitor. The pattern is more characteristic of a guided apparatus than of a natural celestial body. "/" shows its "southerly" trajectory and "//", its "easterly".

DIAGRAM 17

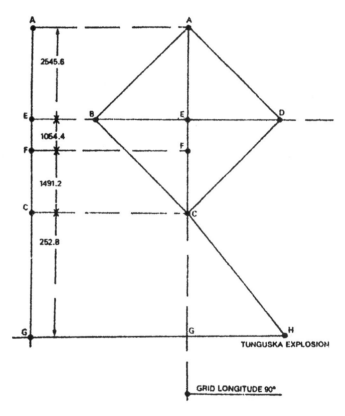

Diagram showing relationship of Tunguska explosion to polar section of UFO grid. Not to scale

The secant of the angle of latitude of the explosion point (60° 55.8') is equal to:

2.0581 (20581) Harmonic

(20581 X 2) squared equals 16943

1695 Harmonic (16944 in later work)

An interesting point which emerges on the map is the actual path of the explosion "object" — usually referred to as a "meteorite." If the phenomenon had been a normal one, that is a meteorite, as has been assumed by most scientists, then the trajectory one would expect would have been a parabolic curve. But the object that blew a great surface scar at Tunguska exhibited no such regularity. It completely ignored all the ground rules laid down for the entry of objects into the earth's atmosphere: it ignored the laws of physics completely.

First of all, it approached from a southerly direction, and when it reached a latitude of about 58°, it suddenly decided to alter course; it veered off to the east for twenty miles or so, whereupon it changed direction yet again, executing a sharp turn to west-north-west, just before the impact which wiped out in a flash millions of trees in the surrounding forest area.

A natural object, whether a meteorite or anything else, and performing in accordance with known laws, could not possibly have carried out such a trajectory. That leaves only one conclusion to a logical mind: the object, whatever it was, was under the control of some sort of intelligence; and the point of impact was not a matter of chance — it was carefully pre-ordained or pre-calculated. This leads me to conclude that what flew over Siberia that day long ago was either a spaceship which blasted something into the grid at that particular point, or else a controlled missile which was exploded in the area for some definite purpose.

If the object was indeed a spaceship which crashed by misadventure, we can understand the situation up to a point. But if the object was a guided missile, another question immediately comes up: why?

Could it have been that as the system was to be reactivated, it was necessary to lay a marker from which all measurements would be taken? The Tunguska explosion in that case, could have been caused by the laying of a colossal survey peg. From this point, any other point on the earth's surface could be electronically calculated.

There are scientists in Russia who say that the explosion near Tunguska in 1908 was atomic in origin, and I find myself in complete agreement. The big question is: how long will it be before the Russians determine just *why* the explosion occurred?

News item from the *Western Leader*, Auckland, dated 17 March 1970:

UFO or?

A mysterious catastrophe took place in the Tunguska taiga, Russian, on 30 June 1908, but it is only now that a plausible theory has been suggested to explain it, says the Novosti news agency.

Albert Zolotov, an engineer-physicist, has devoted many years to the study of news articles about the Tunguska meteorite and has studied the site of the catastrophe, collecting samples and taking photographs.

Recently Zolotov's book on the subject was published. "The Tunguska space body," writes the author, "could not have been a comet, a swarm of particles or a cloud of space dust, nor could it have been an ordinary iron, stone or ice meteorite."

There was, he said, a nuclear explosion at an altitude of three to four miles over the taiga, by a space body 160-230 feet long, travelling at 2300-4500 m.p.h.

23> RUAPEHU ERUPTS

ADRUMMING ON THE ROOF LIKE THE SOUND OF A shower of hail stones was the first indication to the occupants in one of the buildings perched on the slopes of Mt. Ruapehu that something was amiss.

The sound came just on twenty-five minutes after midnight on a chilly miserable night, 21 June, 1969.

It soon became apparent that this was no hailstorm. What was showering down was rocks and debris from the now active crater of Ruapehu, shrouded in thick clouds thousands of feet above. Gargling the millions of gallons of sulphurous water in its crater-lake no longer had the desired soothing effect; the old man had decided that a good cough would shift the abrasive material that had lodged in his throat and was slowly choking up his windpipe.

Ruapehu coughed: showers of rock and debris fell around him, and after a few hours relief was obtained. Drowsiness overcame the giant and once more he quietly drifted off to sleep. The sickness had passed.

The eruption of this volcano, located in the centre of New Zealand's North Island, had been completely unexpected. Scientists received no warning from the electronic gear they had implanted on the summit — the activity had come too suddenly.

With all due respect to those engaged in volcanology in New Zealand's Department of Scientific and Industrial Research, I reiterate something which I have stressed before. A study of the harmonic relationships of the geometric positions of the earth and the sun at the time of volcanic eruptions will yield important findings and point the way to an entirely new system of study.

A complete programme, based on date, time and geometric relationships of earth and sun will enable a scientist, or a layman versed in mathematics, to calculate with extreme accuracy the time when volcanic activity may be expected. The period over which the activity may occur and also the degree of intensity at which it may occur, according to the particular harmonics involved, can be predicted by this method.

I am fully aware that the scientists will treat with scorn utterances of this kind from a mere layman like myself. Volcanologists have built up their particular branch of science over a considerable period of time, yet here am I, an unknown upstart, daring to pull the very foundations from under their precious pile of data.

Gentleman, my apologies. No scientific anarchist, I, If I seem to be rocking your boat a little, it is only in order to shake a few intellectuals into a more wakeful state. As a matter of fact I'm not even particularly interested in the study of volcanoes — I have much too much to interest me in other fields. But I do recommend that just one of you volcanologists, somewhere in the world, takes the trouble to check out my ideas with a computer. If my theory is proved to be correct, then an extensive programme can be planned and carried out, to open up a completely revitalised branch of science.

Let us calculate the harmonic relationship of the latitude position of the sun at the time of the eruption on 21 June, 1969.

Harmonic relationships for light and gravity can be found throughout the whole range of mathematical tables based on angular measurement. These harmonics are the building-blocks of the universe, and are the only values which have such inter-relationships. Who was it that said God made the universe according to the rules of geometry? He was a man with a deep understanding of the fundamental character of Nature.

I have challenged scientists to supply any random values other than those I have calculated for light and gravity, and to try to find similar relationships throughout the tables. So far, to my knowledge, no one has been able to demonstrate that other harmonics are valid.

Analysis of geometric relationships during eruption:

Latitude and longitude of active point below Mount Ruapehu:
    Latitude: 39.28371^0 south / Longitude 175.558333^0 east.

The latitude value 39.28371 creates a harmonic association with the earth's resultant magnetic field:
    3928.371 lines of force per square geodetic inch.

The Sun was passing overhead the following position on the Earth's surface:
    Latitude 23.44^0 north / Longitude 7.219166^0 west.

At this time the Sun position would have been:
    4116.3621 minutes of arc from Grid Pole "B."

The square of 4116.3621 is equal to:
    16944444 harmonic (mass and gravity).

The great circle distance between the Sun position and the active point beneath Ruapehu was:

590335.72 seconds of arc.

The reciprocal of this value is equal to:

1694 (169444 harmonic) (mass and gravity).

The great circle distance between Latitude Sun and Latitude of the active point at Ruapehu was:

62.72371 degrees.

The logarithm of the secant of 62.72371 degrees is:

0.33888

This value divided by 2 is equal to:

0.16944 harmonic. (mass and gravity)

All values calculated by computer.

Again I theorise that all volcanic activity is caused by a geometric imbalance of the universal harmonics which form our physical world.

The scientists can now fight this one out among themselves. I shall be satisfied if they will at least give my theory a fair trial and make an independent check for verification.

24> THE AUSTRALIAN STONEHENGE

U NTIL RECENT YEARS THE VAST AUSTRALIAN outback was thought to have always been a barren, wind-swept sandy desert, devoid of all signs of civilisation. A chance discovery in early 1953 was to change this concept and prove to the world that at some period, way back in what the Aboriginals call the dreamtime, a highly advanced and long-forgotten race had raised constructions there that could be of great scientific importance.

The evidence had been hidden away beneath the sand for centuries and came to light only because a modern-day scientific research team found it necessary to venture into the area in order to probe the secrets of the atom. Ever since the first atomic bombs were dropped on Hiroshima and Nagasaki to end World War Two, the race had been on to discover all that could possibly be known about the structure of matter.

After successful tests at Monte Bello Island carried out by a team of scientists headed by Sir William Penny, it was decided to establish a more permanent test site in south Central Australia.

The person chosen to find and survey the site was a man well used to similar types of operations, by the name of Len Beadell. He had spent months of his life in the Australian outback on surveying expeditions and was chosen as the most experienced man for the job. The trip into the interior was a story unto itself and Mr. Beadell did an excellent job of this in his well-written book called *Blast The Bush*, published in 1967.

The initial site chosen was called "Emu" and needless to say the coordinates of the bomb tower were such that certain harmonics of light were fulfilled to cause atomic disruption of the radioactive material placed upon it.

While preparations were being carried out for the first tests it was decided to send an expedition to survey a more permanent site further south which would be much nearer the trans-Australian railway line. Len Beadell once more led his small team into the desert wilderness in their Land-Rovers to blaze a trail to this new position. During this trip he was the first man in modern times to set eyes on the leftovers of an ancient civilisation on the Australian continent.

I had read Mr. Beadell's book some years before, and had put it aside with an idea in my mind to carry out at a later date some research on the information he gave. During one of my trips to Australia I was shown some photographs which had been taken of the same area.

It was this information that brought my immediate attention to that isolated spot in the desert. On returning to New Zealand I carried out some calculations and decided to contact Mr. Beadell immediately for more accurate information. With his permission I quote from his book: "Just about everyone had a colour camera, and I had a black-and-white-one, so photographs for the recording of our trip were constantly being taken. None of us knew that we were on the brink of one of the most startling discoveries ever made on any of our expeditions past, present, or future, a discovery that would provide ample scope for all our cameras."

The convoy of Land-Rovers had come upon a small claypan nestled among sandhills, and while the others drove their vehicles over it just for the sheer joy of being on a flat surface after hours of struggling up and down sand dunes, Len Beadell decided to do a quiet bit of exploring on his own:

> I did however have a brief scan of the rocky steep bank on the western side to find the best lead out from this claypan. The small plateau beyond was roughly six feet higher than the level of the claypan. Dotted about with casuarinas or sheoaks it looked a very pleasant spot. The shales seemed to have broken away to form an inclined plane which could be used as a ramp slightly to the south of where I was, so I started up and veered towards it to be in position at its base when the others were ready to follow. When they noticed my movement they made towards me so I started the rough shale-strewn ascent.
>
> The moment my vehicle topped the rise to level out again, I saw it, spread out right across my path, extending for at least sixty yards either side. It was almost like a picket fence with posts six feet apart made from slivers of shale. Tingling with excitement I switched off and leapt out of the cabin. Being in so isolated an area it was obviously an ancient Aboriginal ceremonial ground built by those primitive Stone Age nomads in some distant dreamtime. And here we were, surely the first white men

ever to be gazing in awe at the sight, scarcely daring to breathe in order to hold the atmosphere of it all and to prolong the memory of this dramatic moment to its limit.

The others had driven up the rocky incline and had stopped, wondering for a fleeting instant what was the trouble, until they all saw the reason for themselves. We all knew without saying that it was going to cause much speculation and theory, and that we would all be recapturing this scene for years to come. Moved by curiosity we ventured forward slowly on foot, as if we were creeping about an antique egg-shell china-shop....

It was impossible to tell how old the posts were, but they must have been pretty old for they were well-weathered at their base where countless ground thermals and wind currents off the claypan had sandblasted them.

The area was about a hundred and twenty yards long, the main line bearing a few degrees west of north. The individual slivers of grey, water-impervious shale were protruding three feet above the surface of the plateau, and judging by the one or two which were leaning or fallen they seemed to be embedded about a foot or so beneath. Each was comparable in section to its neighbour, measuring four inches by three, very rectangular, and with a perfectly straight long axis. There were about sixty of them about two yards apart. As well as these there were clusters vaguely resembling stocks of hay each made up of one centre "post" of shale with a dozen or so slivers leaning in towards it, the inner ones resting against, and seemingly propping up, the centre; they covered a circle three feet in diameter and were three feet high. On closer inspection they seemed to be rather carefully placed. I counted half a dozen of these clusters in all, one placed at either end of the main line, at its centre and one several yards distant on its own; the other two were on the plateau level on the eastern and western side. One of these was erected about fifteen yards west of the southern extremity but on a raised natural rock dais eight feet higher than the others, and what we took to be the main one of all, was the cluster built roughly a chain west of the northern extremity.

215

At the time of this amazing discovery Mr. Beadell had carried out a hurried survey of the site to record its position for the arm-chair boffins back in civilisation, and it was this information that was necessary for my own research into the possible reason for the remote location of the ancient construction. Len had thought the work had been carried out by an Aboriginal community way back in the distant past, and at that time there was not much evidence to show otherwise. No other explanation would fit the known facts.

The photographs shown to me changed this explanation dramatically.

Over the years, since the original discovery, either nature, due to weathering, or man, due to his insatiable curiosity, had uncovered the sand from a corner of the plateau, and laid bare a small section of stonework which had lain hidden possibly for centuries.

In startling detail the photographs showed a small section of paved surface. The paving stones were large and rectangular in shape and several inches thick. They were very accurately cut and fitted together in an extremely precise tessellated pattern. It was immediately obvious that no primitive race could have had a hand in a construction such as this. The tools necessary to carry out such an operation pointed to a much more advanced type of civilisation being in the area at the time. A find of this nature would be expected more so in Greece, or Rome, than in the Australian outback.

Mr. Beadell described the plateau as being about six feet above the level of the claypan, with a sort of natural ramp on one side, up which he had driven his Land-Rover. This suggests that the stone platform under the sand is the top surface of a construction which is at least a few feet high and possibly of something buried deeper in the drifting sand. The ramp could be the buried remains of a flight of steps perhaps.

Recently Mr. Beadell successfully led another team into the area of the "Stonehenge" site, armed with movie cameras and other gear in order to gather more information necessary for our research purposes. I only wish I could have been one of the party, but my flying commitments with the airline necessitated my remaining in New Zealand.

When discussing the find with him on the telephone, he said he had misplaced the original survey data he had recorded at the time but would replot the position on his maps and send me a set of coordinates which would be within one minute of arc in latitude and longitude. He was true to his word and sent off the data the same day.

The reason I was curious was that the "Stonehenge" site was not far distant from that chosen for the atom test. I had long since discovered the geometric nature of the bomb, which has been verified from scientific sources since I published my findings.

In my earlier publications I had shown a set of harmonics which appeared to fit the geometric coordinates of the bomb site. As time went on and more knowledge became available I became dissatisfied with the initial results and decided to carry out another series of calculations. I thought I had found the most likely combination, then I received a very accurate map through the post, from one of my readers which caused me to check the results once more.

I now believe that the geometric coordinates used were as follows: Latitude: 28° 41' 54.35" south / Longitude 132° 22' 12" east.

DIAGRAM 18

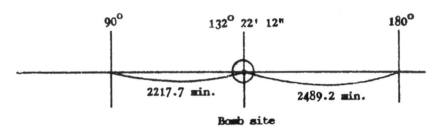

90°   132° 22' 12"   180°

2217.7 min.   2489.2 min.

Bomb site

ATOM BOMB TEST SITE - EMU - AUSTRALIA

Data from the book: "Blast the Bush" By: Len Beadell

The location of the bomb site from map reference:
28° 41' 54.35"S/ 132° 22' 12" E

Bomb site latitude:	28.6984305°
Equal to :	286984305 harmonic
The square root :	169406 harmonic

Displacement from longitude 90° = 2217.7 minutes of arc (great circle)
Displacement from longitude 180° = 2489.2 minutes of arc (great circle)
Total = 4706.9 minutes of arc
(4706.9 X 6 X 6) = 169448.4 Harmonic

In my recent research I have discovered the harmonic relationship of the speed of light and gravity. The indication is that the light geometric changes with the position of latitude in conjunction with the acceleration of gravity. (This will be demonstrated in later publications).

From the latest light and gravity tables:

The light harmonic (gravity) at 28^0 41' 54.35" = 143551 minutes per grid second

Twice the speed of light (2C) = 287102

The square root = 169440845 (16944) harmonic

In each case the geometric harmonics show a close relationship with the unified value of 16944. I believe that an exact match would occur if a star survey of the site position was obtained and the light and gravity tables were corrected by a full computer program.

The 16944 harmonic is now known to be the connecting link between the earth's magnetic field, the speed of light and the acceleration of gravity.

Publications, at a later date indicated that most of the atomic tests were carried out at a place called Maralinga. The position that Len Beadell was heading for on his trip south. The harmonics centered round this position also proved to be extremely interesting. The complete Atlas of Australia shows the position of Maralinga to be:

30^0 09" south / 131^0 35' east.

The great circle distance to Grid Pole "B" in the south proved to be 3240 minutes of arc.

The harmonic 324 is equal to half harmonic 648.

The square root of 648 is equal to 25.455844.

The 25455844 harmonic is related to the earth's magnetic field, as demonstrated in other sections of the book.

If the harmonic 324 is reduced by division by 6 (six times), the resultant harmonic is 6944444, which is the reciprocal of the speed of light.

The "Stonehenge" site was not concerned with the disruption of matter but as it was close to the geometric point necessary to carry out this method of destruction, it could possibly be connected in some way with light harmonics. The ancient site could also have some scientific meaning which would be of great importance to us.

The position supplied by Mr Beadell was:

Latitude 28⁰ 58'S/Longitude 132⁰ 00'E

If we apply these values without any correction, then:

Latitude 28⁰ 58' is equal to:

$28.9666⁰$

If we reduce the harmonic by dividing by 6, we get:

4.82777

The square root of harmonic 482777 is:

6948221 harmonic, which with slight correction would equal the speed of light reciprocal.

The longitude value, in relation to longitude 180⁰ in great circle distance, has a connection with gravitational harmonics which have been discovered in later research. (The value: 2502.35). Also the longitude 132⁰ is displaced 2880 minutes of arc from longitude 180(0). The harmonic 288 is equal to 2C, or twice the speed of light.

Possibly this area will be searched with the appropriate electronic equipment in the future to ascertain whether there is anything hidden away underground. The Stonehenge site could be giving only a hint of what treasures lay beneath the ground for discovery.

Hopefully much more information will be made available about the stone platform in the near future which will help us to probe further into the mystery. So much of this type of evidence is being discovered now that several lifetimes would be necessary to carry out all the research. What we need is a concentration of dedicated scientific minds to spend full time on discoveries of this nature, with complete freedom to pass all their findings on to the public.

MAP 10

This map was originally produced by Len Beadell during the survey of the site for an atomic bomb test. The rough position of the "Native Stonehenge", discovered purely by accident, is clearly shown.

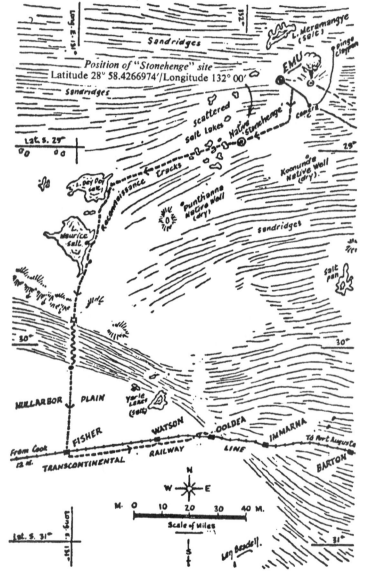

MAP 11

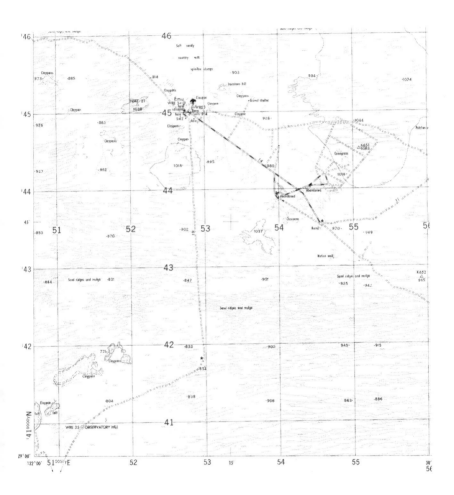

EMU: Atomic Bomb test site

These photos show the cut flagstones uncovered at the Stone-henge platform site discovered by Mr. Beadell. The matchbox resting on the left hand corner of the displaced stone gives some idea of size. It is obvious that this construction was not placed by a primitive race.

25> THE ORGANISATION OF A MIRACLE

WHEN MODERN CIVILISATION, FOR WANT OF A better phrase, first impinged upon the brooding jungles of New Guinea, it inadvertently created new religions.

Primitive tribesmen encountered their first representatives of the outside world, in many cases by courtesy of the airplane. Many missionaries arrived in the bushland outbacks by aircraft; to the native mind these were superior beings who descended in vehicles from the clouds, stepped out, and distributed gifts and medicines.

These strange white beings with their superior powers, their odd clothes, their material benefits, were as gods.

Thus were born the beliefs that have come to be known as "cargo cults."

In the wake of the first airborne missionaries, deluded New Guineans in scattered parts of the territory hacked out rough airstrips in the jungle, hung up tattered rags to represent windsocks, and chanted religious incantations, hoping to entice the gods to come on another visit. No doubt rival tribes adopted differing religious beliefs; one tribe might insist that God was six feet tall, had red hair and a flowing beard; to their rivals across the river, God was a short, plump being in khaki slacks with glasses. None would willingly accept that God was an intangible, a force that has characteristics that are manifested in identical manner to all life throughout the universe; the creative force that permeates all space, all material things; that all beings are cells in the gigantic God-body.

"Ye are gods," Christ said. We are all manifestations of the Creator. And in our turn, to a limited extent, we too can create. When we fully understand the creative force and learn how to apply it we shall create what we now refer to as miracles. Christ insisted that men would, some day, duplicate all the miracles that he performed. Everyone of us has God within himself — a God that is beating furiously from within in an attempt to emerge. Before we can make miracles we shall first have to learn to abide by the teachings of the great religious leaders down through time: God Is Light, this is the fundamental truth. For every speck of material substance in the universe is built up from a particular combination of wavelengths of the creative force, which we call light. God is

Light — Light is God. I hope to demonstrate this truth by unified field equations derived from a study of the UFO grid which envelops this planet.

I have attempted elsewhere to show some possible relationships between UFO phenomena and certain passages of the Bible. The same kind of links have not been ignored by other UFO researchers; the similarities between certain Biblical descriptions and modern reports of UFOs are too marked to be passed over. Again, other writers have shown support for the theory that much in modern religions stems from visits to this planet of superior beings from space in ancient times. Did Christianity, for example, evolve from older religions which in turn had sprung out of cargo cults? There is a great deal of evidence which would indicate that the hypothesis might be a valid one — without in any way denigrating the basic religious beliefs we cling to. On the contrary, a study of the evidence, far from eroding at basic religious tenets, can hardly fail to buttress them up, to give us confidence in their fundamental truth. Some of that evidence, and some of the theories that have been put forward in recent times, we shall look at in this chapter.

It is almost inevitable that a UFO investigator, sooner or later, feels compelled to look at the connections between UFO phenomena and religion. One may satisfy oneself that the connections are there; but to try to encourage this idea in others is fraught with hazards. People of many different races, creeds and cultures have come to an unshakeable belief in the existence of some sort of personal saviour. There are some four thousand different religions in the world; the converts to any one of them will go to any lengths to prove that the followers of the other 3999 are misguided, non- believers of the true God, and beyond redemption. Schisms in the Christian belief have led to some terribly bloody wars during the last two thousand years or so. Where persuasion and argument have failed to win converts from one belief to another, force had been employed almost as a matter of course... What a sorry and divided lot we are!

Here we are, milling around like madmen, searching frantically for something that is right in front of our eyes, always has been, and always will be; the simple truth that we are part of the Creator; this is the meaning behind true phrases such as: "the equality of all men," "all men are brothers," and so on, for as cells among the uncountable billions of cells, we are all aspects of God, God is Us, We are Light.

When we learn how to use the laws of harmony which permeate the whole of Creation, we shall be free to create that which is now unattainable. *We* hold the keys to our own salvation — not some Old Testament figure watching down on us from on high, dealing out punishments and rewards as he sees fit.

Conscience, the laws of cause and effect, the teachings of superior brothers from space — these are the guides.

I believe all this even if you do not, because the evidence I have studied tells me that it is true. Perhaps you condemn me for these beliefs; perhaps you are calling me blasphemer, or worse. I may never know if *all* my beliefs are correct or not; even so, I must be honest with myself, and I must reach my conclusions on the evidence I have before me. One thing I am already sure of: "He" did not create a universe peopled only with sycophants and flatterers; if "He" did, "He" would certainly have become horribly bored with us long ago.

When I began writing my first book I was hesitant about including references to any religion; in fact, I was warned against it. I was assured that readers would be offended, and that the book as a whole would consequently be condemned. I don't deny that the risk of offence is there, although that is certainly not my intention. What I do hope to achieve is the same thing that a friend seeks to do when he calls to a sleeping companion. If I can succeed in jolting some people into a state of wakefulness, even if this means provoking argument and controversy, my intentions will have been successful.

A minister and Biblical scholar, Barry H. Downing also has a degree in physics. When I came across his book, *The Bible and Flying Saucers*, I was understandably surprised. His book, a reverent one for all the eyebrow-raising its title may cause, questions the very foundations of formal religious teachings, and re-interprets the Bible in the light of modern science.

It was this book which recently rekindled my interest in tracing links between modern UFO phenomena and sections of the Bible.

I thought I had been a little controversial when I introduced some material of this kind. Mr. Downing had been much more outspoken, and uses scientific argument to suggest that most of the miraculous happenings related in the Bible were connected with visits to this planet of space people — a superior race sent here to attempt to teach the peoples of earth how to live their lives in harmony with the universe instead of existing in conditions that led to chaos and destruction.

If some of the points I had put forward were ripples in the wind of change, Mr. Downing has produced a veritable tornado. In his book he discusses most of the classical miracles of the Bible which other UFO investigators have considered to be related to the intervention of outer space beings. Some of these events include the Ascension; Jacob's ladder; Elijah being taken up to heaven on a whirlwind; and the experiences of Ezekiel. The Biblical passage which describes the burnished wheels which Ezekial saw in a vision is perhaps the most interesting; the account tallies with many modern-day descriptions of UFOs, complete with passengers. However, I must leave you to study these matters for yourself; a number of books have been published dealing with such correspondences.

Mr. Downing particularly interested me with his explanations of the Exodus. Some months ago it was suggested that I check all the geographic locations of religious significance where miraculous happenings and other events had occurred, from Biblical to recent times, to ascertain whether the actual location had any direct relationship with the occurrence in terms of harmonics.

I did accordingly carry out an approximate check on several places, including Lourdes and Fatima. I found, for example, that all the math incorporated into the geographical position of Bethlehem invariably worked back to unity. Other findings convinced me that geographical positions did have a relationship to particular events and manifestations. We agreed that the whole subject might best be taken up in another work, at a later date, once we have established the existence of the geometric harmonics which connect the physical world, as we know it, to the less tangible worlds reached by harmonic manipulations of light and gravity frequencies.

In any case, my interest was sufficiently aroused after reading Mr. Downing's interpretation of the Exodus that I determined to locate the geometric position of the Red (Reed) Sea where it was closed following the passage of the Israelites in their flight from Egypt. Was it possible that evidence could be found to show that the waters of the sea were parted by an anti-gravity force field, thus allowing the Israelites to cross over on dry ground? Let's quote a passage from Downing's book:

> The Bible narrates that "when the Pharaoh let the people go...God led the people round by way of the wilderness towards the Red Sea," *Exodus 13:17,18.* What is meant by saying that God led the Israelites? Here is the answer:

The "Lord" went before them (the Israelites) by day in a pillar of cloud to lead them along the way; and by night in a pillar of fire to give them light, that they might travel by day and by night; the pillar of cloud by day and the pillar of fire by night did not depart from before the people (*Exodus 13:21, 22*). By means of an unidentified flying object, God led the Israelites from Egypt to the Red Sea.

How does this Biblical UFO compare with modern UFOs? Modern UFOs sometimes exhibit a corona effect, which results in a white, cloudlike halo appearance. Modern UFOs also usually glow in the dark, as the Biblical "pillar of fire" seems to have done. But the difficult question is the significance of the Hebrew term for *pillar*. There are in fact two Hebrew words which have been translated as pillar in the RSV: *'ammud*, and *mazzebah*. In this passage the word *'ammud* is used, which may mean a cylindrical column; thus the implication would seem to be that this UFO looked like a cylindrical column (height not specified), cloud-like during the day, but showing in the dark ...If the Bible is describing a UFO which appears as a cloud-like cylindrical column during the day and as a glowing cylindrical column at night, then this UFO corresponds in description with a class of modern UFOs which have been seen with considerable frequency. Occasionally these cylindrical or "pillar" UFOs seem to act as a kind of "mother ship" for the flying saucer type or class of UFO, which seem smaller in dimension than the pillars from which they come.

This UFO deliberately led the Israelites to the Red Sea, which seemed like a foolish thing to have done, because with the Egyptian army coming up from behind, the Hebrews were literally caught between the Pharaoh and the deep blue sea. The Bible says Pharaoh thought the Israelites were "entangled in the land; the wilderness has shut them in" (*Exodus 14:3*). Pharaoh and his army moved in for the kill with the "pillar" having proved a poor guide unless *the being in charge of the UFO knew ahead of time what would happen at the Red Sea.*

The text suggests that some sort of UFO, totally under its own control, led the Israelites out of Egypt to the Red Sea and then as Pharaoh's army closed in, the UFO moved from the front to the rear of the army of Israel, and kept the two military camps separated during the night. Phase one of the operation involved leading Israel to the sea; Phase Two requires the UFO to keep the camps separated until darkness falls. Now begins Phase Three: "Then Moses stretched out his hand over the sea; and the Lord drove the sea back by a strong east wind all night, and made the sea dry land, and the waters were divided." (*Exodus 14:21*).

I went over these extracts from Downing's book with a recently acquired map from the *National Geographic Magazine* illustrating "The Lands of the Bible Today" (see map 12).

Shown on the map is the traditional route of the Israelites in their flight before the Egyptians. The first point that strikes one is the unusual course followed by the Israelites, considering that Pharaoh's army was in close pursuit. First they headed south-south-east from Raamses to Succoth; then, for some unaccountable reason, they turned back and headed north to the crossing point at the Red or "Reed" Sea. It seems odd that the "Lord" should lead the Israelites into a possible trap of this nature when a free route could have been taken to the south-east, over land which would eventually have led down the eastern side of the Gulf of Suez.

This route would also have been much shorter — unless, of course, as Mr Downing comments, the "beings in charge of the UFOs knew ahead of time what would happen at the Reed Sea". I too believe this to be the case. If the "pillar of cloud" was in fact a cigar-shaped UFO, then the intelligence controlling it had to lead the Israelites to the one place in the area where an unforgettable miracle could be staged, and Pharaoh's army destroyed.

A geographic position had to be selected where all the necessary harmonic coordinates to set up **a force field** with which the seeming miracle could be arranged, were available. And since we in the twentieth century are still unable to duplicate such a feat, a miracle it was indeed.

According to Downing, at the time of the "parting of the waters", the UFO had taken up a position behind the Israelites, who were then on the west bank of the Reed Sea. From this fact we can assume that the cigar-shaped vehicle was positioned a half mile or so from the western shoreline.

I checked the map coordinates for this area and found that the latitude of the crossing from west to east was close to 31 degrees

MAP 12

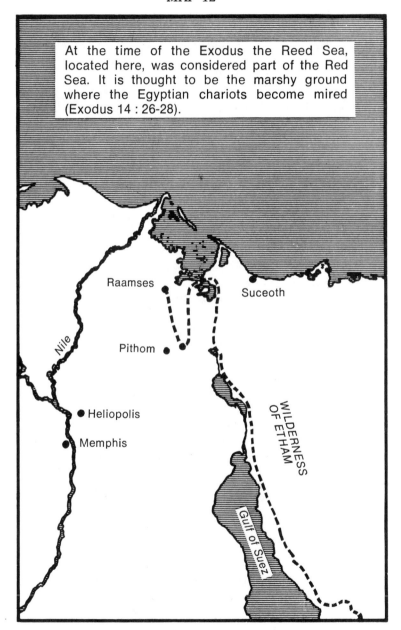

At the time of the Exodus the Reed Sea, located here, was considered part of the Red Sea. It is thought to be the marshy ground where the Egyptian chariots become mired (Exodus 14 : 26-28).

By courtesy of *National Geographic Magazine.*

north. This was an interesting beginning because this angle of latitude is equal to 1860 minutes of arc. The log of 1860 is 2695 which is a harmonic value derived from the unified equation. In my initial publications I used this latitude but with more evidence available at this time I am more inclined to think a latitude of 30⁰ 59' 00.426" would be more appropriate. The displacement from the north pole would then be 59.0165 degrees. The harmonic reciprocal of this value is 169444. Research up to the present time has proved that harmonic is associated with mass and gravity.

The longitude value is estimated to be 32^0 11' 45.1165" which is within seconds of the original calculation. This is equal to 32.195866 degrees. If this harmonic is increased by the multiplication of six, as follows: (32.195866 x 6 x 6 x 6) = 6954307 harmonic, then the speed of light reciprocal is evident.

I now believe that from this position a wedge shaped force field was created and focussed across the stretch of water to the east of the Israelites.

In order for the waters to be parted it must have been necessary to produce such a force field lying along the line of latitude, thus forcing the waters apart and forming a ribbon of dry land by means of which the Israelites could cross over to the eastern shore.

The intensity of the field could have been varied to any desired value, and frequencies necessary to react with the water would first of all have been used to cause the sea to part and allow the Israelites to cross.

Once safely on the eastern shore, the field could have been intensified so that when the Egyptians tried to follow, they and their vehicles would have been weighed down by the gravitational forces directed upon them, stranding them midway across the ribbon of exposed sea bed. At the appropriate moment the force field would have been withdrawn, the water would have flooded back, drowning the army of Pharaoh and destroying its equipment.

The east wind felt by the Israelites to be blowing in their faces all that long night can be explained by the positioning of the UFO behind them. The force field set up would cause atmospheric effects which would certainly have displaced masses of air. The UFO would have been the focal point for the movement of the air masses; in theory, a wind from both the east and from the west would converge on the central point of the wedge-shaped force field. The Israelites would only have been conscious of the wind from the east, blowing in their faces, as the UFO was to their rear, that is, to their west.

If records were available we might find that Pharaoh's army experienced strong winds blowing up from behind them.

Did an inscrutable but almighty God cause the "Reed" Sea to part? Or did some highly advanced beings perform a scientific "miracle" for us, knowing that some day we would be able to go to the records and understand for ourselves how it had been done? The miracle was a masterly production; intentionally, perhaps, it was one that could never be forgotten by the human race. Would a just God have destroyed an entire army in such a horrifying way? I think not. But a superior race may have done so, if the action suited their purpose, whatever that may have been.

DIAGRAM 19

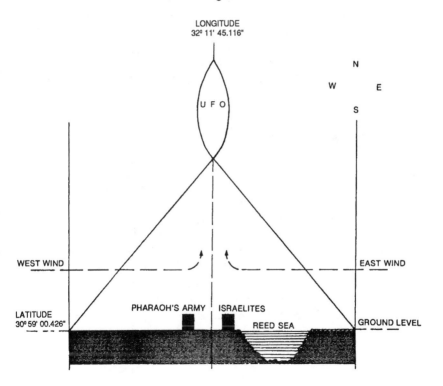

Exodus
The making of a Miracle

26> THE DIMINUTIVE MAN OF MYSTERY

HE WAS A SMALL, FRAIL MAN, NOT MORE THAN 100 pounds in weight. He came to the United States in 1912 from near Riga, in Latvia, where he was born on a farm in the district of Metei.

Almost as though he were making for one particular point on the map, he passed through California, Texas and Florida. He moved south almost to the tip of the Florida peninsula, right at the edge of the Everglades. There, at a point where US Highway No. 1 now runs, about twenty-five miles south of Miami, he took up the life of a recluse.

His name was Edward Leedskalnin.

Until the day of his death — 7 December, 1951 — he lived a life of secrecy; he undertook and carried out a colossal building project the like of which the world has never known. He worked alone, and with simple tools and pulleys. Today scientists confess they are still baffled; for he moved great stones hewn from coral rock; he hoisted massive blocks, set up fantastic edifices, including an obelisk weighing more than twenty-eight tons; all alone, without the aid of machinery.

In his later years the Latvian was to make this claim:

"I have discovered the secrets of the Pyramids, I have found out how the Egyptians and the ancient builders in Peru, Yucatan and Asia, with only primitive tools, raised and set in place blocks of stone weighing many tons."

A colonel of the United States Army Engineers, Carrol A. Lake, has written of the wonders that Leedskalnin built: "Leedskalnin proved for all the world to see today, that he knew the construction secrets of the ancients. He quarried and moved into place, alone and without modern machinery, stones weighing twice the weight of the largest blocks in the Great Pyramid. In all he cut and placed over 1,000 tons of coral rock, the greatest achievement in all history by one man. Here is one of the great wonders of the world, ranking with the pyramids of Egypt, with Stonehenge in England, with the fabulous Temple of Jupiter at Baalbek near Damascus in Syria, with the great mysteries in stone on Easter Island."

It was natural for this army engineer to associate Coral Castle, as it is now known to thousands of visitors each year, with the wonders of the ancient world which he listed. There is every reason to believe that Baalbek and Giza are positions on this planet where some curious physical conditions prevail. I have also noted an apparent connection between these sites and the energy grid which encompasses this globe; Stonehenge too, falls within this grid.

No one ever saw Leedskalnin at work when he was engrossed with his constructions in the 1920s. He built a wall of stone slabs, each of several tons, rising to a height of eight feet around a courtyard. Within this he erected a two-storeyed tower, the ground floor of which became a workshop and storehouse. He used the upper storey as his living quarters.

But from the simple tools he left behind, some conjectures have been made about his working methods. It appears that he would drive a wire cable several feet into the rock with an iron stake, attaching the other end of the cable to an apparatus that he moved backwards and forwards in a sawing motion until a cut was achieved reaching the depth of the driven cable. A second cut made in the same manner would then be made at a distance determined by the size of the slab he required. Next he would cut a trench between the two cuts, several feet in depth, and set into it a row of flat chisels; by hammering each in turn the block would ultimately break free from the bedrock. With the help of a tripod made of logs and a hoist, he would then put a sling around the slab and little by little raise it from the ground by using jacks and wedges. With his own arrangement of pulleys, it is said, plus the use of rollers, he would coax the slab into its final position.

But when it comes to the moving of blocks weighing up to thirty-five tons, this explanation is obviously not good enough. Says one American writer, Vincent H. Gaddis, "What mystifies the engineers is how equipment of this nature and size could possibly be enjoined to support the tremendous weights that Ed raised in the air to high levels or stood upright. There is no doubt that he applied some principle in weight lifting that remains a secret today."

Leedskalnin worked on his project for twenty-five years. Coral Castle is on a ten-acre site. There is a tower containing 160 tons of coral rock, made from individual blocks weighing nine tons. Behind the massive walls of the tower are fantastic pieces of furniture and movable objects, including a bed that could be raised to the ceiling. There are rocking chairs made of rock, weighing thousands of pounds, but so delicately balanced that they move at the touch of a finger. Great crescents top walls in the garden which rise to twenty feet in height; there is a 28.5 ton obelisk reaching for the sky. There is also a polaris telescope carved from coral rock, rising to twenty-five feet, and weighing nearly thirty tons. There is a circular hole bored through it, near the top, within which are wires crossing at right angles. Several feet away is a lower stone with a similar hole and a similar "gun-sight". By lining up the crossed wires in the lower stone with those in the obelisk, a direct sighting of the North Star is obtained.

The Latvian's interest in astronomy is further evidenced by the representations of the moon and the planets along the rear wall of the courtyard — and also by a unique sundial which tells time to within two minutes of accuracy all year round.

Entering Coral Castle, visitors pass through a swinging gate — a triangular stone block weighing three tons. In the centre rear wall of the courtyard there is a nine-ton stone gate so perfectly pivoted that a child can make it swing around.

Leedskalnin's secrets have never been plumbed. When asked directly by visitors how he had created his marvels, his only reply would be to the effect that he was privy to the secrets of the ancient Egyptian pyramid builders.

A remarkable man in every respect, and one too little known outside his adopted Florida, Leedskalnin also undertook studies and experiments in magnetic current, an interest which reminds us of that other mysterious genius who emigrated to America from Europe, Nichola Tesla. Leedskalnin developed a number of theories related to the field of magnetism, claiming that they were more accurate than any prevailing ideas on the subject; he published booklets on his studies at his own expense. His theory on cosmic force is along the lines of Einstein's unified field theory.

In a pamphlet which he published in 1946, he wrote: "The north and south poles are the cosmic force. They hold together the earth and everything on it, turning the earth around on its axis."

And, in a newspaper article, he declared: "Every form of existence, whether it be rock, plant or animal life, has a beginning and an end, but the three things that all matter is constructed from have no beginning and no end. They are the north and south poles' individual magnets, and the neutral particles of matter. These three things are the construction blocks of everything."

It came as no great surprise to me that the site of Coral Castle is mathematically related to the world energy grid, as are the other remarkable structures which, however, date back from ancient times. After a series of calculations I came to the conclusion that Ed Leedskalnin had not moved on to the Florida site by chance.

The initial check I made to ascertain the position of Coral Castle, published in my earlier works, was Latitude 25⁰ 28' north, longitude 80⁰ 27' west — as near as I could pinpoint the position on my maps. This geometric position was extremely close to one that would be ideal for setting up harmonics related to gravity and light harmonics.

More recent information gives the position as 25⁰ 29' 09" north, 80⁰ 26' 08" west.

In my initial publication I stated that the direct latitude value of the site set up a gravitational harmonic, but further investigation has indicated that a modification of this view is necessary.

When the geometric pattern is projected onto a flat plain, as in Diagram 20, then the coordinates projected from Coral Castle to the zero degree and ninety degree longitude lines, where they pass through the equator, yield harmonics related to light and gravity. The angle 0 as shown in the diagram, is equal to 69.4 degrees and the square root of the longitudinal distance of 4826.133 minutes of arc is a value of 69.4: close to the speed of light harmonic reciprocal of 69444. My latest research shows that this harmonic is also related directly with gravitation. The pattern suggests a dimensional relationship between spherical and flat plain geometry.

The fact that Leedskalnin had access to secret knowledge is much more evident in the relationship of Coral Castle to the world energy grid system. Normal latitude and longitude, on the earth's surface, is not coincident with latitude and longitude related to the energy grid, due to the fact that the Polar positions are off-set. In the case of energy grid pole "B" the position is 694.4 minutes of arc displaced from the north geographic pole, on normal longitude 105 degrees west. (Geometrically opposite on normal longitude 75 degrees east in the southern hemisphere). It would appear that zero longitude, grid "B", is coincident with 105 degree longitude (normal) in the northern hemisphere.

This is, no doubt, confusing to the reader, but a study of the grid polar diagrams should help to make this clearer.

I now have more modern equipment to work with and a computer calculation indicated that the direct great circle distance between Coral Castle and grid pole "B" in the north is 3246.4847

DIAGRAM 20

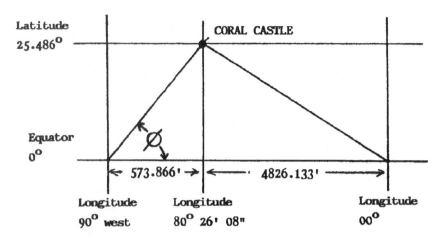

The geometric position of CORAL CASTLE

minutes of arc. It is therefore a simple matter to calculate the grid latitude which passes through the Coral Castle position: Latitude 35° 53' 30.9".

The circumference, in minutes of arc, or nautical miles, relative to the grid equator, at this parallel of latitude, is 17,498.685 minutes. This is equal to: 1,049,921.1 seconds of arc, relative.

If we subtract this value from the circumference around the grid equator we have:

1,296,000 − 1,049,921.1 = 246,078.9 seconds of arc difference.

If we subtract the difference of 246,078.9 from the circumference 1,049,921.1, we have 803,842.2 seconds.

(803,842.2 X 60 Harmonic)	=	48230532
The square root	=	6944.8205

A few hundred feet correction in the position of Coral Castle would give the 69444 harmonic exactly.

The great circle displacement of Coral Castle from grid longitude zero, at the same grid latitude, is just on 22.275 degrees relative.

DIAGRAM 21

CORAL CASTLE and the WORLD GRID

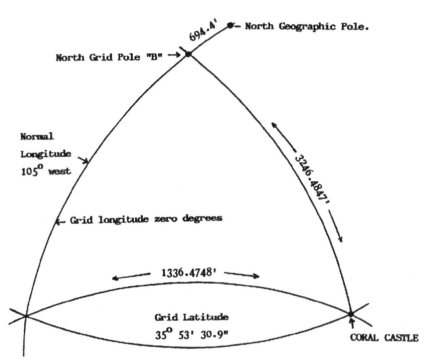

1336.4748'   = 22.27458 degrees
(22.27458 ÷ 60)   = 0.371244

The reciprocal harmonic of 0.371244 is equal to:
2693645 harmonic: Derived from the unified
equation in recent research.

(22.275 divided by 60 harmonic) = 0.37125 harmonic.

The 37125 harmonic is the reciprocal of the geometric harmonic derived from the unified equation: 26936: (in recent research).

Leedskalnin's remark that he was privey to the secrets of the ancient Egyptian pyramid builders points to another remarkable seeming coincidence.

The computed great circle distance from the Great Pyramid in Egypt to Coral Castle is 5650 minutes of arc, or nautical miles.

5650 minutes is equal to 94.16666 degrees.

As we work in 90 degree arcs to calculate most of the geometric harmonics it is necessary to subtract 90 degrees form 94.16666 degrees to ascertain the harmonic evident in the second sector.

$$(94.16666 - 90) = 4.16666 \text{ degrees.}$$
$$(4.1666 \div 60) = 0.0694444 \ (694444 \text{ harmonic})$$

This I believe is sufficient to show that Mr. Leedskalnin knew what he was about when he searched out this area to establish his stone Garden of Eden. He knew secrets that some of our scientists would give their right arm for.

At certain positions on the globe there are localities where the forces of gravity can be manipulated by the application of certain geometric harmonics. Coral Castle, I believe, occupies one of these positions. We already know for certain a little about other areas of gravity abnormality. Many of them exist deep within the oceans; modern navigational charts show ocean areas where the sea is above sea level — as much as 250 feet or more above normal sea level. Apollo Ten astronauts found abnormal gravity conditions on the moon — causing their frail craft to buck and tumble in totally unpredictable fashion.

Where these geometric conditions exist, it is evidently possible for people who have the knowledge to use gravitational forces to construct great buildings of massive material. Stonehenge, the ancient pyramids, the temple at Baalbek, and perhaps the pyramids in Central and South America were the results of a combination of knowledge and gravitational abnormalities.

27> BITS AND PIECES

L ITHIUM
   The Marshall Cavendish book on *The Atom* states: "One isotope of lithium has three protons and three neutrons in its nucleus, giving a mass number of 6. But the atomic weight of lithium is 6.94 because of a significant contribution by an isotope with three protons and four neutrons: that is, a mass number of 7. The average of these two isotopes is 6.94 rather than exactly 6.5 because there is much more naturally occurring lithium 7 than there is lithium 6."

We can see from this the reason why lithium has become a very important element on the world market. The atomic weight of 6.94 is the harmonic reciprocal of light speed 144. This makes the element ideal for the construction of extremely efficient batteries. (The batteries used in the lunar module and other space research vehicles are of the lithium type.) The element is also used in many other types of modern electrical apparatus.

Atom Bomb Tests
   In my first two books I pointed out that the harmonic geometrics of the earth are a necessary factor in the successful detonation of an atomic-type device. Certain points on the earth must be selected because of their harmonic geometric location. It was shown that the islands of Bikini and Eniwitok in the Pacific were used because the latitudes were 695 minutes of arc north of the equator. This gave the scientists perfect positions to set up bomb apparatus tuned to the reciprocal of the speed of light (694.444 harmonic). Successful detonations devastated the islands, proving that the scientists knew what they were up to.

   Closer to home and more recently, the French have been causing ill feelings in the Pacific by the use of Mururoa Atoll for their testing programme. Why don't they carry them out in France or somewhere close to their own shores, is the argument, instead of harassing the friendly peoples of the Pacific?

   The reason is that they can't as the proposition is a geometric one. The following may point this fact out once again. In 1973, during all the protests and opposition to the tests, a small news item appeared in the Auckland *Sunday Herald* on 7 October, headed ANTARCTIC BASE FOR N-TESTING (by Gilbert Sedbon, Paris NZPA — Reuter): "France may use the Antarctic island of Kerguelen — about 2500 miles south-west of Perth — as its new nuclear testing base. Work is now proceeding on the island for a possible relocation of France's huge new 'World Strategy' base in the Indian Ocean. If the French government decides to switch to underground nuclear tests because of world public opinion over its use of Mururoa Atoll it is possible that the Antarctic base may be used. The French have already built a space telecommunication station on Kerguelen Island which will serve as a direct link with their nuclear submarine fleet."

The latitude and longitude of Kerguelen Island:
Latitude 49^0 30' south/longitude 69^0 30' east

Latitude 49^0 30'	=	49.5^0
Displacement from the equator	=	49.5^0
Displacement from the south pole	=	<u>40.5</u>
Difference		<u>9.0^0</u>

If we shift the harmonic by division of 6 (4 times); then the speed of light reciprocal, harmonic 69444, is evident.

Grid latitude, which is offset from normal geographic latitude, is: 61^0 00' 00" south.

If we shift the harmonic by division of 6 (2 times),The harmonic 169444 becomes evident, which has relationships with mass and gravity.

Longitude 69^0 30'	=	69.5'
Harmonic 695 (6944)	=	Reciprocal of the speed of light

It is obvious from the above geometrics that a position chosen near the centre of Kerguelen Island would be ideal for the carrying out of atom tests, when correlated with my previous publications and recent findings. Is it necessary to show more evidence?

Headline AUCKLAND STAR 1 August 1974

SCIENTISTS FIND NEW ELEMENT

Moscow — Wednesday: Soviet scientists working at the Nuclear Research Institute at Dubna have discovered a new element with the atomic number of 106, Tass reported today.

The news agency said the scientists bombarded lead nuclei with accelerated ions of chromium-54 to produce the new element, which divided in radioactive decay in less than one-hundreth of a second.

The search for new elements is carried on mainly as a test of scientific theory and has little practical value. The elements are created in very small amounts and often have an extremely short life-span before radioactive breakup.

But according to scientists there is a theoretical possibility that some elements with higher atomic numbers may be more stable and of value — for example, as improved sources of neutrons for use in atomic fission.

What an idiotic statement to make — that the search for new elements of higher atomic number is of little practical value! The search for these elements is of the utmost importance for the advancement of science.

It is possible that the heavier elements will be found deep down towards the centre of the earth when our technology is advanced enough for us to reach for them.

Headline AUCKLAND HERALD 16 October 1975

HEAVY HOLES IN SPACE

An American astronomer has produced rare visual evidence of the presence deep in space of a "black hole", a mysterious object where time and space are distorted.

Black holes whose existence is largely theoretical are stars collapsing under intense gravitational forces, sucking in nearby material and emitting powerful X-ray pulses....The black hole is thought to be between 16 and 32 kilometres across but it is so compressed that a pin-head of its material would weigh millions of tons.

Could it be that the so-called black holes are the gateways between the universe and the anti-universe? The raw material that is necessary for the creation of matter may pass back and forth through small areas of space such as this, in a pendulum-type motion, to alternately form the universe and anti-universe. The action would take place, of course, over millions of years in terms of human time.

A UFO which hovered over the radio masts of Mt. Victoria, Wellington, on 31 May 1965. This object was seen by dozens of witnesses in the vicinity of the airport and as far away as the central city area. The weather on this particular day was filthy, and flying conditions were minimal. However I had been able to take off from Wellington airport less than half an hour before the UFO appeared.

The object was first sighted about 3:55 pm and was observed for over half an hour. It was first seen to descend from the clouds over Mt Victoria. It was generally oval in shape, but appeared to change in outline quite rapidly, as if it were tumbling. It hovered over the northern face of Mt. Victoria for about ten minutes, then rose into a low stratus cloud layer covering Wellington Harbour. It appeared almost immediately farther north over Point Jerningham, the northern part of Evans Bay, then shortly after this it was seen again over Mt. Victoria. It was approximately 20 feet in width or diameter, and greyish-white in colour. It was seen by experienced personnel in the airport control tower and by numerous witnesses around Wellington city. I understand that at least six people in Broadcasting House, Bowen Street, which is about two miles distant, also saw this strange object.

A report was given on the television news but so far as I know the newspapers were silent and the whole affair was quietly forgotten.

During the last nine months, a football-shaped UFO has been seen on many occasions in the Wellington area and this could very well be the same one seen over Mt. Victoria. I anticipate it will continue to be seen until its job is done.

And now a report from the Wellington *Evening Post*, dated Friday 21 May 1976:

P.O. WORKERS' ELEVATED VIEW OF UFO

An unidentified flying object (UFO) was reported this morning by Post Office workers who say they watched it for about five minutes from their cafeteria on the twelfth floor of Post Office Headquarters in Waterloo Quay.

"We stood at the window and watched for about five minutes," said a spokesman for the twelve people. "The object appeared as a dark mass at first, then changed shape and kept disappearing and re-appearing. Basically it was oval in shape and hovered above Mt. Kau Kau, to the left of the transmitter [TV transmitting mast]. It seemed to vary in size at first then steadied, and from then appeared as a thick mass."

So there we have two similar reports eleven years apart, 31 May 1965 to 21 May 1976. Has it completed its job yet, or can we expect another visit?

28> COINCIDENTAL PATTERN OF OIL WELLS

SCIENTISTS REPORT ON KAIPARA HARBOUR UFO

POSITION 1965

Map 13 is a copy of my original grid map showing the positions of recent drill sites off the west coast of New Zealand, indicating another amazing coincidence. Each of these drill sites has been abandoned as a dry hole, and as being of no further use to the oil companies. Possibly a bright mind could find some other use for the holes and make use of their peculiar geometric positioning.

The key to the following positions as shown:
A UFOs plotted from radar screen at Mangere Airport as previously described.
B Moa 1B.
C Maui 2.
D Tasman 1.
E Drill site off Albatross Point.
F Maui 4.
G Possible future drill site (prediction by us).
H UFO position published *Harmonic 33* 1968.
I Plotted position latitude $39^0\ 24'$.
J Cook 1.
K Distance $D - E$, $E - I$, equals 2C/4.
L Position of UFO activity at Port Underwood reported by Mr. and Mrs. C. H. Harris in *Harmonic 33*, 1968.

The copy of a letter is that received from an American scientist, Mr. J. Jackson, who resides in Auckland city. The letter refers to a survey carried out over the position where I observed the Submarine Unidentified Object in the Kaipara Harbour in 1965. This was the position published in *Harmonic 33*, and the point from where all my research originated.

I was informed by Mr. Jackson that there is now a hole in the harbour bed approximately one eighth of a mile wide and over one hundred feet deep. I feel that this proves that there was indeed an object carrying out some secret project at this point five years ago.

MAP 13

COINCIDENTAL PATTERN OF OIL WELLS

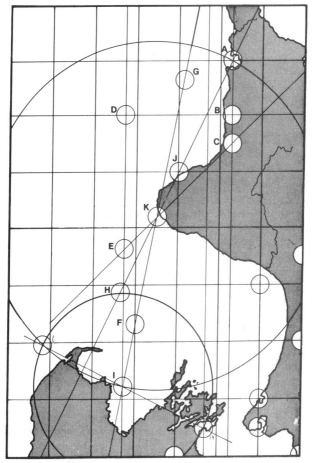

Section of original UFO grid showing surprising relationship of drill sites off the West Coast of New Zealand.

In August 1970, some months after a copy of this map had been lodged with a New Zealand Government agency, the Marine Department issued a warning to shipping advising that marker buoys had been placed at a position of 39° 24′ south, 173° 46′ east. This position coincides with position K on my original map. I believe that this proves, without any doubt, that scientists are fully aware of the geometric principles governing the unifield equations established in this book.

KAIPARA HARBOUR, N.Z.

Position lat : 36° 29'S   Weather : Fine, Clear, Cloud
         long : 174° 19.25E   9/10 Wind N 2/3
                                                     Sea Confused
                                                     Bar 30.35 A.T. —
                                            State of Tide : On flood

Date : 5th September 1969
Time : 12.00 hrs / 12.27 hrs N.Z.S.T. East Bound

When passing over this area (speed 7 kts) the depth sounder, while
indicating an average depth of 40/50 ft., the meter needle commenced to
swing back and forth from ∅ to 120 (extent of range scale) violently, this
continued until the black beacon was abeam. The meter now acted normally.
I swung around and returned to this area immediately and the meter carried
on the same way. Then carried on up the main channel to Shelly Beach.
(Distance 6¼ miles). The depth sounder acted normally the balance of the
trip.

Checked Sounder : Accuracy near enough to maker's claim.
                   Marlin M.I.20 model.
                   8 months old 200 khz Batteries O.K.
                   All connections O.K.
My son, Karl, aged 7½, said that the meter "was swinging around like mad".
The sounder has never done this before.
The magnetic compass was stable.
Written at 14.00 hrs at Shelly Beach.

                                            J. Jackson
                                               5.9.69

*Report from the Chief Engineer of the Ministry of Works,
Auckland, regarding the position in the Kaipara Harbour where
the submarine type object was observed*

29> WAKE UP, EARTH!

I AM CONVINCED BEYOND ANY REASONABLE DOUBT that space is the home of countless billions of intelligent beings. Among those billions there must be a great percentage of entities whose physical appearance is similar to ours. The human form is a highly efficient mechanism and a design team would find it very difficult to make any improvements. On earth we have many variations of this form but basically we are all very much the same.

Because of the growing mass of evidence that indicates we are not the sole owners of the universe, the probability that we will meet a traveller from some other part of our galaxy who looks much like we do is ever increasing. The acceleration of technical knowledge in recent times makes this prospect almost a certainty in the near future. Anyone who is interested enough to search through all the available evidence in the world today will find to his astonishment that there are very strong indications that contact with alien intelligences has already been accomplished by a number of individuals throughout history. These contacts have invariably been treated by the authorities at the time with ridicule or hostility. The contacts which they have been unable to hush up have been written into religious tracts as visitations by angels, or various emissaries of the gods who supposedly rule the heavens. Every method possible has been used to make certain that the public at large is kept ignorant of the fact that we are not alone.

The reason for this massive con job is not completely clear, but possibly greed, and a fear by the comparatively small group of people who decide our destiny that they will lose control of the ordinary individual, like you and me, if the truth is known, ensures that the evidence is suppressed.

One of the main arguments brought up in recent years as the increasing number of sightings of strange objects in the sky has aroused public interest, is that if "they" exist why is it that astronomers, or other scientific people, do not see them? In actual fact, many of these people *have* seen unexplainable objects in the sky, and out in space. Unfortunately they would probably lose their jobs if they made too much of a fuss about it. In the early stages of my own research I was threatened with this very same thing, but common sense prevailed and I am still happily flying aircraft for a living and, as far as I am aware, within certain bounds, am in control of my own destiny. How long this will last is probably debatable.

Mr. William Moser, president of the British Astronomical Association and general secretary of UFOIC Sydney, has brought attention to the fact that a great number of men of science have observed strange occurrences throughout recorded history. He lists some thirty-odd cases of sightings by astronomers and scientists dating from 7 February 1802 to 23 August 1966 in the newsletter of July/August 1973. The objects varied from cigar-, disc- and ovoid-shaped, and with sizes from three metres to two kilometres in diameter; both stationary and moving. This is only a small percentage of sightings which can be found by searching through old records. The general UFO-type publications list many of these.

I believe that researchers like myself read all this mass of material and get to the stage where they say to themselves "OK, I know they are out there and that every now and then a contact takes place. But what is to be done next?"

The obvious thing to do, as I have attempted to show in my writings, is to find scientific evidence which will help us to emulate the activities of the intelligences which we are continually observing invading our airspace. The time is past when long lists of sighting reports and unsubstantiated speculation will help us to advance our own knowledge, or to make progress. This information is essential in the early stages of a research project, but eventually we have to stop gathering new data and start using the stuff to form the basis of a new science. This is my main objection to many of the large international UFO organisations scattered round the world. Since the late 1940s they have gathered together massive amounts of evidence of UFO activity and related data. Their boards of directors and consultants list dozens of names of scientists, mathematicians, physicists, astronomers and academics in all fields. Besides this they have direct access to computer facilities into which they can feed the truckfuls of information they have collected, hopefully to come up with some sort of intelligent analysis. Years have gone by yet nothing has happened — so far as the public are aware. I am very surprised, and very suspicious. As an individual with access to none of this sophisticated knowhow and technical machinery, I have been able to discover many areas where a small amount of research should bring a great spin-off of new knowledge. I am, perhaps, tenacious in my efforts to discover new concepts, but I have only an average education and level of intelligence. It is quite obvious to me that many of these organisations are not making known their findings and that the public are being kept blissfully in the dark.

Wake up, Earth! We are being taken for a ride and the time has come to demand the truth.

As I have pointed out earlier in this book, if space is being traversed by vehicles controlled by advanced intelligences, we would expect to intercept some sort of communication signals which are obviously being passed between the space vehicles and various bases scattered round the cosmos. Initially the interception of such signals would probably be accidental, as we would not be sure of the electronic principles behind long-distance communications over the millions of miles of space. Eventually, after scientific analysis, the concepts would be understood and a full-scale project could be contemplated which would hook us into the galactic switchboard. And this I believe is exactly what has happened.

As I was nearing completion of this book I received another letter from Mr. Cook of Derbyshire, England. My writings have sparked him off on an independent line of calculations and from the information received from him it appears that he is on the way to opening up more areas for serious research. He decided to take a close look at some radio signals that were received from space in 1928, using the basis of harmonic mathematics that I formulated in my original work.

The radio signals were recorded in the 1920s by Norwegian, Dutch, and French experimenters. It was suggested in recent years that the long-delayed echoes of equally-spaced radio signals transmitted from earth could be interpreted in the form of a code. A Mr. D. A. Lunan, a graduate of Glasgow University, carried out an analysis along these lines and concluded that the echoes were being broadcast from a space probe in orbit somewhere in the vicinity of our moon.

The theory is that if an advanced civilisation wished to contact us, they would leave a space satellite in earth orbit, waiting quietly through the centuries until our technology reached the stage where we were able to interrogate it. I believe that the space probe is out there, and that it is programed to teach us how to get out into space and join the galactic community.

Mr. Lunan suggests that the signals identify the probe's origin as the double star Epsilon Bootis and puts its arrival in earth orbit at somewhere around 13,000 years ago. Another investigator made the comment that such probes might listen for our radio signals and repeat them back to us after obvious delays, such as those reported in the 1920s. It is thought that the device is still in orbit waiting for its secrets to be unlocked.

The APRO *bulletin* of March/April 1973 states:

> American experimenters Taylor and Young first reported echoes coming from apparent distances of 2900 to 10,000 km in 1927. Halls, an engineer, reported to Carl Stormer of Oslo that echoes of 3 seconds delay had been heard at Eindhoven, Holland. On 11 October 1928 Carl Stormer, with Halls, helped by Van der Pol transmitting from Eindhoven, picked up 3-second echoes on 31.4 meters, which changed to echoes varying from 3 to 15 seconds (signal pulses were transmitted at 20-second intervals). Echoes were received in the following delay sequence: 8, 11-15, 8, 13, 3, 8, 8, 8-12, 15, 13, 8, 8. In two cases two echoes were heard 4 seconds apart.
>
> To the author the series of 3-second echoes without doppler shift constitute the statement: "Here I am in the orbit of your moon," while the varied series means something much more elaborate.
>
> He constructed a graph and plotted the delay time of each echo of the Van der Pol series against its position in the sequence presenting double echoes on the same line ... When delay time was graphed horizontally the result was a striking resemblance to the constellation Bootis. Bootis was missing, but when the 3-second point was transferred from the left of the vertical barrier formed by the 8-second points it completed the constellation figure by marking the position of Epsilon Bootis...This is interpreted to mean that Epsilon Bootis is the origin of the probe.

I do not wish to disagree with Mr. Lunan's interpretation of the space signals when subjected to this type of analysis. What I do believe however is that the received signals, and others waiting to be triggered, are for the purpose of teaching us scientific knowledge pertaining to the universe itself. Many different types of information are sure to be coded into the system.

I had heard of the radio signals and Mr. Lunan's work, but up until recently I had not spent any time in trying to decipher them. I was occupied with so many other interesting projects that I shelved this particular line of thought for some future date. That was until I received the letter from Mr. Cook.

He had found many interesting mathematical associations between the space signals and my harmonic calculations. The most important and interesting piece of information that he passed to me was that the transmission which triggered the space echoes was broadcast on 31.4 metres and that when this wavelength was converted into minute of arc value to compare it with grid harmonics the answer was .016944 minutes of arc!

This was an amazing piece of news. The signals were tuned to the most important harmonic of 16944, as shown in other sections of my work. This must be a universal wavelength which will plug us into the space network. Did someone know something as far back as 1928, and are we about to make a serious attempt to communicate, as evidenced by the massive radio grid being constructed in the United States.

Are we receiving other signals from the heavens which to us could be classed as divine?

There are many powerful religious groups in the world, each of them vying for the minds of man and promising various states of salvation or damnation for those of us who choose or reject their particular doctrine. It is very difficult for the ordinary person like me, who has a belief in some overall divine intelligence controlling the universe, to sort out which particular religious group is nearest to the truth. After all, if we, as individuals, are going to place our souls in the hands of one of these groups, we want to be very sure that they are not going to mess about with them. Out of all the thousands of religions there can only be one which is treading the path to absolute truth — maybe none of them are. We shall only be sure when we pass from this life and have a look for ourselves. In the meantime we can only choose the particular group that suits us best, or remain out of them all and search for truth in our own way.

My attention has recently been drawn to one of the major religions of modern day, as a result of my delving into the mathematical mysteries of the universe. *Time* magazine published an article on this religion in the issue of 16 September 1974, headed "Behind The Temple Walls." Some statements in the article are as follows:

To people of other faiths, the Mormon temple is an impenetrable place of mystery...only Mormons in good standing can participate in the Holy "ordinances" that are performed in the temple precincts, or even visit the rooms where they are performed....

Although the exterior of the temple is striking — 288 ft tall from the ground to the tip of the angel Moroni's trumpet and encased in 17,300 square feet of gleaming white Alabama marble — the interior does not inspire awe. Divided into dozens of rooms on nine levels, the temple has nothing comparable to the great nave and towering sanctuary of a traditional Christian cathedral. Indeed the Mormon temple is not built for regular worship (that purpose is served by thousands of local "ward" meeting houses) but for "temple work" — the performances of various church duties and doctrinal study. To the outsider the rooms seem to serve a function rather than majesty.

Has divine guidance had a hand here and inspired elders of the church to design a temple that reaches 288 feet into the air, to broadcast the voices of us mortals to the gods in the heavens? Out of curiosity I wondered if divine guidance had had any influence in the actual placing of one of these temples in a geometric sense. From my own work I had discovered that geometric location on the structure of the earth had profound effects on physical manifestations. Possibly the spiritual part of our nature could benefit by the effects of specific geometric location.

On 20 April 1958 a Mormon temple was dedicated at Temple View, Hamilton, New Zealand. My wife and I had been taken on a conducted tour of some parts of this temple shortly before it was closed off from public view. What we saw of the interior structure was very impressive, but in some ways strange to us, not being familiar with the Mormon beliefs.

I checked the placement of the Temple on a survey map and the following coordinates were evident.

Latitude: 37° 49' 40" south / Longitude 175° 13' 28" east.

I have shown in my earlier works that this position could be associated with grid harmonics but now that I have access to much more accurate computers I was able to discover a quite startling fact.

But first an extract from the book, "Essentials in Church History", by Joseph Fielding Smith regarding the Survey for the Temple Block at Salt Lake City.

The Place for the Temple. — During the westward journey the building of a temple was a constant theme. On the evening of the 28th of July, President Young and the apostles with Thomas Bullock, the clerk, walked from their camp northward to a spot between the forks of City Creek, and there President Young designated a site for the building of a temple. Waving his hand he said: "Here is the forty acres for the temple, and the city can be laid out perfectly square north and south, east and west."

Orson Pratt's Survey. — The survey of the city was made by Orson Pratt. His line was on the southeast corner of the Temple Block. Beginning at that point the city was marked out into blocks of ten acres each. It was decided by the brethren that instead of using forty acres for the site it would be better to have that block conform in size with the others. According to Orson Pratt's calculations, the latitude of the north boundary of the Temple Block was 40 degrees, 35 minutes and 34 seconds. The longitude was 111 degrees, 26 minutes and 34 seconds west of Greenwich. The altitude was 4,300 feet above sea level. Later government observations varied from these of Elder Pratt but slightly.

From the above it seems that the Temple Block was surveyed very accurately.

I had a hunch that if I checked the geometric placement of the New Zealand Temple in relation to the First Temple in Salt Lake City, on the computer, something interesting might turn up — and it did.

The great circle displacement, in seconds of arc between the two Temples is :

371244 seconds.

With a margin of error of a few hundred feet.

My latest book, "The Bridge to Infinity, Harmonic 371244" will show that this is the reciprocal harmonic of the value 2693645 derived from the unified equation — according to the speed of light at the

253

Earth's surface 143,795.77 minutes of arc per grid second. Have the Mormons been given the secrets of the unified field?

Other geometric areas on the earth's surface which I have mentioned before in my writings are those where the normal gravitational fields are grossly distorted. These small localised positions have been of great interest to scientists in recent years and no logical explanation has yet been given for the queer physical effects experienced within the boundaries of an "anomaly area". If a plumb-bob is suspended within the distorted field it will not hang vertically but at an angle; people who walk into such an area start walking with a lean on; light itself appears to be distorted, and photos taken of objects within the influence of the gravity-warp from outside the area, show all sorts of queer effects. Depending on position, for instance, objects can appear either physically elongated or shortened. According to reports at least seven of these areas have been located on the North American continent.

More information is gradually filtering out regarding these anomaly areas and I have discovered several mathematical leads in connection with the effects which I intend to follow up in later research. One of the best-known anomalies is called the Oregon Vortex, the position of which is given as 42^0 29' 40" north/123^0 05' west. The area is circular with a diameter of just over 165 feet. A series of force-lines has been discovered passing through the circle, running east-west and north-south, five lines one way and six the other. The given information does not indicate how the position was calculated; whether by map reference, or by a very accurate star survey.

I am not completely happy with the accuracy of this position so I will leave the analysis of the associated geometric harmonics until a later date. However the great circle displacement of the position from longitude 180 degrees, at the same latitude, is very close to 41.1636 degrees. The square of this value being the 169444 harmonic.

A theoretical diameter for the area which would be very close to the given value of around 165 feet 4 inches would be 165 feet 3.76524 inches. This would give a conversion diameter of 163.13859 geodetic, or grid, feet. Converted to grid inches we have 1957.6631 geo/inches. The volume of a sphere with a diameter of 1957.6631 grid inches equals 3928371000 cubic grid inches. This would be a harmonic of the resultant field strength of the Earth (3928.371 lines of force per square geodetic inch) as shown in my earlier work. This rough calculation would indicate that a spherical field is being produced in the gravity anomaly area, harmonically tuned to the magnetic field of the Earth.

The force-lines discovered passing through the area could have some connection with the harmonic of the speed of light. I found that if I divided the number of force-lines east-west by those north-south, 5 divided by 6, the value was .83333 repeating. The square of this figure is .694444 repeating — the reciprocal of 144 (the harmonic of the speed of light). The distorted optical effects in the area could be controlled by this factor.

It is my hope that at some time in the future arrangements can be made to visit one of these areas and to have accurate measurements taken with all the necessary scientific instruments. The relationship with the grid structure can then be thoroughly investigated by use of computers and harmonic mathematics.

My studies have led me up many paths over the last few years and helped me to understand that the universe and all things in it are inter-related. If the unified equations which I have formulated prove to be valid, or even partly valid, when checked by the academics, then the time I have spent on my research will be of some value.

If what I have written is sufficient to prove that not all knowledge can be found in the standard textbooks, and others are encouraged to carry out independent research, I shall be happy.

The most important aspect to be aware of is that we have neighbours out there, and that we must change our attitudes if we wish to join them.

Wake up, Earth! We are about to be taken out of isolation!

INDEX

Decagon 76,77
Deland, John D. 141, 142
Department of Scientific and Industrial Research 134, 210
Dick, William 160
Dolmens 168
Dow, John 186, 187
Downing, Barry H. 225, 226
Dougall, W.K. 187
D'Urville Island 15, 20, 21, 22, 23, 24

Edison 101, 102
Einstein 5, 6, 38, 69, 234
Elijah 226
Eltanin, survey ship 25, 26, 27, 28, 55
Emu, Atom Bomb test site 213, 217, 221
Eniwetok 48
Exodus 226, 227, 228, 229, 231,
Ezekial 226

Fatima 226
Fesenkov, Professor 204
Flindt, Max 201
Formation of matter 10, 76, 125, 162
Fort, Charles 1
Fort Lauderdale, Florida 123, 127
Franklin, Paul 186, 187
Fuller, Buckminster 163

General Electric Company 103
Geodetic foot 74, 75
Geykin, M. Dr. 160
Goncharov, Nicholai 93
Gramme machine 100
Grand Bahama Island 125
Grand Hotel, Invercargill 134
Gravity acceleration 39, 48, 205
Great Asaco Island 125
Greek foot 74
Grid Poles 29, 39
Gris, Henry 160

Leedskalnin, Edward 232, 233, 234, 235, 238
Lemay, General Curtis 4
Lepunov, B. 204
Light, speed of xiii, 5, 6, 7, 10, 11, 13, 23, 29, 36, 37, 39, 40, 41, 48, 65, 66, 67, 69, 71, 72, 74, 75, 81, 86, 87, 96, 109, 114, 115, 116, 120, 122, 127, 142, 160, 161, 170, 179, 205, 218, 219, 230, 235, 239, 240, 253, 255
Lithium 239
Llano Uplift, Sanguine site 119
Lockwood, Don 188
Lourdes 226

Magnetic lines of force 81, 82
Magnetic prospecting 81
Magnetron 80, 81
Magnifying transmitter, Tesla 111
Mallery, Captain A. H. 89
Makarov, Valery 93
Maralinga, Atomic Bomb test site 218
Mathews, Ellis E. 194, 195
Megalithic mile 75
Megalithic yard 75
Mercators plotting chart 20, 23
Michel, Aime 22, 23
Mitchell, John iii, 75, 86, 87
Mikhalevsky, I. V. 160
Moon Base xvi
Monte Bello Island 213
Morozov, Vyacheslav 93
Morgan, J. P. 110
Mormons 252, 254
Moser, William 248
Moses 228
Multiple Wave Oscillator 157, 158
Mundrabilla xv
Mururoa Island xvi, 45, 239, 240
Musical Harmony 86

National Academy of Sciences 3
National Investigations Committee of Aerial Phenomena 3

THE ANTI-GRAVITY HANDBOOK
edited by David Hatcher Childress, with Nikola Tesla, T.B. Paulicki, Bruce Einstein, Albert Einstein and others

The new expanded compilation of material on Anti-Gravity, Free Energy, Flying Saucer Propulsion, UFOs, Suppressed Technology, NASA Cover-ups and more. Highly illustrated with patents, technical illustrations and photos. This revised and expanded edition has more material, including photos of Area 51, Nevada, the government's secret testing facility. This classic on weird science is back in a 90s format!
• **How to build a flying saucer.**
•**Arthur C. Clarke on Anti-Gravity.**
• **Crystals and their role in levitation.**
• **Secret government research and development.**
• **Bruce Cathie's Anti-Gravity Equation.**
230 PAGES. 7x10 PAPERBACK. ILLUSTRATED. $14.95. CODE: AGH

ANTI–GRAVITY & THE WORLD GRID

Is the earth surrounded by an intricate electromagnetic grid network offering free energy? This compilation of material on ley lines and world power points contains chapters on the geography, mathematics, and light harmonics of the earth grid. Learn the purpose of ley lines and ancient megalithic structures located on the grid. Discover how the grid made the Philadelphia Experiment possible. Explore the Coral Castle and many other mysteries, including acoustic levitation, Tesla Shields and scalar wave weaponry. Browse through the section on anti-gravity patents, and research resources.
274 PAGES. 7x10 PAPERBACK. ILLUSTRATED. $14.95. CODE: AGW

ANTI–GRAVITY & THE UNIFIED FIELD
edited by David Hatcher Childress

Is Einstein's Unified Field Theory the answer to all of our energy problems? Explored in this compilation of material is how gravity, electricity and magnetism manifest from a unified field around us. Why artificial gravity is possible; secrets of UFO propulsion; free energy; Nikola Tesla and anti-gravity airships of the 20s and 30s; flying saucers as superconducting whirls of plasma; anti-mass generators; vortex propulsion; suppressed technology; government cover-ups; gravitational pulse drive; spacecraft & more.
240 PAGES. 7x10 PAPERBACK. ILLUSTRATED. $14.95. CODE: AGU

QUEST FOR ZERO-POINT ENERGY
Engineering Principles for "Free Energy"
by Moray B. King

King expands, with diagrams, on how free energy and anti-gravity are possible. The theories of zero point energy maintain there are tremendous fluctuations of electrical field energy embedded within the fabric of space. King explains the following topics: Tapping the Zero-Point Energy as an Energy Source; Fundamentals of a Zero-Point Energy Technology; Vacuum Energy Vortices; The Super Tube; Charge Clusters; The Basis of Zero-Point Energy Inventions; Vortex Filaments, Torsion Fields and the Zero-Point Energy; Transforming the Planet with a Zero-Point Energy Experiment; Dual Vortex Forms: The Key to a Large Zero-Point Energy Coherence. Packed with diagrams, patents and photos. With power shortages now a daily reality in many parts of the world, this book offers a fresh approach very rarely mentioned in the mainstream media.
224 PAGES. 6x9 PAPERBACK. ILLUSTRATED. $14.95. CODE: QZPE

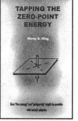

TAPPING THE ZERO POINT ENERGY
Free Energy & Anti-Gravity in Today's Physics
by Moray B. King

King explains how free energy and anti-gravity are possible. The theories of the zero point energy maintain there are tremendous fluctuations of electrical field energy imbedded within the fabric of space. This book tells how, in the 1930s, inventor T. Henry Moray could produce a fifty kilowatt "free energy" machine; how an electrified plasma vortex creates anti-gravity; how the Pons/Fleischmann "cold fusion" experiment could produce tremendous heat without fusion; and how certain experiments might produce a gravitational anomaly.
180 PAGES. 5x8 PAPERBACK. ILLUSTRATED. $12.95. CODE: TAP

THE FREE-ENERGY DEVICE HANDBOOK
A Compilation of Patents and Reports
by David Hatcher Childress

A large-format compilation of various patents, papers, descriptions and diagrams concerning free-energy devices and systems. The Free-Energy Device Handbook is a visual tool for experimenters and researchers into magnetic motors and other "over-unity" devices. With chapters on the Adams Motor, the Hans Coler Generator, cold fusion, superconductors, "N" machines, space-energy generators, Nikola Tesla, T. Townsend Brown, and the latest in free-energy devices. Packed with photos, technical diagrams, patents and fascinating information, this book belongs on every science shelf. With energy and profit being a major political reason for fighting various wars, free-energy devices, if ever allowed to be mass distributed to consumers, could change the world! Get your copy now before the Department of Energy bans this book!
292 PAGES. 8X10 PAPERBACK. ILLUSTRATED. BIBLIOGRAPHY. $16.95. CODE: FEH

THE HARMONIC CONQUEST OF SPACE
by Captain Bruce Cathie
Chapters include: Mathematics of the World Grid; the Harmonics of Hiroshima and Nagasaki; Harmonic Transmission and Receiving; the Link Between Human Brain Waves; the Cavity Resonance between the Earth; the Ionosphere and Gravity; Edgar Cayce—the Harmonics of the Subconscious; Stonehenge; the Harmonics of the Moon; the Pyramids of Mars; Nikola Tesla's Electric Car; the Robert Adams Pulsed Electric Motor Generator; Harmonic Clues to the Unified Field; and more. Also included are tables showing the harmonic relations between the earth's magnetic field, the speed of light, and anti-gravity/gravity acceleration at different points on the earth's surface. New chapters in this edition on the giant stone spheres of Costa Rica, Atomic Tests and Volcanic Activity, and a chapter on Ayers Rock analysed with Stone Mountain, Georgia.
248 PAGES. 6X9. PAPERBACK. ILLUSTRATED. BIBLIOGRAPHY. $16.95. CODE: HCS

THE ENERGY GRID
Harmonic 695, The Pulse of the Universe
by Captain Bruce Cathie.
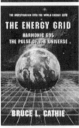
This is the breakthrough book that explores the incredible potential of the Energy Grid and the Earth's Unified Field all around us. Cathie's first book, *Harmonic 33*, was published in 1968 when he was a commercial pilot in New Zealand. Since then, Captain Bruce Cathie has been the premier investigator into the amazing potential of the infinite energy that surrounds our planet every microsecond. Cathie investigates the Harmonics of Light and how the Energy Grid is created. In this amazing book are chapters on UFO Propulsion, Nikola Tesla, Unified Equations, the Mysterious Aerials, Pythagoras & the Grid, Nuclear Detonation and the Grid, Maps of the Ancients, an Australian Stonehenge examined, more.
255 PAGES. 6X9 TRADEPAPER. ILLUSTRATED. $15.95. CODE: TEG

THE BRIDGE TO INFINITY
Harmonic 371244
by Captain Bruce Cathie

Cathie has popularized the concept that the earth is crisscrossed by an electromagnetic grid system that can be used for anti-gravity, free energy, levitation and more. The book includes a new analysis of the harmonic nature of reality, acoustic levitation, pyramid power, harmonic receiver towers and UFO propulsion. It concludes that today's scientists have at their command a fantastic store of knowledge with which to advance the welfare of the human race.
204 PAGES. 6X9 TRADEPAPER. ILLUSTRATED. $14.95. CODE: BTF

THE TESLA PAPERS
Nikola Tesla on Free Energy & Wireless Transmission of Power
by Nikola Tesla, edited by David Hatcher Childress

David Hatcher Childress takes us into the incredible world of Nikola Tesla and his amazing inventions. Tesla's rare article "The Problem of Increasing Human Energy with Special Reference to the Harnessing of the Sun's Energy" is included. This lengthy article was originally published in the June 1900 issue of *The Century Illustrated Monthly Magazine* and it was the outline for Tesla's master blueprint for the world. Tesla's fantastic vision of the future, including wireless power, anti-gravity, free energy and highly advanced solar power. Also included are some of the papers, patents and material collected on Tesla at the Colorado Springs Tesla Symposiums, including papers on: •The Secret History of Wireless Transmission •Tesla and the Magnifying Transmitter •Design and Construction of a Half-Wave Tesla Coil •Electrostatics: A Key to Free Energy •Progress in Zero-Point Energy Research •Electromagnetic Energy from Antennas to Atoms •Tesla's Particle Beam Technology •Fundamental Excitatory Modes of the Earth-Ionosphere Cavity
325 PAGES. 8X10 PAPERBACK. ILLUSTRATED. $16.95. CODE: TTP

ETHER TECHNOLOGY
A Rational Approach to Gravity Control
by Rho Sigma
This classic book on anti-gravity and free energy is back in print and back in stock. Written by a well-known American scientist under the pseudonym of "Rho Sigma," this book delves into international efforts at gravity control and discoid craft propulsion. Before the Quantum Field, there was "Ether." This small, but informative book has chapters on John Searle and "Searle discs;" T. Townsend Brown and his work on anti-gravity and ether-vortex turbines. Includes a forward by former NASA astronaut Edgar Mitchell.
108 PAGES. 6X9 PAPERBACK. ILLUSTRATED. $12.95. CODE: ETT

THE FANTASTIC INVENTIONS OF NIKOLA TESLA
by Nikola Tesla with additional material by David Hatcher Childress
This book is a readable compendium of patents, diagrams, photos and explanations of the many incredible inventions of the originator of the modern era of electrification. In Tesla's own words are such topics as wireless transmission of power, death rays, and radio-controlled airships. In addition, rare material on German bases in Antarctica and South America, and a secret city built at a remote jungle site in South America by one of Tesla's students, Guglielmo Marconi. Marconi's secret group claims to have built flying saucers in the 1940s and to have gone to Mars in the early 1950s! Incredible photos of these Tesla craft are included. •His plan to transmit free electricity into the atmosphere. •How electrical devices would work using only small antennas. •Why unlimited power could be utilized anywhere on earth. •How radio and radar technology can be used as death-ray weapons in Star Wars.
342 PAGES. 6X9 PAPERBACK. ILLUSTRATED. $16.95. CODE: FINT

One Adventure Place
P.O. Box 74
Kempton, Illinois 60946
United States of America
Tel.: 815-253-6390 • Fax: 815-253-6300
Email: auphq@frontiernet.net
http://www.adventuresunlimitedpress.com
or www.adventuresunlimited.nl

ORDERING INSTRUCTIONS

✓ Remit by USD$ Check, Money Order or Credit Card
✓ Visa, Master Card, Discover & AmEx Accepted
✓ Prices May Change Without Notice
✓ 10% Discount for 3 or more Items

SHIPPING CHARGES

United States

✓ Postal Book Rate { $3.00 First Item
50¢ Each Additional Item
✓ Priority Mail { $4.00 First Item
$2.00 Each Additional Item
✓ UPS { $5.00 First Item
$1.50 Each Additional Item
NOTE: UPS Delivery Available to Mainland USA Only

Canada

✓ Postal Book Rate { $6.00 First Item
$2.00 Each Additional Item
✓ Postal Air Mail { $8.00 First Item
$2.50 Each Additional Item
✓ Personal Checks or Bank Drafts MUST BE
USD$ and Drawn on a US Bank
✓ Canadian Postal Money Orders OK
✓ Payment MUST BE USD$

All Other Countries

✓ Surface Delivery { $10.00 First Item
$4.00 Each Additional Item
✓ Postal Air Mail { $14.00 First Item
$5.00 Each Additional Item
✓ Payment MUST BE USD$
✓ Checks and Money Orders MUST BE USD$
and Drawn on a US Bank or branch.
✓ Add $5.00 for Air Mail Subscription to
Future *Adventures Unlimited* Catalogs

SPECIAL NOTES

✓ RETAILERS: Standard Discounts Available
✓ BACKORDERS: We Backorder all Out-of-
Stock Items Unless Otherwise Requested
✓ PRO FORMA INVOICES: Available on Request
✓ VIDEOS: NTSC Mode Only. Replacement only.
✓ For PAL mode videos contact our other offices.

Please check: ☑
☐ This is my first order   ☐ I have ordered before

Name			
Address			
City			
State/Province		Postal Code	
Country			
Phone day		Evening	
Fax			

Item Code	Item Description	Qty	Total

Please check: ☑   Subtotal ➡
Less Discount-10% for 3 or more items ➡

☐ Postal-Surface   Balance ➡
☐ Postal-Air Mail Illinois Residents 6.25% Sales Tax ➡
(Priority in USA)   Previous Credit ➡
☐ UPS   Shipping ➡
(Mainland USA only) Total (check/MO in USD$ only) ➡

☐ Visa/MasterCard/Discover/Amex

Card Number

Expiration Date

10% Discount When You Order 3 or More Items!

Adventures Unlimited, Pannewal 22,
Enkhuizen, 1602 KS, The Netherlands
http: www.adventuresunlimited.nl